Y0-BSN-102

Informatics in Higher Education

IFIP – The International Federation for Information Processing

IFIP was founded in 1960 under the auspices of UNESCO, following the First World Computer Congress held in Paris the previous year. An umbrella organization for societies working in information processing, IFIP's aim is two-fold: to support information processing within its member countries and to encourage technology transfer to developing nations. As its mission statement clearly states,

> IFIP's mission is to be the leading, truly international, apolitical organization which encourages and assists in the development, exploitation and application of information technology for the benefit of all people.

IFIP is a non-profitmaking organization, run almost solely by 2500 volunteers. It operates through a number of technical committees, which organize events and publications. IFIP's events range from an international congress to local seminars, but the most important are:

- the IFIP World Computer Congress, held every second year;
- open conferences;
- working conferences.

The flagship event is the IFIP World Computer Congress, at which both invited and contributed papers are presented. Contributed papers are rigorously refereed and the rejection rate is high.

As with the Congress, participation in the open conferences is open to all and papers may be invited or submitted. Again, submitted papers are stringently refereed.

The working conferences are structured differently. They are usually run by a working group and attendance is small and by invitation only. Their purpose is to create an atmosphere conducive to innovation and development. Refereeing is less rigorous and papers are subjected to extensive group discussion.

Publications arising from IFIP events vary. The papers presented at the IFIP World Computer Congress and at open conferences are published as conference proceedings, while the results of the working conferences are often published as collections of selected and edited papers.

Any national society whose primary activity is in information may apply to become a full member of IFIP, although full membership is restricted to one society per country. Full members are entitled to vote at the annual General Assembly, National societies preferring a less committed involvement may apply for associate or corresponding membership. Associate members enjoy the same benefits as full members, but without voting rights. Corresponding members are not represented in IFIP bodies. Affiliated membership is open to non-national societies, and individual and honorary membership schemes are also offered.

Informatics in Higher Education

Views on informatics and non-informatics curricula

IFIP TC3/WG3.2 International Conference on Informatics (computer science) as a Discipline and in Other Disciplines: what is common?
17–20 August 1997, Enschede, The Netherlands

Edited by

Fred Mulder
Faculty of Engineering
Open University, Heerlen
The Netherlands

and

Tom van Weert
Director of School of Informatics
University of Nijmegen
The Netherlands

Published by Chapman & Hall on behalf of the
International Federation for Information Processing (IFIP)

CHAPMAN & HALL
London · Weinheim · New York · Tokyo · Melbourne · Madras

Published by Chapman & Hall, an imprint of Thomson Science,
2–6 Boundary Row, London SE1 8HN, UK

Thomson Science, 2–6 Boundary Row, London SE1 8HN, UK
Thomson Science, 115 Fifth Avenue, New York, NY 10003, USA
Thomson Science, Suite 750, 400 Market Street, Philadelphia, PA 19106, USA
Thomson Science, Pappelallee 3, 69469 Weinheim, Germany

First edition 1998

Printed in Great Britain by Athenæum Press Ltd, Gateshead, Tyne & Wear

ISBN 0 412 80790 4

A catalogue record for this book is available from the British Library

∞ Printed on acid-free text paper, manufactured in accordance with ANSI/NISO Z39.48-1992 (Permanence of Paper).

CONTENTS

INTRODUCTION

These proceedings are the result of a working conference of Working Group 3.2 (University Education) of the International Federation for Information Processing (IFIP). Its title was: "Informatics (computer science) as a discipline and in other disciplines: what is in common?".
It took place in an excellent setting: the Faculty of Informatics of the University of Twente in the Netherlands. A working conference like this one allows in-depth treatment of the conference theme by selected experts in the field coming from all over the world. The result is presented to you in these proceedings.

This book is of interest to teachers of informatics (computing science) in higher education, both in informatics programmes and in other disciplines. And also for curriculum designers dealing with informatics curricula or curricula in other disciplines involving informatics.

The first theme in the book is the discipline of informatics itself. It is considered to be a merge of what traditionally (at least in the USA) is called computer science, computer engineering and information systems. The number of informatics studies and educational programmes has rapidly grown all over the world. The spectrum by now is very broad, varying from generalized to more specialized contents, from theoretical to more applied programmes, and from monodisciplinary to multidisciplinary approaches. The question is: What is informatics precisely and how do we teach this?

The second theme in the book deals with the relation between informatics and other disciplines at the higher education level. All disciplines are undergoing profound changes because of informatics and its related Communication and Information Technology (CIT). The question is: What informatics concepts, methods and techniques form the hard core needed in every other discipline?

These proceedings have three parts in which both themes are addressed:

Part1 Discussion papers (an editorial paper and focus group reports developed during the conference).

Part 2 Full invited papers

Part 3 Short papers

We thank the Programme Committee for developing a programme which resulted in such an interesting book.

Fred Mulder
Tom van Weert

PROGRAMME COMMITTEE

- Tom van Weert, Netherlands (Chair)
- Fred Mulder, Netherlands (Vice-Chair)
- Monique Grandbastien, France
- Anneke Hacquebard, Netherlands
- Peter Ho, Australia
- Gerrit van der Hoeven (Chair Organizing Committee), Netherlands
- Doris Lidtke, USA
- Ken Robinson, Australia
- Joe Turner, USA
- Jan Zabrodzki, Poland

PART ONE

Discussion Papers

1

Towards informatics as a discipline: search for identity

Fred Mulder, editor
Faculty of Engineering (Informatics), Open University, PO Box 2960 6401 DL Heerlen, The Netherlands, e-mail: fred.mulder@ouh.nl

Tom van Weert, editor
School of Informatics, Faculty of Mathematics and Informatics University of Nijmegen, PO Box 9010, 6500 GL Nijmegen The Netherlands, e-mail: school@cs.kun.nl

Abstract

A changing discipline like informatics can be questioned with respect to its identity and its core concepts and skills. This concern is being expressed by the focus group papers and has led to this editorial paper. We discuss the different paradigms or views with respect to informatics that can be identified and comment on the resulting fragmented approach of the discipline. We advocate a more integral, generic and coherent approach. And we present some preliminary thoughts and notions as input for a search for the identity of the discipline, resulting in a first draft working definition for informatics as a discipline.

Keywords

Informatics, other disciplines, curriculum (general), taxonomies, educational profiles, professional profiles

Informatics in Higher Education F. Mulder & T. van Weerts (Eds.)

1 A CHANGING DISCIPLINE

Informatics is a young discipline and has already seen many changes in its young life. Since the first electronic computer was introduced for performing numerical calculations, a lot has changed. Turing and Church have given informatics a theoretical fundament based on the concept of algorithm. The technology of informatics has developed from calculating device (number processor), via automating device (data processor), information system (information processor) to personal tool (interactive information processor) and intelligent agent (interacting knowledge-based process).

At the basis for this development is the stored program computer which can change its own program and therefore can adapt its behaviour. Application of informatics turns out to be possible and feasible in areas which are not immediately and directly associated with just data or information processing. We are moving from a world of information processing in which the concept of the algorithmic process was central, to an even richer world of interaction in which the concept of interacting processes is central. By this the fundaments of the discipline are changing.

2 IDENTITY AS A COMMON CONCERN

This book, being the proceedings of the IFIP/WG 3.2 Working Conference held in August 1997 at the University of Twente in the Netherlands, contains three so-called focus group papers, which are the result of the focus group discussions at the conference. A common area of discussion and concern in these papers is the identity of informatics as a discipline and the related allocation and demarcation of a conceptual core of informatics for both informatics majors and noninformatics majors. We illustrate this by quoting from the focus group papers below.

An ongoing identity crisis for informatics
There is considerable variance in what is perceived to be the discipline of informatics. This results in a lack of professional identity: the public does not really know what informatics is about and the business community frequently does not recognize informatics as a discipline in its own right. Unlike disciplines such as medicine and law, it is not possible to state a simple mission for informatics in terms of its role in society. At the heart of this problem is the rapid expansion of the field, the lack of agreement on what constitutes the core of the discipline and the need to produce a coherent integrated body of knowledge and skills concerned with systems design and implementation. Rapid changes that have made computing accessible to noninformatics professionals have raised questions about what the discipline of informatics is and will the discipline continue to exist.
(Turner and Hughes *et al.*, 1998)

The future
Changes to the environment of both informatics and education have raised many challenges which must be addressed by those involved in informatics education. Is informatics education a discipline in crisis? If the discipline does not respond in an appropriate manner to the rapidly changing environment this may well be the case.
(Turner and Hughes *et al.*, 1998)

Informatics as an amalgamation of various fields
The broad field of informatics has increasingly been defined to be an amalgamation of the fields of computer science (CS), information systems (IS), software engineering (SE), and computer engineering (CE). Informatics may be seen then as computing in a very general sense. Yet though the term is in fairly wide use, there has been given no attention to those core concepts of informatics that would be essential for the development of relevant curricula. By its very definition, we see that the core concepts of informatics are in the intersection of the core concepts of CS, IS, SE and CE, respectively.
(Lidtke and Myers *et al.*, 1998)

Controversial proposals?
The listing of the preceding core topics, concepts, and experiences (.....) has been influenced by the personal knowledge and experiences of the focus group members, representing the various subfields of informatics. But this list is not simply the reflection of current practice that is common to all those subfields. Indeed, in places we advocate topics that may not be part of the current curriculum or knowledge base of one or more classes of informaticians. Thus we assume that some of the preceding may be quite controversial.
(Lidtke and Myers *et al.*, 1998)

Introductory informatics for all students
Therefore we have concentrated on developing a proposed conceptual core for an introductory informatics course. We strongly advocate that this core knowledge should be learned by both nonmajors and majors in informatics, since these fundamental informatics concepts are relevant to virtually all students in the modern academic world.
(Grandbastien and LeBlanc *et al.*, 1998)

Programming or not?
Conversely, we think it quite possible that a course based on this core might include no programming at all. We do believe though that such a course should include a 'construction experience', that is students should be required to get experience constructing formal problem solutions by doing one or more of: writing algorithms, creating spreadsheets, programming in visual languages, etc. As suggested by the previous point, we believe that courses based on this core can

have a wide variety of implementations. The level of detail to which these concepts are developed and the methods used in the course might depend significantly on the audience.
(Grandbastien and LeBlanc *et al.,* 1998)

3 PARADIGMS IN ISOLATION OR IN COHERENCE?

Computing as a discipline

The paper 'Computing as a discipline' by Denning *et al.* (1989) was a major breakthrough in that it attempted to describe the discipline in terms of different styles of thinking and working (paradigms). Three paradigms were identified: theory (rooted in mathematics), abstraction (rooted in science) and design (rooted in engineering). The discussion on how to view our discipline has been continued in a special issue of ACM Computing Surveys (1995) by quite a range of distinguished authors.

We see a multi-view approach both in the paper and in the discussion, but also a clear focus on the areas traditionally called 'computer science', 'computer engineering' and 'computing', excluding other closely related areas. The area of 'information systems', for example, is not explicitly considered, although there are definitely strong connections with the areas mentioned.

Scientific leadership

Suppose that we would ask seven scholars to give their view and definition of the discipline of 'informatics'. Try to guess their answers, if these seven would be, for example, Gene Amdahl, Gordon Davis, Peter Denning, Edsger Dijkstra, Edward Feigenbaum, David Parnas and Josef Weizenbaum. Now suppose that we would lock them in a room - with Bill Gates as technical chairman - under the condition that they only may come out with an agreed definition or description of the discipline of informatics and also with an outline for an academic educational programme incorporating different paradigmatic views. Would there be any chance of success? And would the same experiment with seven physicists, or seven economists, or seven psychologists proceed in a comparable way?

This thought experiment illustrates the fragmentation inherent to our discipline. Views of the discipline are strongly dependent on the specific scientific leadership involved.

Scientific communities

Suppose now, we do the same experiment with representatives of different scientific communities, for example the USA-organizations ACM (Association for Computing Machinery), IEEE (Institute of Electrical and Electronics Engineers) and AITP (Association of Information Technology Professionals) and the international organization IFIP (International Federation for Information Processing). One may expect a better result since these organizations have demonstrated joint efforts in developing curricula. ACM and IEEE have presented in 1991 their common model Curriculum'91 for 'computing'. ACM and AITP (as well as AIS - Association for Information Systems) have come up with their IS'97 model curriculum for 'information systems' in the beginning of 1997. And IFIP published an update of its modular curriculum on 'computer science' in 1994.

One could question, however, whether a merge of these efforts would be conceivable and valuable in view of a future (re)definition or (re)description of the discipline of informatics.

Informatics: a fragmented adhocracy?

'Can the field of MIS (Management Information Systems) be disciplined?' is the title of a paper by Banville and Landry (1989). In this paper Kuhn's model for the development and progression of science and the role of paradigms is denounced. Not any science can be forced into the 'monistic' view of normal science which is modelled on the 'queen of sciences', physics.

Banville and Landry argue extensively that MIS is an example of a scientific field that can be characterized as a 'fragmented adhocracy'. It is a scientific field which requires a pluralistic view in which several paradigms coexist. Does such an approach not only apply to MIS, but also to the broadly based discipline of informatics?

4 FROM COMPUTING TO INFORMATICS AS A DISCIPLINE

Computer science, computer engineering, information systems, software engineering, artificial intelligence, telematics, multimedia, those are all fields that constitute - in full or in part - informatics as a broad discipline and contribute to it. Rather than having this diversity resulting in 'scientific disintegration' a more integral, generic and coherent approach is needed in the context of scientific and technological progress, acknowledging of course the coexistence of the distinguished fields. Since these fields on their own are linked to a wide variety of other disciplines, scientific leaps are conceivable and well-conditioned on the basis of multi- or interdisciplinary work.

The development of such an integral approach is urgent, as the focus group papers in this book show. The editors of the conference book have decided to add this 'editorial paper' in which some preliminary thoughts and notions are presented that might contribute to a fruitful search for the identity of the discipline of informatics.

Various approaches

In this search one can choose different approaches. We list some of these below and refer - if possible and useful - to papers contained in this conference book.

- **Taxonomies:**

various specific classification systems used for literature (or for curricula) can be compared and balanced (see, for example, the papers by Mulder and Hacquebard, Sheridan and White).

- **Curricula:**
  different characteristic (model) curricula from various organizations and countries can contribute to make the position of a broad informatics curriculum clearer (we refer to the papers by Duchâteau, Geissinger *et al.*, Gupta, Juliff, Ohiwa *et al.*, Robinson, Shackelford and LeBlanc, Vollmar and Gruska).
- **Classes of problems:**
  one could think of the following classes of problems, all to be solved through methods and techniques of informatics: calculation, administration, reasoning, retrieval, communication, information, simulation, controlling, organization, foundation, and what is more (no specific papers to be referred).
- **Processes:**
  several kinds of processes can be distinguished and associated with various intended activities for informaticians (see the papers by Van Weert, Wupper and Meijer).
- **Professional profiles:**
  professional as well as educational profiles can clarify questions with respect to the variance in the discipline and its practitioning (see, for example, the papers by Lidtke and Mulder, Van der Kamp, Van Leeuwen and Smeets).
- **Core concepts and skills:**
  thinking about core concepts and skills is an important key in the search for the identity of the discipline (see the three focus group papers).

Extending the variety in views

The discipline of 'computing' was described in Denning *et al.* (1989) according to three different paradigms or views, as mentioned before:

- theory (rooted in mathematics);
- abstraction (rooted in science);
- design (rooted in engineering).

In describing 'informatics' as a discipline we should modify and extend on these three paradigms or views. We propose a first attempt here - quite open to discussion - with the following five views:

- theory (linked not only to mathematics, but also to linguistics and philosophy);
- empiricism (linked not only to science, but also to psychology and economics);
- design (linked not only to engineering, but also to management science);
- ambiguity (linked to psychology, philosophy, economics and social sciences in general);
- application (linked to technology in general and social sciences in general).

A working definition for informatics

The discipline of 'computing' was defined in Denning *et al.* (1989) as follows:

> 'The discipline of computing is the systematic study of algorithmic processes that describe and transform information: their theory, analysis, design, efficiency, implementation and application. The fundamental question underlying all of computing is: "What can be (efficiently) automated?"'

Again, we propose a first draft working definition for the discipline of 'informatics', which hopefully will contribute to a fruitful discussion:

> 'The discipline of informatics deals with
> the manipulation of *objects*
> with the aim to solve a *problem,*
> specified by a *requirements analysis*
> under a given set of *constraints,*
> resulting in a maintainable working *system*
> with an *automated* component,
> in which *men and machine* interact adequately.'

Clearly this draft working definition abstracts from specific processes such as:

- program specification, software engineering and programming software systems;
- information analysis and the design and implementation of information systems;
- configuration specification and the design and construction of computer systems.

By using the generic term 'objects' the draft working definition - one could say - is object oriented, which is not meant to be limitative with respect to object oriented methods and techniques, but rather serves as a generalization for other familiar terms, such as 'data structures', 'entities', 'records', etc.

The problems to be solved can be of any of the different classes that we have distinguished before. The result should be a maintainable working system which implies attention for system exploitation. Also note the emphasis on the interaction between men and machines.

5 CONCLUSION

The discipline of 'computing' seemed well-defined in 1989 in the paper by Denning *et al.* But now we are moving to a discipline (which we have denoted by the common European term 'informatics') with a somewhat different identity. This editorial paper is meant to state questions to be resolved in this respect and to present some ideas as input for an ongoing discussion.

6 REFERENCES

ACM Computing Surveys (1995), **27** (1).

Banville, C. and Landry, M. (1989) Can the field of MIS be disciplined?. *Communications of the ACM,* **32** (1), 48-60.

Denning, P.J., Comer, D.E., Gries, D., Mulder, M.C., Tucker, A.B., Turner, A.J. and Young, P.R. (1989) Computing as a discipline. *Communications of the ACM,* **32** (1), 9-23.

Grandbastien, M., LeBlanc, R.J., Jr *et al.* (1998) A common core for noninformatics majors, in *Informatics in higher education: Views on informatics and noninformatics curricula* (eds. F. Mulder and T.J. van Weert), Chapman & Hall, London.

Lidtke, D.K. and Myers, P. *et al.* (1998) A common core of concepts for informatics majors, in *Informatics in higher education: Views on informatics and noninformatics curricula* (eds. F. Mulder and T.J. van Weert), Chapman & Hall, London.

Turner, A.J. and Hughes, J. *et al.* (1998) Informatics education: trends, problems and the future, in *Informatics in higher education: Views on informatics and noninformatics curricula* (eds. F. Mulder and T.J. van Weert), Chapman & Hall, London.

7 BIOGRAPHY

Fred Mulder is working at the Dutch Open University from its start in 1983 and is full professor in informatics education since 1991. From 1993 till 1996 he was dean of the Faculty of Engineering. He holds degrees in chemical engineering (Bachelor), applied mathematics (Engineer) and theoretical chemistry (Ph.D.). After a postdoc research project in Canada, he went to teach informatics and mathematics in higher professional education, prior to his OU career. He has served on various national committees, such as the quality audit committees for informatics programmes at universities as well as higher professional institutes and committees for informatics at secondary schools. He is representing The Netherlands in the education committee TC3 of IFIP.

Tom J. van Weert is director of the undergraduate School of Informatics (Computing Science) of the Faculty of Mathematics and Informatics of the University of Nijmegen, The Netherlands. He also teaches management of large software projects to informatics students developing real software applications in multi-disciplinary teams. Previously he has worked in teacher education, teaching mathematics and informatics, and prior to that as a computer system engineer in an academic environment. His background is in applied mathematics. He has been active within several IFIP Working Groups and is currently chair of IFIP Working Group 3.2 on university education.

2

Informatics education: trends, problems and the future

Focus group
Joe Turner (USA; chair), John Hughes (AUS; rapporteur), Adrie Beulens (NL), Betsy van Dijk (NL), Sally Fincher (GB), Tsurayuki Kado (J), Ken Robinson (AUS), Ad Sanders (NL), Deny Smeets (NL), Erkki Sutinen (FIN), David White (NZ) and Hanno Wupper (NL)

Abstract

In the late 1980s there was a widespread belief in the informatics education community that informatics curricula were maturing and that the rate of change would slow down. However, the rate of change in informatics programs is as rapid as ever. In this focus group paper we examine the current state of informatics education and identify some of the stimuli for change and hindrances to change as well as future trends within and impacting informatics education.

Keywords

Informatics, informatics majors, curriculum (general), role of CIT, academic requirements, business and industry requirements

1 CURRENT STATE OF INFORMATICS EDUCATION

The environment in which informatics education finds itself today can be characterized as follows.

An ongoing identity crisis for informatics

There is considerable variance in what is perceived to be the discipline of informatics. This results in a lack of professional identity: the public does not really know what informatics is about and the business community frequently does not

Informatics in Higher Education F. Mulder & T. van Weerts (Eds.)

recognize informatics as a discipline in its own right. Unlike disciplines such as medicine and law, it is not possible to state a simple mission for informatics in terms of its role in society.

At the heart of this problem is the rapid expansion of the field, the lack of agreement on what constitutes the core of the discipline and the need to produce a coherent integrated body of knowledge and skills concerned with systems design and implementation.

Rapid changes that have made computing accessible to noninformatics professionals have raised questions about what the discipline of informatics is and will the discipline continue to exist.

A danger of isolation

There is a perception that informatics wants ownership of everything to do with 'computers' and 'information', that it is internally focused and is not interested in applying its knowledge and skills.

Changing roles for informatics graduates

As users have become more empowered by access to powerful software tools, applications-generation software and subject-oriented software, the need for informatics graduates as intermediaries in developing many computer systems has diminished and their role has changed. Nonetheless, demand for informatics graduates remains high.

Changing learning environments

There is a change away from traditional modes of teaching towards more flexible student-centred approaches to learning. Students want access to learning modes which allow them to learn with fewer time and space constraints, and to build their own curriculum with access to many sources of education material.

Learning is seen as an ongoing process, life-long learning is the expectation of every professional.

Informatics education is notoriously slow at adopting information technology to support teaching and learning. Other disciplines are much more adventurous in using computers in teaching.

An increasing widespread global information infrastructure

Students increasingly have access to a global information infrastructure through the world wide web and Internet. This not only provides students with access to large amounts of information (including educational material, courseware etc.) but also with a powerful means of communicating with their teachers, their peers and with others.

2 MOVING INFORMATICS EDUCATION FORWARD

Successes of informatics education

Informatics education has been by-and-large successful in meeting its responsibilities to industry. Principal among these successes are:

- production of competent technical practitioners for society;
- introduction of professional issues into the curriculum;
- responding to the needs of industry and collaborating with industry.

The discipline has been doing a fairly good job of teaching micro-concepts, perhaps not as good a job at macro-concepts, and the field is progressing more quickly in macro-concepts.

Stimuli and obstacles

There are numerous forces acting on informatics education, many are stimuli for change (both from within the discipline and from within society and the profession), others are obstacles which hinder progress. The ultimate direction informatics education takes will depend on the resolution of the forces emanating from stimuli and obstacles.

Stimuli for change include:

- changing technology in hardware, information services and information infrastructure;
- changing learning receptivity of students;
- changing expectations and attitudes of students;
- increased expectations of and dependence on informatics by society;
- changing needs and expectations of business, industry, employers;
- globalization.

Obstacles against change include:

- fear of the consequences of change by students, faculty, administrators;
- resource availability to support change implementation;
- established procedures and structures inhibiting development;
- availability of qualified faculty;
- overloaded faculty;
- inadequate reward structure for faculty;
- lack of recognition of problems by faculty;
- lack of common terminology.

3 CHALLENGES

Arising from changes to the societal, professional and educational environment and from an examination of the stimuli for and obstacles to change, are a number of challenges for informatics education. The ability of informatics education to successfully address these challenges will largely determine the future health of the discipline.

The challenges are:

- to clarify the identity of the informatics discipline on its own, with respect to other disciplines and with respect to public perception;
- to find the correct balance between teaching theory and principles (the foundations needed for long term use to enable graduates to apply knowledge in new situations) and skills (to make students immediately useful on graduation);
- to achieve adequate and appropriate rewards for teaching faculty in informatics, recognizing that faculty in informatics education particularly have to cope with the rate of change of the discipline and expansion of subject matter of informatics (with a consequent impact on the curriculum), in addition to changes in educational practice;
- to overcome conservatism with respect to the development of learning; particularly by seeking out ways of using information technology to support the teaching of informatics;
- to understand and clarify employers' expectations of graduates and ensure that there is a realistic match between expectations of graduates and employers;
- to meet industry demands for an increase in the quality of software systems by instilling professional responsibility and accountability in graduates;
- to maintain adequate levels of IT infrastructure, particularly in terms of global information infrastructure;
- to recognize the growing impact of globalization in business and the role to produce graduates with an awareness of globalization and the informatics skills necessary to achieve these business objectives;
- to collaborate and communicate with other disciplines and domains.

4 TRENDS

Four areas have been identified in which trends in informatics education are perceived:

- forms of teaching;
- changes in the profession;
- impact on the curriculum through changes in technology;
- changes in the context of the educational experience.

Forms of teaching

There are two aspects to this trend:

- the form of teaching;
- reflection on the role of the teacher.

It is a positive sign that informatics educators are increasingly reflecting on their own professional practice, on how they teach.

Among the trends in forms of teaching are:

- project orientation;
- problem based learning;
- flexible learning;
- project work with external problems.

Trends which impact on the role of the teacher include those intended to:

- help the students analytically and critically evaluate information provided (for example, from the world wide web);
- find out the personal talents of the student and help the student in planning their personal curriculum;
- rethink the process of assessment from traditional grading to profile and portfolio-based criteria.

Response to changing needs of employers and the profession

With the external societal forces there is no longer a single job market. Computer scientists and information specialists will have so many different kinds of tasks and working areas that it will become inevitable to educate students for several different kinds of professions (as in the medical world, which has specialists, general practitioners, nurses, physiotherapists, etc.). This is exemplified by:

- the growth in use of engineering paradigms in informatics;
- a process and systems orientation in building software;
- the importance of information modelling and a re-orientation towards information as the central concept;
- the different range of skills needed in practitioners working as consultants.

Impact on the curriculum through changes in technology

Programming will be emphasized less, component-based systems will be emphasized more. There will be an increased emphasis on information modelling. With the changes in hardware there will be a re-evaluation of the importance of continuous mathematics. The external global information infrastructure will continue to raise the importance of information networks.

Changes in the context of the educational experience

There is a trend in teaching (reflecting the profession's expectations of graduates) towards focusing on the different needs of each student and towards an increased emphasis on professional preparation and life-long learning. Projects will be so large that teamwork is inevitable. Teachers have responded by including experiences such as teamwork, case-based, problem-based and project-based learning. This trend must be tempered by the necessity to balance (and assess) team and individual working.

The identification and specification of problems requires ability to communicate with clients from outside the profession. Besides technological knowledge and skills, interpersonal skills will therefore become more important. Technology and society will keep changing and developing which necessitates life-long learning.

5 THE FUTURE

Changes to the environment of both informatics and education have raised many challenges which must be addressed by those involved in informatics education. Is informatics education a discipline in crisis? If the discipline does not respond in an appropriate manner to the rapidly changing environment this may well be the case.

3

A common core of concepts for informatics majors

Focus group
Doris Lidtke (USA; chair), Paul Myers (USA; rapporteur), Lillian Cassel (USA), Gopal Gupta (AUS), Anneke Hacquebard (NL), Fred Mulder (NL), Sigrid Schubert (FRG), Diane Schwartz (USA), Nobumasa Takahashi (J), Henk van Leeuwen (NL) and Stanislaw Waligorski (PL)

Abstract

The core concepts of informatics can be located in the intersection of the core concepts of the constituting and amalgamating fields of computer science, information systems, software engineering and computer engineering. In this focus group paper we present a core of both concepts and skills in eleven categories, ranging from information modelling, formalism and system design to social/ethical implications and (inter)personal skills.

Keywords

Informatics, informatics majors, curriculum (core)

1 INTRODUCTION

The broad field of informatics has increasingly been defined to be an amalgamation of the fields of computer science (CS), information systems (IS), software engineering (SE), and computer engineering (CE). Informatics may be seen then as computing in a very general sense. Yet though the term is in fairly wide use, there has been given no attention to those core concepts of informatics that would be essential for the development of relevant curricula. By its very definition, we see that the core concepts of informatics are in the intersection of the core concepts of CS, IS, SE and CE, respectively.

Informatics in Higher Education F. Mulder & T. van Weerts (Eds.)

The following is an attempt to identify such a core. Of course it is worth pointing out that these core concepts are not identical, for instance, to the ACM Curriculum '91 (influenced by Denning's paper, 'Computing as a discipline'). For though the terms used there seem to be broad, the emphasis is actually on computer science alone. Here we share with Curriculum'91,however, the emphasis on core concepts and experiences that should be incorporated into the curriculum as a whole. The topics below are thus not intended to represent individual courses in any particular sequence.

2 CORE CONCEPTS AND SKILLS

The headings below are the broadly stated concepts and issues proposed as constituting the common informatics core in a very general sense. For each heading there are sufficient details and examples for clarifying and explaining the concepts. These indicate the sorts of knowledge and skills needed as a basis on which to build the 'whole person' who will become an informatician.

Representation of information

Perhaps the most fundamental concern of the field is information (hence the very term *informatics*). And whatever the domain of discourse, to enable manipulating (computing) and communication requires that the information be represented symbolically.

Examples are: symbols; various natural languages; sound, colour, etc.; bits and bytes; encryption and compression.

Information modelling

Manipulating information (or its representation) is important precisely because we obtain understanding of some situations or phenomena. Whenever anyone writes a program or designs a system to solve a problem, he or she is modelling the world (or a specific domain).

Critical to the discussion of information modelling is an appreciation of the complexity of the phenomena to be modelled. Such attention will reveal certain inadequacies and difficulties in the very paradigm of informatics: data collection, ambiguity, effects of policy and social parameters, information loss, etc. Other relevant topics include: abstract data types, object orientation, databases.

Formalism

Information modelling requires underlying formalism, i.e. the manipulation of *forms* that represent information about a domain.

Tools and symbol systems of particular importance to informatics include: discrete mathematics, logic, artificial language(s) and awareness that computing systems are vast compared with previous modes of mathematical modelling.

System design

The various fields of computing have always been involved with the construction of systems. Perhaps due to increasing awareness of engineering methodologies, more recent attention has been given to elements of good design (e.g. the emergence of the discipline of software engineering).

Most relevant in this area is the system life-cycle: without advocating a particular life-cycle model, attention should be given to requirements analysis, design, implementation, testing and validation as well as maintenance. Other important topics are: documentation, human-computer interaction, security, quality.

Algorithmics

It is a truism that computing is accomplished by algorithms and data structures. So awareness of key concepts in the design and analysis of algorithms is core to any computing discipline.

Pertinent knowledge and skills include: complexity (time and space), comparing algorithms, selection and design of algorithms, data structures.

Software development

Hands-on experiences in the methods of programming are taken to be core experiences, though they may be interpreted quite broadly and not strictly limited to standard programming languages.

Topics here include those very programming methods (e.g. programming paradigms, case tools, database systems, spreadsheets), modularity, reuse.

Capabilities and limitations of computing

It goes without saying that all computing practitioners need a keen appreciation of the capabilities of the computing paradigm: they will be adding to those capabilities during the course of a career. In addition the 'whole person' practitioner should be at least aware of limitations of the paradigm, from both theoretical and pragmatic points of view.

Examples include breadth and scope of feasible applications (perhaps achieved through student research projects and reports), noncomputability (the halting problem), infeasibility (the travelling salesman problem). We make a note here that there is no need to know these last two examples very deeply; they are often presented to educated lay readers without appeals to such deeper concepts as Church's thesis or NP-completeness.

Social and ethical implications

While often acknowledged as important for the computing professional, there never seems to be sufficient time in a curriculum to tackle concepts in these areas.

Possibly through seminars, case studies, role-playing, field trips and guest speakers, formal attention must be given to such topics as privacy, intellectual property, professional issues, access equity, codes of ethics, social change.

Computer systems and architectures

Core knowledge includes awareness and demonstrated abilities concerning the diverse parts of a computer system such as hardware, systems software, networks, embedded systems, tools, comparison and evaluation. Also included are important computer applications such as spreadsheets, databases, world wide web.

Personal and interpersonal skills

It has been stated that the era of the solo asocial programmer has come to an end. Through a maturing of the field, as well as the awesome complexity of the problems to be solved, effective team work has become crucial in the construction of the resulting extremely complex systems.

So skills are needed in such areas as communication, team work, critical thinking, leadership, working with users, interdisciplinary environments, written specifications and documentation, dealing with ambiguity.

Broad perspectives

Some knowledge and understanding may not be directly relevant to the design of a computing system yet is still considered as core to informatics. This would be similar to an acknowledgement that a solid grounding in the liberal arts is core to any educated person. One should be aware that informatics has a very rich and lengthy history (far predating electronics and involving some of the giants of the world's intellectual heritage) and exceedingly deep philosophical implications.

Relevant topics for this awareness might include: history, philosophy, artificial intelligence and cognitive science, theoretical foundations (see also capabilities and limitations of computing above).

3 CONCLUSION

The listing of the preceding core topics, concepts, and experiences (not constituting specific courses in a curriculum) has been influenced by the personal knowledge and experiences of the focus group members, representing the various subfields of informatics. But this list is not simply the reflection of current practice that is common to all those subfields. Indeed, in places we advocate topics that may not be part of the current curriculum or knowledge base of one or more classes of informaticians.

Thus we assume that some of the preceding may be quite controversial. But controversy stimulates further deliberation and discussion, and is the enemy of complacency. As ours is still a young, growing, and rapidly changing field, we might all agree that lazy complacency is to be avoided at all costs.

4

A common core for noninformatics majors

Focus group
Monique Grandbastien (F; chair), Richard LeBlanc (USA; rapporteur), Hubert Christiaen (B), Charles Duchâteau (B), Peter Juliff (AUS), Hajime Ohiwa (J), Harriett Taylor (USA), Eric van Ammers (NL), Piet van der Kamp (NL) and Roland Vollmar (FRG)

Abstract

Virtually all students in modern higher education programs should be exposed to informatics, not only in its applications but also in its core concepts. In this focus group paper we propose an introductory informatics course with six important themes, covering the full breadth of the discipline. The course can be implemented in various ways, depending on the audience. In any case there should be 'construction experience' and problem solving activity. This can be achieved through the conventional programming approach, but equally through alternatives that are more attractive for noninformatics majors.

Keywords

Informatics, other disciplines, noninformatics majors, curriculum (core)

1 QUESTIONS FOR CONSIDERATION

The question regarding a common informatics core for noninformatics majors can be translated in the following practical questions:

- what is the conceptual core of informatics?
- should their be a separate course or approach for science and engineering majors?
- who should do the teaching and what training should students have?

Informatics in Higher Education F. Mulder & T. van Weerts (Eds.)

- when is the right time for an informatics course?
- what tools should be used for practical work?
- what can students be expected to know before they begin an introductory informatics course?

All questions in the list above depend on the first question: What is the conceptual core of informatics? Therefore we have concentrated on developing a proposed conceptual core for an introductory informatics course. We strongly advocate that this core knowledge should be learned by both nonmajors and majors in informatics, since these fundamental informatics concepts are relevant to virtually all students in the modern academic world.

Thus, we recommend that most (or all) higher education programs include an introductory course in informatics.

2 PROPOSED INTRODUCTORY INFORMATICS COURSE

The core of the introductory course, proposed in this focus group paper, is intentionally described in general terms in order to cope with the many contexts in which it could be implemented. Among the various constraints that may have to be faced in implementing such a course, are:

- the inability to rely on any prerequisites;
- the limited duration of the course;
- limitations on the quantity and nature of practical experiences that can be included.

The proposed core consists of the following themes:

- information processing as a formal process;
- functional model of a computer system;
- concepts of computer-based communication;
- problem specification, modelling, representation, limitations and validation;
- potentials and limitations, fundamental as well as practical, of computer-based technologies;
- the computing perspective.

Information processing as a formal process

Students should develop an understanding of how informatics deals with formal processing (by programs) of digitalized information (data). A program provides a formal set of rules for manipulating information. Though information in the real world may take many physical forms, it must be coded as discrete values in order to allow formal processing by a program.

Functional model of a computer system

A student should be able to describe a functional (conceptual) model of a computer system which embraces the following.

There is a hardware component, including:

- a processor which executes instructions as directed by the software;
- an internal memory which is transient and represents an area where data may reside temporarily to be processed by instructions (a program);
- an internal permanent storage medium (hard disk) for permanent storage of software and data;
- a screen, keyboard, and other devices for user interaction.

and there is a software component, including:

- system software, such as the operating system, which controls and coordinates all of the activities of the computer;
- application software, which carries out tasks specifically chosen by users.

Concepts of computer-based communication

Since computer-based communication has become a pervasive way of interaction, it is important that students understand the conceptual workings of such communication systems, including how information goes from an input device to a computer, from a computer to an output device, and from a computer to (potentially) many other computers through networks. Simple notions of coding and decoding and of the need for standards to make communication systems work should be included.

Problem specification, modelling, representation, limitations and validation

Students should achieve understanding of the fundamentals of problem specification and modelling. These include both the designation of some set of tangible and observable aspects of the real world together with their relationships in order to describe a problem (specification) and the recognition of the information needed to describe the mechanisms held responsible for these relationships (modelling). Finally, issues of model representation and the limitations on model fidelity that are a consequence of discrete modelling should be included, along with the need to validate the meaningfulness of models.

Potentials and limitations of computer-based technologies

Computer-based technologies are founded in principles that induce limits to their applicability. The concept of an algorithm (rules for formal processing) embodies the range of potential applications and also provides a basis to understand the limitations of the technology, as expressed in our knowledge about complexity and computability. Students should be familiar with these concepts and be able to relate them to applications in their own disciplines. They should also understand where limitations on the performance of computer systems are of a more practical nature, such as the lack of success so far in creating computer systems that can mimic human perceptual capabilities (vision, speech understanding) in any general way. The issue of correctness should also be introduced, as it relates to specification, modelling, algorithm design and implementation.

The computing perspective
The design of algorithms is a basic methodology not only for solving problems, but also for obtaining a basic scientific understanding of various phenomena, problems and processes. Recent attempts to develop information processing models of physical, chemical, biological, economic and social aspects of the world have shown such modelling to be an important new paradigm to attack problems that could not be handled adequately before.

Students should obtain experience with construction of algorithmic models so that they can understand and utilize this computing-inspired way of thinking about the world, just as previous generations shared a common understanding of mechanistic models.

3 CONSIDERATIONS FOR REALIZATION

Abstraction
The use of abstraction for complexity management is a pervasive technique in informatics. It is expected that students will be exposed to it and will apply abstraction repeatedly in the process of mastering the concepts described above.

Programming or not?
The most common form of introductory informatics course today is one in which students learn to program. A course that focuses primarily on students developing programming skills in a particular language will most likely succeed in transmitting major aspects of this core. However, it is by no means obvious that it will necessarily transmit the entire core. Conversely, we think it quite possible that a course based on this core might include no programming at all. We do believe though that such a course should include a 'construction experience', that is students should be required to get experience constructing formal problem solutions by doing one or more of: writing algorithms, creating spreadsheets, programming in visual languages, etc.

Implementations depending on the audience
As suggested by the previous point, we believe that courses based on this core can have a wide variety of implementations. The level of detail to which these concepts are developed and the methods used in the course might depend significantly on the audience (such as, informatics majors alone, informatics and other technical majors, engineering majors, nontechnical majors, business majors, or a mixed class). It is particularly important that the construction experience involves tools and problems appropriate for the composition of the class.

Attention for implications of various kind

There are numerous ways to include considerations of social, ethical and human-computer interaction issues related to information technology. For example, a discussion about why some applications are harder to use than others can call attention directly to interface design issues. That might lead to consideration of the implications of substitution of an automated system with a restricted interface (e.g. voice-mail) for a more flexible and responsive person (e.g. a receptionist). An introductory course should take good advantage of this opportunity to increase students' awareness of the relationship between these issues and technical concerns more naturally associated with an informatics course.

4 CONCLUSION

Informatics for all students and optional specializations

Fundamental informatics concepts are relevant to most (if not all) students in the modern academic world. Understanding of these concepts would provide a valuable foundation even for those students who will only be users of computer technology, particularly as modern applications provide increasing capabilities for user-level customization. Many students, however, will want to go beyond knowing only these fundamentals. Appropriate paths might include deeper development of modelling, design and programming skills in courses taught within an informatics department or development of discipline-specific informatics skills through courses in their own majors.

Informatics to be included in secondary school programs

There are many different situations regarding informatics courses in secondary schools. Because of the lack of consistency among these courses and their uneven availability to students, most introductory courses in higher education must begin from scratch. We recommend that secondary education moves rapidly toward inclusion of some informatics basics and experiences, based on our recommended core, on which higher education courses could rely.

Who should do the teaching?

Finally the question remains on who should teach the introductory informatics courses. For the introductory course as outlined above, instructors must clearly have informatics knowledge; specialized expertise in a particular noninformatics discipline is not enough. In addition, instructors must have sufficient conceptual background to help the students abstract the core concepts from particular examples.

PART TWO

Full Papers

5

Computing and education at the university level

Lillian N. Cassel
Department of Computing Sciences, Villanova University
800 Lancaster Avenue, Villanova, PA 19085-1699, USA
e-mail: cassel@vill.edu

National Science Foundation, Education and Human Resources
Division of Undergraduate Education, 4201 Wilson Boulevard
Arlington, Virginia 22230, USA, e-mail: lcassel@nsf.gov

Abstract

This paper places the modern university education system in a context derived from its full history. It examines where university education in general, and computing education in particular, are and where they are heading. By placing the current situation in historical context, we see the relevance of changes in society. And these changes create a need for determining what is appropriate for education. Education in computing faces the same need for change as all other disciplines. At the same time computing faces unique challenges which must be addressed. The paper proposes a model for university computing education to carry it into the new millennium.

Keywords

Informatics, other disciplines, university education, professional training, continuing education, curriculum (general), role of CIT, academic requirements, business and industry requirements, educational profiles

Informatics in Higher Education F. Mulder & T. van Weerts (Eds.)

1 WHERE WE COME FROM

When taking a look at the discipline of computing (computer science, informatics, computer engineering, information systems or sciences - whatever we call it) and its relation to other disciplines, let us first take a brief look at our common history. Let us ponder where we are going by considering where we have been (see in the references under 'History').

1.1 Higher education begins

Our university educational system is ancient, deriving from Greek traditions. Socrates used a method of dialogue, of questions and answers, to bring his students to an understanding of truth. The first school for higher education in the Western world was formed by Plato to continue the educational methods of his teacher, Socrates. Plato's Academy was established in Athens in 387 BC. The Academy was a state of mind for inquirers and their teachers, not a place of stone and wood. Teachers were masters in philosophy and mathematics; students and masters pursued greater understanding through discussion and debate.

Aristotle, one of the students of the Academy, created the basis for scientific enquiry, which is still used today. His interest in science expanded the scope of higher education. Aristotle's Lyceum, established in Athens in 335 BC, was dedicated to the pursuit of science and the preparation of students to continue scientific inquiry. The Socratic method of questions and answers continued as the means to learning.

1.2 The liberal arts

By the end of the Greek period, the basic division of subject matter in advanced education corresponded to the seven topics that would later be called the liberal arts. These are the 'practical skills' of Grammar, Rhetoric, and Dialectic which provided the ability to speak, to persuade and to interpret the ideas of others; and the more theoretical pursuits of Arithmetic, Music, Geometry, and Astronomy. Conflict between the practical and the theoretical is not new; we just change our ideas about what falls into each of those categories.

The Muslim capture of Alexandria marked the end of the Greek supremacy in learning and in Western culture. When the Muslims also learned, from a Chinese prisoner, how to make paper, there was a momentous opportunity for the advancement of learning. The great library at Alexandria provided content; paper provided a powerful dissemination mechanism. The Arabs established learning centres throughout their empire. Learning became accessible to more people and was decentralized. Subjects taught under Arab rule included algebra, trigonometry, geometry, physics, chemistry, astronomy, medicine, logic, ethics, metaphysics, grammar, prosody (study of poetic structures), law, jurisprudence and theology. The Arabs assimilated knowledge from all the cultures with which they had contact and disseminated it through their empire. . The improved distribution technology and access to knowledge by more people led inevitably to a significant change in education as it was practised at that time.

As the Arabs were pushed out of Europe, scholarship focused on the task of translating, organizing, copying and sorting the accumulated materials. Scholars were burdened with an early version of information overload. Without organization and methods to access what was needed, the accumulated knowledge of the ages would have had limited value. From study of the earlier works of Plato the liberal arts re-emerged as the meaning of advanced learning. The practical verbal skills, the 'trivium', were recognized as important for practitioners of law, business and politics. The less practical skills, the 'quadrivium' were all related to mathematics. The utilitarian pursuits of medicine and architecture were too specific and practical for the kind of general, broad preparation represented by the Liberal Arts. Such specific training for a limited career path was not the goal of liberal arts education. At that time most higher education took place in Cathedral schools.

1.3 The first universities

The first universities began to appear soon after the turn of the first millennium. The universities were small, independent communities of scholars attached to a host town. The world's universities were a kind of global community. A degree study begun at one university would often be finished at a different one. This implies, of course, a common understanding of or a good bit of flexibility in what is meant by degree requirements. Students had much more power in these early universities than they do now. Students found a master from whom they wished to study. The number of students a master could attract directly determined the income the master received. The student could move at will to another master to study a different subject or just to improve the learning opportunity.

In Medieval times research was not a significant activity in universities. People were fully engaged in understanding, translating and discussing the knowledge they had received from the Ancient Greeks, the Arabs, Asia and from Christian Theology. There was not a general feeling of there being more to learn. Full command of this body of knowledge was considered a sufficiently challenging intellectual activity.

The European Renaissance of the 15th and 16th centuries was a time of rebirth of intellectual life. There was prosperity, which allowed more leisure for study and contemplation; it was a time of discovery of new lands, which challenged beliefs about the world and generated new questions as well. The fall of Constantinople sent manuscripts into Europe, opening new opportunities to investigate classical philosophy and learning. Despite vehement opposition, the humanities entered the university curriculum. And there was also the printing press making the distribution of knowledge easier than ever before.

The international mobility of scholars faded in the Renaissance, as strong nationalistic identities were forged in Europe. Perhaps the ready access to information in books made travel less important. Perhaps nationalism, competition in exploration and conquest made people associate closely with one location and stay there. As mobility of scholars faded, so did the sense of a global community of scholars.

By the 18th century the Enlightenment and the Industrial Revolution spawned the interest and need for science as a topic of study. As the Industrial Revolution brought factories and assembly lines, study also became closely regimented. Preparation for work in the industrialized world called for homogeneity, ability to fit into the mould and work in a complex system that allowed little room for individuality. In industrialized societies education was another system to produce a product: a worker who fits into a well-defined role, who has well-understood responsibilities and needs very specific skills. In a society dominated by the factory as a production model, students might be viewed as raw material to be processed into a desired end product. As in a factory, each student goes through an identical process with an inspection occurring periodically throughout the production process. Products that do not pass inspection are discarded or recycled. Products that pass inspection pass on to the customer who knows exactly what to expect from the product.

In every age many factors determine what constitutes an educated person: the perception of the range of subjects suitable for study changes according to the needs of the society for educated people and the availability of materials determines where scholars congregate and how many centres of learning exist. History shows that the introduction of new subjects occurs more quickly in society, business, industry and government than in the universities.

2 WHERE ARE WE NOW?

After nearly a thousand years the university system needs to change. In some ways change may take us back to some of the characteristics of early universities. Global communities of scholars are again the norm, but without the need for physical mobility. Once again education needs to look at the needs of society. For what types of work do we prepare our students? The Information Age demands knowledge workers who are able to learn, able to apply their knowledge in new situations, able to work with others and to use the best abilities of each person in addressing complex problems. Once again the needs of society combine with a radical new way to distribute knowledge. This makes us rethink what is education at the university level. How do we define an educated person in these times?

We, who are scholars in the subject of computing in its broadest sense, are faced with many questions. Some of these we share with our colleagues in other disciplines. Some of them are specific to our discipline. Like the humanities and the sciences before us, our subject is not readily accepted as a vital component of an educated person. We suffer from the attitude of people who think they know all about computing because they can use word processors and spreadsheets, and can surf the Web happily for hours. Often our subject is considered trivial as a result of the success of those of our colleagues who work diligently to make common tools easy to use.

2.1 Computing and information in the core of education

What does our discipline offer to the common core curriculum of an educated person? How much do people need to know about computing to participate fully in the Information Age? What do we add to the intellectual content of a university education? The new age, the Information Age, requires individuals who can acquire information (relatively easy), judge the value of the information (harder) and convert the information into knowledge to apply in a variety of situations (there's the rub).

Our concern with the changes affecting education is twofold. Like in other disciplines we need to redefine what we mean by 'educated'; we must consider what we offer in the core curriculum. Equally important, however, is the impact of the products of our field on the very nature of the university. We have created the Information Age and we, like all university subjects, must re-examine the way we define education and the way we and our students approach learning. It is no longer desirable to have people work in lockstep, to discard those that do not come successfully through the production process.

Not only is there need for a different product, there is need for a very different way of producing a product. In fact 'product' is a very wrong word, for our educated person is never complete. Information resources increase at a great rate and opportunities to use information profitably and beneficially will continue to develop. Education must be a continuing affair, never ending. In this context, what does a degree mean? What do we certify? What possible meaning is attached to grading? Of what significance is the fact that a student was able to retain a set of definitions or other facts long enough to pass an exam? How do we describe what that student can do? How do we determine that the student is ready to move into a different phase of life, where work and family and education are intermixed in some proper proportion? Once our students have graduated to that new time of life, how do we help them continue to learn? What is our role in their ongoing education? We cannot expect people to stop work to take years of study to prepare for a new field or a new direction in an old field. Even the concept of a course, as we know it, may be unreasonable. Yet, updating and even changing our speciality must occur throughout life. We need education to be available to learners when and where they are ready to learn. How will we integrate that into our notion of a university?

2.2 What should a university be now?

What is a university as the new millennium approaches? What are the role of research and the place of education? All of us are learners. Faculty learning is called scholarship and research. It is a large part of the business of professors. Students are learners also. They are not as advanced in their learning as their faculty, but they are on the same path. The methods that faculty members use to learn need to be taught to their students. Teaching these methods is the major responsibility of faculty to their students. Students should be engaged in research suited to their level, so that they can develop the skills and habit of learning.

Sitting through a class does not constitute learning. How do we know when learning has occurred? We know it by the evidence of accomplishment. Some things are easy to measure. If the learning involves a skill, we can test the skill. If the learning involves the ability to address a class of problems by invoking appropriate tools and applying suitable knowledge to develop a reasonable solution, then testing means posing suitable problems. Our students need to know some facts, of course. But facts separated from the context in which those facts are meaningful are not going to lead to learning and understanding. We need to introduce facts when they are meaningful. We need to develop a set of problems that establish the need for the facts. We need to teach our students to recognize what they need and how to obtain the relevant information.

2.3 Are professors on the path to extinction?

Some people say that the job of the professor is in jeopardy; that we will have all our courses on the World Wide Web and there will be nothing left for us to do. These people have not developed Web-based courses, tried to use them in effective instruction, tried to keep them current, tried to do all that while dealing with the questions students generate. The job of the professor may not be in jeopardy, but university teaching staff faces a number of challenges in the near future:

- redefinition of success for students;
- integration of effective tools into the teaching process where the technology enhances the education of students;
- reaching students in time and place when the learners cannot be in the same location as the professor;
- maintaining currency in rapidly changing disciplines;
- locating and evaluating relevant information in the vast amount of material now readily available.

What is the significance of the Web and Web-based courses with respect to the role of the professor? Is teaching staff still important in the process of learning? It has been possible for a motivated learner to study without taking formal courses. Multimedia based courses may have more to offer than the standard textbook, but I maintain that for effective learning something more is needed. Call it a class, call it a community: most people benefit from being part of a group of learners. They need someone to turn to for discussion and confirmation of their own progress. They need guidance on what to do next and how to put the pieces together.

Interaction between faculty members and students, and among students themselves will certainly change over time, but it will not go away.

Lectures will likely become very unusual, rather than standard practice. Faculty members will spend more time as guides in learning and as developers of learning modules, than they will spend in preparing and delivering lectures. They will design courses from materials developed only in part by themselves and mostly developed by others. But each course will continue to reflect the experience and the preferences of the faculty member who charts a path through mountains of interesting, relevant material. Many alternative paths will be charted to fit the needs of students with different goals.

3 CHALLENGES TO HIGHER EDUCATION

Let us consider some of the challenges put to university faculty in this time of change for universities and in the nature of higher education.

3.1 Evaluating learning

Peter Denning (1997) speaks of the new kind of teacher as a 'course manager and a coach rather than an information transmitter'. He speaks of the distinction between 'knowing how' and 'knowing about' expecting a much greater emphasis on certification of competence in specific areas of expertise. While the term certification is unpopular with many faculty members, the idea of students gaining proficiency, which is the ability to demonstrate that they are capable of doing something as a result of their education, has merit. If we consider the task of faculty members as guiding students toward a type of understanding that includes the ability to apply what they have studied in a variety of relevant situations, we are not talking about training in the use of tools. We are talking about what an educated person should be. If a course of study is designed to bring students to a level of competence on which they are capable of applying specific knowledge and are capable of continuing to advance in their understanding of that specific area, then courses are naturally going to change.

Evaluation of student performance is an area ripe for change. If our goal is to bring all our students to a level of proficiency, why are we talking about grade inflation? Why is it taken for granted that some students will fail and that, if there are not enough failures, then our standards are too low? I do not mean to imply that grade inflation does not happen. However, we need to redefine our goals and the way we measure our accomplishments so that appropriate levels of achievement for every student are the surest sign of success in any educational enterprise.

What would happen if we banish the bell curve from our idea of learner evaluation? Is it really meaningful to compare the best performer in a poor course to a mediocre performer in a very challenging course? Suppose that instead we expect some students to take longer or to put in more effort to achieve a goal, and that the goals of different individuals will vary. To use the terms in Bloom's taxonomy of the cognitive domain: some students may be satisfied with knowledge, others will strive for comprehension, application, analysis, synthesis or evaluation (see 'Bloom'). Suppose that accomplishment in a course of study means to first set learning goals and then to document the level of achievement acquired in each of the course goals? Suppose that, instead of success or failure, we report the level of achievement of each student in each of the goals of the course.

3.2 Use of technology and tools

At this time, we have two strong pressures for change in education. There is:

- a need for students to prepare for a different type of work environment than was the norm in the past;
- available technology to completely revise the way we conduct learning activities.

With the need for change and the tools for change in place, faculty members are expected to use the tools wisely to bring about the needed changes.

Of course there is limited connection between the technology and the need for change; the relation between the two is that technology brought about changes in the work environment which led to demands for change in education. By some logic this might imply that the same technology should be applied to bring about the changes in education. The problem with this association of ideas is that the technology may be applied in education because it is available and good for some things, and therefore presumed good for education. As we move the professor off the podium and look to technology to provide much of the information content for our courses, we must take the time and effort to evaluate what works well and what does not work well. We need to analyse what we expect of our students and use research findings on learning to tell us what supports student learning and what hinders it. We must set recognizable goals and test ourselves to be sure that we are achieving those goals.

There is an important distinction between teaching about technology and teaching with technology. We must carefully consider what our discipline has to offer to the formation of an educated person in these times. At the same time we must look at what computing, communication and information technologies can contribute to the learning environment of our own students.

In what way might technology help in learning?

Many examples exist of how technology may help in learning and more are emerging. The vast information resources of the World Wide Web provide easy access to more information and more expertise on any number of subjects than will ever be found in a single library. The volume of information is expanding rapidly. There are problems, of course. Much of the information on the Web is useless or worse. There are difficulties in finding the best available information, because the

Web needs many more tools to support searching and retrieving relevant information. Web resources that are available on one day may be inaccessible on another. The challenges are substantial, but the value of this information source is undeniable.

Technology can assist group work. Teams can work together on a joint project, learning to cooperate as well as to solve a problem. Technology supports merging work, maintaining traces of work done, scheduling and planning. Technology allows an absent member of a team to follow the work of the group through e-mail, discussion groups and dynamic Web pages. Teams may be formed from students and faculty members at a number of institutions spread around the world. The group dynamics may be challenging, but the opportunities to explore collaboration at that level are there to be used.

Technology supports experimentation. In computing, appropriate experiments might allow students to test the running time of different classes of algorithms, clearly seeing that the Big-O notation has significance. Other experiments could stress potential solutions to problems, such as network configurations, division of work over parallel processors, capability of expert systems and others.

In what way might technology help in management of learning?
Perhaps technology can also be employed to make significant changes in the way we manage classes. If keeping track of individual progress of students taking different paths through course material is too burdensome, technology may be used to keep the records and monitor progress.

Perhaps more interestingly, technology can allow groups of students to have access to experts in a topic area beyond the faculty of their own institution. Students in one institution could work with students in a different type of institution to share their knowledge and learn from each other's experiences and insights.

Technology, and particularly the World Wide Web, may well redefine the notion of a textbook. Instead of a fixed ordering of a specific set of topics, a textbook could be constructed by a faculty member from modules generated by a number of different authors. The order, scope and depth of the material could easily be tailored to the specific goals of a group of students and their teachers.

Perhaps for some students it is appropriate to return the responsibility for student learning to the students themselves. A student could put together a set of resources, seek guidance from faculty in many locations and present a portfolio of accomplishments as evidence of achievement. Perhaps faculty members will once again be rewarded based on the number of students they attract?

3.3 Asynchronous and distance learning

Currently, student study is organised into courses and there is usually one faculty member or a group of faculty members who teach the course. However, there are many reasons to consider the idea of students studying at a distance and asynchronous to any class schedule. The need for updating knowledge or learning about a new field is common for today's workers. It will become more important as knowledge workers struggle to maintain currency and keep up with changes in career needs. Already census figures show that the average age of university students is increasing; one in every four US college students was at least 30 years old in 1993 according to US census figures (see 'Chronicle').

Most workers will not be able to leave the job for a prolonged period of time to pursue further education. In many cases, even taking a course is difficult. Many people travel in their work and must miss classes; others are immersed in projects that demand their full attention, or must share in family responsibilities that make class attendance and study difficult for prolonged periods of time. Many people must maintain their current work schedule while achieving the education needed to move into a different field of work. Does the university have a place in this education? Can technology help? Progress has been made in accommodating students at a distance. A number of universities have incorporated distance education into the mainstream of their education activities. Conferences are held and a Web-site serves as clearinghouse for relevant materials in issues involved in distance learning (see 'Distance Education Clearinghouse').

The problems related to asynchronous learning are not as well understood. Most courses have a specific beginning and ending time and a set of expectations, which must be met in that time. Building flexibility into a schedule so that people who work in jobs with cyclic schedules of busy and light times, or people who must face unpredictable schedule changes, can meet course requirements is difficult. Technology will not be enough to solve this type of problem. It is something that requires determination to accommodate variations in lifestyle and available time. It will require a plan that recognizes that some people require pressure to get to the end of a task, and some have a tendency to go on and on without feeling satisfied with their accomplishments. Technology can provide the course material at any time and place the student needs it, and can track progress of the student through the material. Technology can allow the student to interact with others at the same stage in the course, wherever they may be located, and can provide access to a faculty guide at any time. The harder problems have to do with acknowledging the human tendencies that make such learning difficult and with finding solutions that work for as many people as possible.

3.4 Maintaining currency

If knowledge workers in general will be hard pressed to stay current, the challenge will be just as real for the teaching staff. Putting course materials on the Web or embedding them in CD ROMs or other media will not address all course development needs. Materials must be reviewed and revised regularly. Materials displayed on the Web are very visible, and will make potential students well aware of the care with which a course is maintained.

Web and other hypermedia offer an opportunity for faculty to use their time and energy in pursuing better ways to present lessons, in developing new learning experiences and in incorporating new thoughts and recent developments into their course presentations. Because hyper media allow modification of individual modules without disturbing other sections and allow changes in the links that shape the overall structure of the course, the evolution of a course structure and content presents virtually unlimited possibilities.

Students who study with a faculty member will contribute to the structure and content of the course also. They will discover resources; they will add their opinions and observations, experimental results, even their project presentations. Their legacy will be part of the course materials that future students will see. The professor will guide students through the wealth of material associated with the course, providing navigational assistance and some structure where needed.

With all this material on the Web, does the professor serve a useful purpose? I believe the role of the professor will change, but will become more critical to student success. The professor will lecture only rarely. Students will get specific content from presentations available from the Web or other media. They will learn from interaction with the professor and with other students and with individuals in many locations who have expertise in the subject matter. The professor will be responsible for managing the student progress, making sure that the paths taken are directed toward a predetermined goal. The professor will be the producer and maintainer of the course materials. That does not mean that every professor will be an expert in multimedia development or a writer of source material on every subject taught. It does mean that the professor will monitor the content of courses, will review the relevance of the modules and judge them for currency and continuing relevance in the context of changing needs. The professor will select materials that present ideas well and which assist students in their learning. The professor will also assign tasks that guide the student learning experience and evaluate progress relative to the course goals.

Many teachers will develop excellent materials for presenting specific concepts. They will create laboratory exercises, experiments and experiences of every sort to support learning. They will incorporate the latest research into their materials so that the student experience is related to the newest results in the discipline. What will happen to those outstanding materials? Will only the students who study with that professor see them? This makes no more sense than having a textbook only used by the students of the expert who produced the book. Once these materials are developed, they will be available for use by other faculty members teaching the same material. The mechanism for this sharing might parallel the publication and sale of textbooks or licensed software.

The problem of maintaining currency is acute in our discipline, of course. We are young; the field is growing rapidly. We are closely related to the technology that changes so fast that new products are obsolete almost before they are on the market. We tend to think that we have a special problem in keeping up. Other fields are subject to change as well. All the sciences have been changed by significant discoveries in recent years, which have put new perspectives on some old ideas and have shown others to be clearly wrong. In fields such as the humanities, there are new interpretations of old works and new forms of expression (often made possible by our technology) to explore. All forms of knowledge are evolving. All education requires constant effort to keep current with new developments, to help our students to explore what is new and learn from the past, and to be prepared to deal with what will come. If our course materials are going to become multimedia Web-based presentations, there is a great deal of work to do to develop them, keep them up to date and keep them evolving, both to stay current in the discipline and to make the best use of the new technology.

4 PROPOSAL FOR A NEW MODEL OF FACULTY TEACHING

Consider a new model of university teaching. Suppose that a faculty member who has a wonderful way to present a topic, spends the time and effort to encode that presentation, puts it onto the Web or some other medium and posts notice of its availability. Others learn of it and want to use it. They license the use of the material. A course might consist of modules created by several people merged by a professor with a creative view of how the material should be combined and presented to students. Just as a person counts the number of times a publication is cited to see how the research community values his or her work, teaching faculty members will count the number of others who integrate his or her modules into their courses. Let us reward faculty members who make it their primary task to make advances in the way students learn. Let us judge the person who produces first-class learning modules which are cited by other faculty members as worthy as the person who publishes an advance in knowledge in the field.

We have heard the cute phrases: 'Guide on the Side to replace the Sage on the Stage'. Let us go back to the primary purpose of the university: a place where scholars search for truth. Let us have the courage to tell our students that we are all students, all seeking. That we learn from them as we help them learn. Scholarship is the business of every faculty member. Some faculty members spend most of their time in research, in solving problems in the discipline. Others focus on bringing knowledge of the field to learners. Both must be growing in knowledge and understanding in their discipline. These two paths are both important parts of the university. These are different, but connected. The teacher must be aware of the changes in the discipline. The teacher will learn and advance in the field as a consequence of the teaching activity. The teacher's learning and discoveries will be reflected in the learning materials developed for use by students and other teachers. The person who focuses primarily on research must also contribute to the teaching enterprise, but perhaps in a different way. Instead of the burden of papers to grade and even course work to prepare, the researcher serves as a content specialist, a resource to whom the students and teaching faculty may turn when their questions call for this level of expertise. The students will also conduct experiments, participating in some way in the research activity of the department. There must be close interaction between the teaching and the research arms.

In this model, everyone is a learner: a seeker after truth in the Socratic model. The role of the researcher is to pursue the discoveries that advance knowledge in ways that will not happen in private industry. The role of the teacher is to disseminate that knowledge to others. Often those others will be the ones to put those advances to work in business, industry, government and society. Neither role is valuable without the other. People must overlap, having some part in each responsibility, but focusing on what they most enjoy and on what they are best suited for.

5 CONCLUSION

The modern university system began at the turn of the first millennium. As the second millennium approaches, we have all the factors in place for major changes in higher education. We should expect:

- a return of a global community of scholars, including students as well as faculty members, both teachers and researchers;
- a system of evaluation of our students which describes their level of achievement and does not aim for failure for anyone;
- learning as a never-ending part of life and work;
- faculty work less oriented toward lectures and exercises, and more directed towards the development and evolution of effective learning materials;
- improving tools which will facilitate student learning and also will challenge faculty members to appropriate use;
- learning which is not constrained by semester schedules and classroom locations;
- evaluation that demonstrates capability which will stay with the student beyond the test time.

For the discipline of computing there is the potential of a special position in the description of an educated person. Just as the core of the Liberal Arts focuses on the essential skills of communication: the ability to speak, to persuade and to interpret the words of others, an educated person should be able to discover, validate and apply relevant information for the task at hand. What we provide is central to the core of an education.

Web-based materials represent a monumental advance in the distribution of knowledge, an advance as profound as the invention of paper and of the printing press. But, having the distribution vehicle does not mean an end to a problem; it means a new challenge. Talented educators will need to revise their methods of guiding students toward learning. They will be challenged to produce suitable experiences to support learning, to generate the need for the facts in reasonable doses, to make the connections and to generate the excitement of learning that makes the student keep going.

A current advertisement shows a grandfather and a child on a bicycle with training wheels. The learner has been practising. Now the training wheels come off. The grandfather holds the back of the bike to steady it. Just at the right time the grandfather takes away his hand. The bike rider goes off on his own, shaky at first, but full of the joy of the new ability. This is our position with our students: to guide them with training wheels when they need them, to recognize when they are ready to go off on their own, to give them the balance and the push to get started, and to see them off on a lifetime of adventure made possible by the start we gave them.

6 REFERENCES

Bloom
http://weber.u.washington.edu/~krumme/guides/bloom.html, or *http://www.fwl.org/edtech/blooms.html.*

Chronicle, The Chronicle of Higher Education Academe Today Fact Files, September 1, 1995
http://www.chronicle.com/che-data/infobank.dir/factfile.dir/students.dir/5kid.html.

Denning, P. (1997) How we will learn, in *Beyond Calculation. The Next Fifty Years of Computing* (ed. P. Denning and R.M. Metcalfe). Copernicus, Springer-Verlag, New York.

Distance Education Clearinghouse
http://www.uwex.edu/disted/home.html.

History, The History of the Ideas of a University
http://quarles.unbc.edu/ideas/gen/history/history.html.

7 BIOGRAPHY

Lillian N. (Boots) Cassel is professor of computing sciences at Villanova University, USA. Her doctoral thesis is from the University of Delaware and her special interest within the computing sciences is information access in networked systems. She is currently on leave from Villanova to spend two years at the National Science Foundation in Washington as program director in the Division of Undergraduate Education. Dr. Cassel served as chair of the ACM Special Interest Group (SIG) in Computer Science Education in 1993-1997 and is a member of the SIG-Board. She is on the Technical Editorial Committee of IEEE Network magazine.

Teaching informatics to nonprofessionals: why, what and how?

Charles Duchâteau
CeFIS, Facultés Universitaires Notre-Dame de la Paix
Rue de Bruxelles, 61, B-5000 Namur, Belgium
e-mail: charles.duchateau@fundp.ac.be

Abstract

Informatics is now fifty years old. Initially, only professionals used computers and it was quite easy to determine what the profile of these professionals was and, by consequence, to train them. Ten years ago a new reality appeared: nonprofessional users and thousands of software tools. As a consequence computer use is now appearing as a new field with its own mental representations, procedures and concepts. Several terms have been suggested to name this new domain: 'informatics technology', 'information technology', etc. There are links between this new field and informatics, but there are also many differences. In short: what must a user know about informatics systems, what concepts and principles make up the new discipline of 'informatics for users'?

Keywords

Informatics, university education, noninformatics majors, curriculum (core), role of CIT

1 INTRODUCTION

Let us first try to answer the question: 'why teach informatics to students in universities, who will be only users?'. Maybe we do not have to teach anything. Maybe, using a computer is only a matter of basic skills. In this paper the reasons for teaching 'something about informatics for users' will be compared with the traditional reasons put forward for teaching mathematics or physics to students whose primary interests are for example biology or pharmacy. For this comparison

Informatics in Higher Education F. Mulder & T. van Weerts (Eds.)

we in any case have to find and highlight the basic principles and concepts of 'informatics for users'. What are the unchanging features which characterize the vast field of computers use? What is the basic knowledge required for efficient and creative uses of different software tools? What are the real mental models allowing users to adapt to new tools and environments?

The second section of the paper will try to pick up some of these fundamentals. For example:

- data processing by a computer is always a formal process (in the word 'informatics' we should read 'form' and not 'information');
- computers do not process information, but work with a representation in numeric code of this information;
- the only thing the user is faced with is the pair: computer plus software.

The third section will present some ideas for teaching these basic principles.

- Basic principles from which users can infer and explain the behaviour of 'informatics systems' which very often are expressed by short sentences or slogans like 'the computer does not exist', 'do not speak about "information", only about "form"', 'to program is to have it done by...', 'informatics is not computer science'.
- Simple questions like 'from where do in fact the programs come which make my computer work?', 'what does the computer send to the printer?', and 'under what conditions can information be processed by a computer?'.
- Main threads which allow us to present various features in a coherent and consistent way (like the definition of a computer).
- Deductive reasoning which leads to important conclusions.

In conclusion the paper will show that these issues are brand new and that, as teachers, we will gain by an exchange of our experiences, trials and questions.

2 A TEACHER HAS TO TEACH!

One may ask: 'Why all these questions?'. Because a teacher has to teach! Whatever the answers to the questions mentioned above, whatever my opinion about the necessity of teaching the basics of computer science in some university study, I still have to teach every week first year students in biology, geography or pharmacy. My task is 'to talk about computer science without including any programming practice'. As a consequence in my teaching I have had to answer all these questions concerning teaching of 'informatics for end-users' to people who would not become computer scientists. At the moment I am in charge of a thirty hour course (two hours a week, for three months) complemented with fifteen hours of laboratory work supervised by a colleague. The students are in their second year of biology, geography or geology. I also teach a fifteen hour course (without laboratory work) to first year students in pharmacy. Both groups consist of more than one hundred students. The conditions are typical of first year classes: I am not able to control the environment and the schedule in which the students will be brought into contact with computer science or at least in contact with computerized environments. I can only teach in a very classical way, with students sitting in a lecture hall for 55 minutes of informatics, after 55 minutes of physics and before 55 minutes of botany. A teaching assistant is in charge of exercise sessions: groups of twenty students spend two hours in a computer room (two students per computer) and discover the basic skills of word processing and spreadsheets.

3 ARGUMENTS FOR INCLUDING 'INFORMATICS' IN FIRST YEAR

Only fifteen years ago informatics was still excluded from the first year university curriculum, but today the situation is quite different. Above and beyond local circumstances and priorities reasons have been and are still put forward by academic authorities to include informatics in the curriculum. These reasons have changed with time. Not all of them have the same importance and not always the same persons have put them forward.

The 'electron microscope' argument

Firstly, informatics courses are motivated by computer use. This reason is similar to requiring physics classes for learning how to use a microscope efficiently. The argument goes: users must know the laws and principles underlying the functioning of an electron microscope in order to be able to understand how it works. As a matter of fact, physics programs generally contain an 'alibi chapter': 'Principles of the functioning of the electron microscope'. This argument is important and is worth some discussion. It is embarrassing when we have to talk - just like with microscopes - about 'the principles underlying the functioning of a computer'. According to the level of description principles of this functioning come under physics, electronics, algebra, algorithmics, etc. Or under what we find in most of the books about internal architecture (processor, memory, etc.) or global architecture (central processing unit, mass memory, etc.). These material descriptions are insufficient for the users to understand how their favourite word processing software works. As a consequence they lack coherent and efficient understanding.

A description which only deals with the computer itself cannot be satisfactory because the computer does not exist on its own (see also below). What the user is faced with is a duo 'computer plus software' where software takes very different forms: The computerized system used by a musician is completely different from the one used by an architect or a secretary.

However, the electron microscope argument is a very important one: it offers us the opportunity to state general principles which explain and underlie any use of an informatics system (computer plus software). If we are not able to discuss these principles, then 'informatics for users' could be a myth.

The 'it is essential for future classes' argument

This is also a traditional argument to justify first year programs. They have to study mathematics because of the physics classes et physics in order to understand some parts of the chemistry classes, and chemistry because they will have biochemistry the following year.

The reason justifying my informatics class to biology students is that they will have a class about a statistical package after the first year. The mathematics class might well be more elaborate than needed to understand the physics class, and the physics class more elaborate than needed to understand the chemistry class.

The 'it is necessary in professional life' argument

Tomorrow, my first year students in pharmacy will have to work with computers in their dispensaries, so we have to train them in the use of computers and learn them to deal with hardware and software providers. However, computer scientists using the computing systems of today have not received the corresponding training during their studies. And the long period of time till the training can be used in the professional life speaks for a training stressing principles and unchanging features, focusing on analysis rather than on description.

The 'today it is part of basic academic culture' argument

This is a common argument for university first year. Computer science now has its own place in the university; other departments recognize this new field and give it some room in their curriculum.

The 'it is formative' argument

This argument is similar to the one which ascribes a formative character to the learning of mathematics or physics. It is often used in a defensive way: 'Even if it does not sound useful to you, it is formative'. This argument has been used in the case of a course focusing on programming, not for its direct or future usefulness (few biologists or pharmacists will have to program), but for its formative side. I have earlier discussed this (Duchâteau, 1990), as other researchers have done before me (Arsac, 1980). It is a valid argument, even if formative and transferable effects can only be noticed after long (Romainville, 1989). This argument, however, becomes shaky and irrelevant if you leave out the algorithmic part in the informatics course for users.

The 'informatics deals with old issues' argument

As I am going to try to show, informatics, when taught in an appropriate way, allows treatment of central issues in other disciplines in a simple and operational way. 'Information' and 'knowledge', or 'form' and 'meaning' are for example at the heart of linguistics, even if the terms 'signifier' and 'signified' are more common. Semiology is also a concern of computer science, just as 'artificial intelligence' raises philosophical questions. This seems to me to be the main reason for teaching informatics: it deals with problems as old as and suggests specific answers: what is 'meaning', 'intelligence' or 'conscience' (Hofstadter and Dennet, 1987)? What is 'to give a name' (Arsac, 1987)? what is a 'sign'?

Does this justify a place for informatics in university curricula? The answer probably depends highly on what we mean by 'informatics' in this context. I will discuss this in the second part of my paper.

4 NEW DEMANDS FROM OTHER DISCIPLINES

Since informatics classes were started in 1983, two major changes can be noticed.

- Initially, the informatics course for biology, geography and geology students was optional at the end of the fourth year (last year of the program). The course was moved forward to the second year and has become compulsory.
- Initially it was essentially devoted to algorithmics (Duchâteau, 1990). Later on, I was asked to choose more useful contents, dealing with end-users needs. Which in one word means to pass from 'informatics for computer scientists' to 'informatics for users'.

This change is revealing. The key factor in this change is the appearance of the end-user concept linked to software developments in the middle of the eighties. From then on the computer is in a position of secondary importance; software tools now have primary importance. See for a discussion of development stages Van Weert and Tinsley (1994).

Advocated as main characteristics of the use of software tools were: simplicity, efficiency, easiness of use, user friendliness. But these claims were false. The main difficulty was not to find the on-off switch, it was not 'easier than driving a car'. You have to know some essential principles to deal with the multiplicity of software and computerized environments. So we have to find and teach these basic principles in 'informatics for users'.

5 METHODOLOGY

In a course the organization of contents and the methodology used are essential. The 'informatics for users' course is structured around the following.

- Important explanatory principles from which consequences which end-users notice can be easily inferred. Frequently, these principles take the form of slogans or brief assertions:
  - > do not talk about 'informatics' but about 'in**form**atics!';
  - > the computer does not exist;
  - > for **everything** it does the computer needs a program!

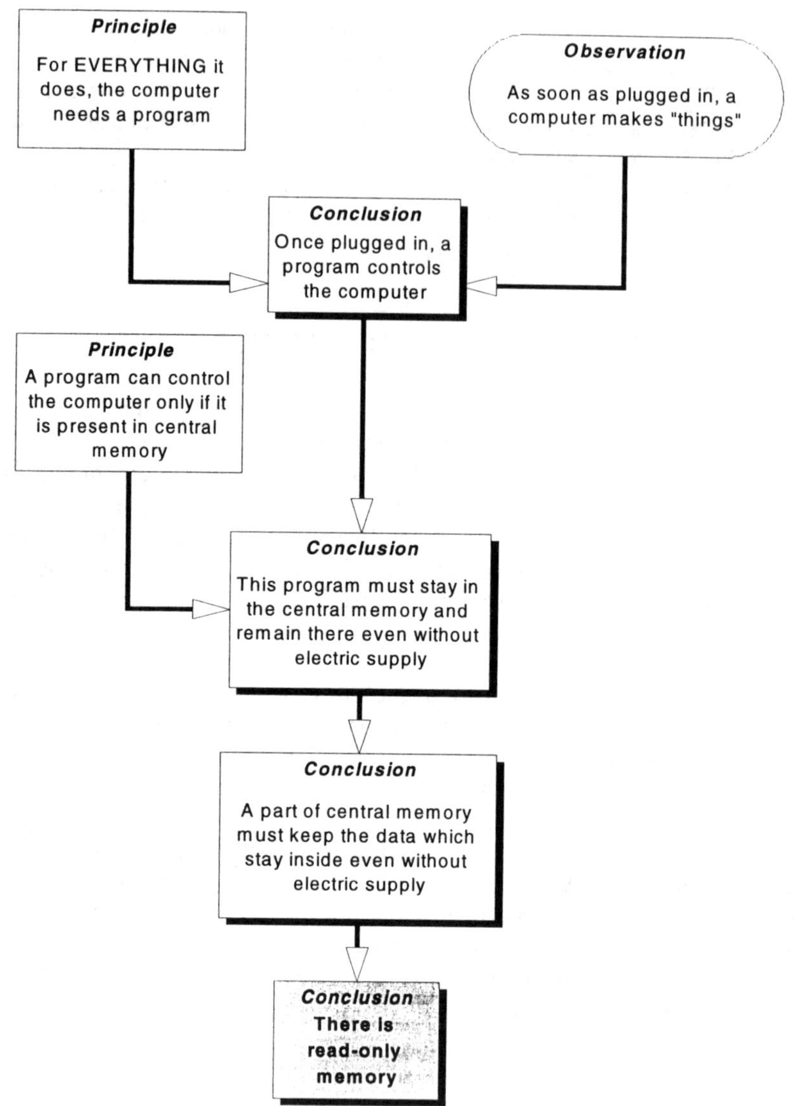

Figure 1 Example of a deductive thought process.

> to **program** is only 'to have it done by';
> if informatics is the science of computers, then meteorology is the science of thermometers.

- Easily understood questions which lead to important facts. For example:
  > where do the programs which are loaded into central memory and which run the computer come from, really?

> what information, whatever its form, needs to be processed by a computer?
> what does the computer send to the printer?

- Main themes which will allow a coherent presentation of the main aspects. For instance, the definition of a computer: 'machine, to process information, in a formalist (formal) way, as long as it is told how to do it'. Or the evolution of programming languages from three different points of view: how is data to be processed specified, what are the basic actions and how are these specified and how are these scheduled?
- Deductive thought processes which starting from stated principles will lead to interesting conclusions to posed questions (see Figure 1).

6 CONTENTS

An incomplete definition of the computer is the skeleton of the first parts of the course: 'machine, to process information, in a formalist (formal) way, as long as it is told how to do it'. The different parts of this definition are scheduled in the way described below

'to process information'
(see Figure 2)
'in a formal way'
(see Figure 3)

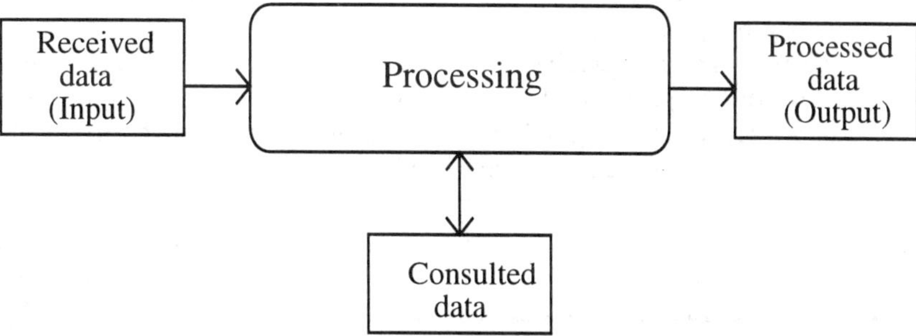

Figure 2 Information processing.

	Formal or easily formalised process	Hardly formalised process / non formalisable process (Meaning, signification, ...)
Processing dealing with numbers		
Processing dealing with language		
Other		

Figure 3 Classification of information processing.

An operational criterion is put forward in order to classify information processing on a continuum (see Figure 4).

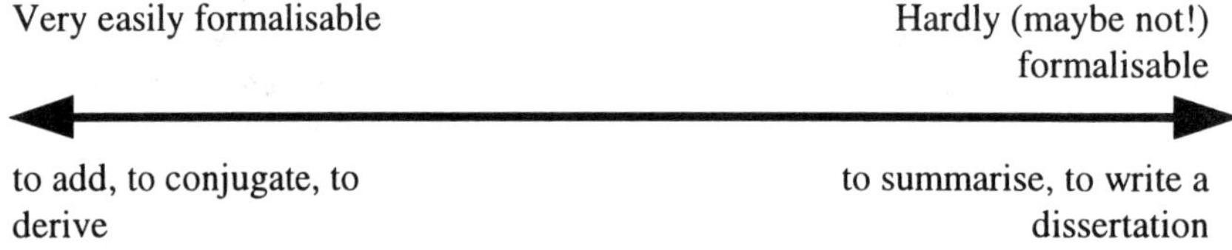

Figure 4 Information processing continuum.

This is the 'my Spanish friend criterion': the difficulty of explaining different forms of information processing to this friend, allows us to assess the difficulty of formalization of this processing. Following a definition of informatics is suggested (as a slogan): 'the point of informatics is to transform formalizable processes into formalized processes'. We will be faced with the problem of the intelligence needed to successfully carry this out (see Figure 5).

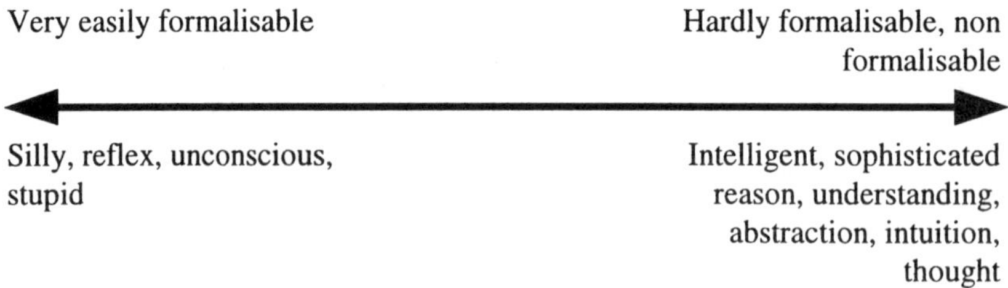

Figure 5 Information processing and intelligence.

'information'

For a piece of information to be processed we have to be able to represent it, to code it as a finite set of integer numbers. This is going to lead to text coding (ASCII or ANSI code), to the coding of real numbers (floating point representation), to the coding of pictures (bitmap or object-oriented coding), to the representation of sounds (sampling and analogue/digital conversion) and the functions of input or output peripherals (coding and decoding). Also problems around optical character recognition and speech recognition are discussed. The whole section results in a final statement: 'We are leaving an analogue era to enter a digital one. And the computer is both the reason for and the means of this transition'.

'as long as it was told how to process'

For everything it does, the computer needs a program (= processing instructions). It is essential that the end-user knows that a computer does not exist on its own. That during a single session of computer work the machine does not change, but the second element, the program, changes several times, sometimes surreptitiously. These observations lead to meaningful consequences. For example, it is impossible to indicate a key on the keyboard which has always the same effect when you press it. 'When using a computer system, nothing is always valid' (this is another important statement). Later we will draw other consequences from these principle: the need for a bootstrapping program in the read-only memory and the need for an operating system to load applications into the random access memory. It is also important to present the programmer's point of view; he is the one who has to create and to provide processing instructions to the computer. The job of a programmer is not 'to do', but 'to have it done by...'. As you could guess, the short sentence 'as long as it was told how to process' covers the whole universe of programming, where you have nothing to do, but where everything has to be done by...

'machine'

The main question here is: How does Figure 2 change when dealing with hardware? Figure 6 shows the two things the computer needs: data to process and programs explaining how to process these. I also discuss, stressing their coding or decoding function, various input devices: keyboard, mouse, scanner, microphone and analogue/digital converter. And output devices: screen, printer. The time has also come to give some assessment details about the processor and the central memory and to tackle operating principles, without too many technical details. The usual jargon has to be defined : bit, byte, binary coding, etc.

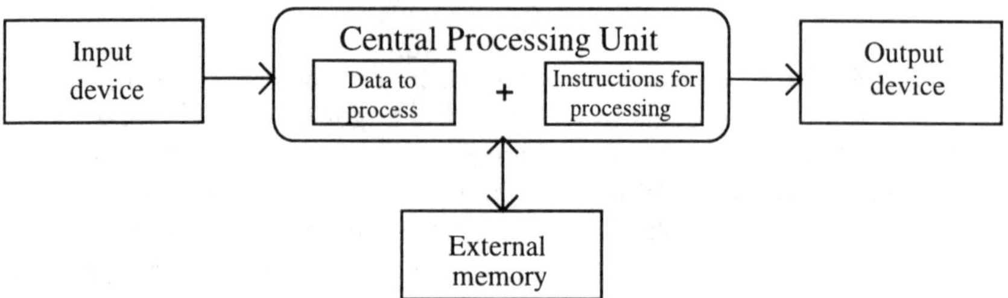

Figure 6 The machine.

Of course this is not the end of the course. There is a section dedicated to the evolution of programming languages and dealing with the specific difficulties of programming. See Duchâteau (1990). Another section is devoted to the history of computer science and focuses on micro-computing. See Duchâteau (1992). Software (operating systems, application software) is also dealt with, stressing the evolution of user interfaces.

7 CONCLUSION

I hope I have shown the spirit of the course and the way it is taught. I hope I have answered, at least partially, the question regarding the definition 'informatics for users'. Maybe the knowledge and mental representations which end-users need can only be learned through actually using computer systems (Duchâteau, 1994). In any case, many teachers in university first year courses are faced with the same content and methodological issues. I have tried to contribute to a joint reflection, which is more than ever necessary.

8 REFERENCES

Arsac, J. (1980) *Premières leçons de programmation*. Cedic / Nathan, Paris [in French].

Arsac, J. (1987) *Les machines à penser. Des ordinateurs et des hommes*. Editions du Seuil, Paris [in French].

Duchâteau, C. (1990) *Images pour programmer. Apprendre les concepts de base*. De Boeck-Wesmael, Bruxelles [in French].

Duchâteau, C. (1992) *L'ordinateur et l'école ! Un mariage difficile ?*.CeFIS, Facultés Universitaires Notre-Dame de la Paix, Namur [in French].

Duchâteau, C. (1994) Faut-il enseigner l'informatique à ses utilisateurs?, in *Actes de la quatrième rencontre francophone de didactique de l'informatique*, AQUOPS, Montréal [in French].

Hofstadter, D. and Dennet, D. (1987) *Vues de l'esprit. Fantaisies et réflexions sur l'être et l'âme*. InterEditions, Paris [in French].

Romainville, M. (1989) Une analyse critique de l'initiation à l'informatique : quels apprentissages et quels transferts ?, in *Actes du colloque francophone sur la didactique de l'informatique*, Editions de l'Epi, Paris [in French].

Tinsley, D. and van Weert, T. (eds.) (1994) *Informatics for Secondary Education. A Curriculum for Schools*. Unesco, Paris.

9 BIOGRAPHY

Charles Duchâteau was born in 1946 in Belgium. After studying to be a primary school teacher, he undertook a degree in mathematics at the Catholic University of Louvain and then a Ph.D. (about incomplete information differential games) at the University Notre-Dame de la Paix in Namur. It was within the Mathematics Department of this university that he founded the CeFIS (a centre for the training of teacher in informatics). He is now member of the Education and Technology Department. His research field is that of informatics didactics and the meaning of the elements constituting an 'Information Technology Culture'.

7

Informatics: the core and the presentation

Helen Geissinger
Instructional Media & Design P/L, PO Box 112, Brunswick Heads
Australia 2483, e-mail: 100235.3713@CompuServe.com

Peter Ho
School of Computer Science and Engineering
University of New South Wales, Sydney, Australia 2052
e-mail: Peter.Ho@cse.unsw.edu.au

Ken Robinson
School of Computer Science and Engineering, University of New South Wales, Sydney, Australia 2052, e-mail: kenr@cse.unsw.edu.au

Abstract

This paper puts forward a core curriculum and suggests ways to present it in support of the authors' basic premise: that informatics should be part of every curriculum. So many daily routines in the world have become dependent on computer functions that people have a responsibility to understand how they work and take an informed interest in what they do. They also must be able to visualize computer work for the future so that they can help prepare their professions and occupations such that people will still have meaningful work in coming generations.

Keywords

Informatics, context of informatics, curriculum (core), role of CIT

Informatics in Higher Education F. Mulder & T. van Weerts (Eds.)

1 INTRODUCTION

Informatics has to do with the ways in which computers operate and with the data these provide, as well as with the transformation of that data into information by interpreters, whether human or other computer applications. People need to understand this connectionbetween computers and humans because the presence of computerized functions is becoming so pervasive in the world in both developed and less-developed countries, even though people living in remote villages may not perceive it. Humankind has the potential to manage its collective life better, if this connection is understood and used beneficially. There are many issues involved, such as impacts on social life and the need for people to develop critical faculties in relation to technical information, as well as ethics and privacy concerns, the social use of computer tools and the quality of decision-making based on computer-provided information. These issues will not go away. People want computers to further their aims, whether professional, in the business or the public sector, but they do not want their thinking and decision-making to be subordinated by computerized procedures.

2 INFORMATICS IN THE CURRICULUM

A quick survey of employment advertisements for lecturers in informatics for tertiary institutions shows that the topics such people must be able to teach are technical in nature, such as systems analysis and computer networking. They do not appear to require the teaching of a wider sense of the discipline, e.g. the quality and effectiveness of networked communications or the necessity for the inclusion of a wide spectrum of users when a system is to be designed.

There are of course exceptions to this general situation. For example, one alternative is provided by an Australian university for computing science students. The students in that program are required to complete satisfactorily 21 computing and project units and 5 non-computing units. (Nunn *et al.*, 1995). One of the noncomputing electives is a first-year subject titled 'Technical Communication' in which the curriculum is based on cognitive learning theories and helps students engage in meta-cognition through facilitated experiential learning. The faculty has deliberately chosen to align the competencies for employment identified by a governmental committee with the principles of lifelong learning outlined in another government report. These are used in the curriculum development so that students are made aware of the parameters provided by these two studies and are asked to engage in learning activities which will help them realize the extent and meaning of those ideas. The meta-cognitive activities make it likely that learners will think more deeply about the subject material they will study in other parts of the program. Unfortunately it is an elective rather than a core subject and possibly may attract fewer students once its novelty has worn off. On the other hand one of its outcomes may be a desire expressed by successful students that it become a core subject.

Informatics touches on many concerns which are fast becoming a larger part of today's professions. Such an issue is making computer functions more sensitive to human needs and more responsive to the various users of a system. Grémy and Bonnin (1995) documented the development of an automated health information system (AHIS) in a large hospital in France and found that a climate of what they term 'social debate' has arisen around the functions of this system. The earlier introduction of AHISs in hospitals is described as 'brutal', because the systems were designed to meet the needs of certain user groups (such as doctors) and did not meet the needs of other groups such as hospital administration or allied health departments. Grémy and Bonnin note that: '...things happen as if citizens had lost their blind faith [in] the link between happiness and technical progress. They now claim the right to intervene...into the evaluation process of the technical objects.' (page 28). The authors have seen almost violent confrontations among groups which use the AHIS and either find the system works well or does not, according to their experiences. They suggest that the design of any AHIS must centre on the needs of all the groups which will use it, rather than on those advanced by prominent stakeholders.

3 THE CORE

Whether or not there are common elements which must be taught to all groups of learners is debatable, especially as the uses are so varied. One could possibly distinguish between the needs of learners in developed countries, where computer use is widespread, and those of learners in less-developed countries where often computerized elements are invisible to those impacted by them. However, students in those countries who will become the future decision-makers, need to understand computers and see how these can accomplish useful things for their nations; they also need to realize how decisions made elsewhere, but impacting locally, may be based on computer analyses. The distinction between learners' needs in developed nations compared with those of less-developed states therefore probably has to do with quantity and not quality. This means that there is an informatics core which is universal while the supporting components vary according to the needs of the particular learner group.

The authors of this paper suggest that the core of informatics topics must include the following:

- technical aspects: hardware and software functions and capabilities;
- current computers applications (contextual examples);
- likely computer applications of the future;
- social impacts and issues.

Technical aspects
Learners in every discipline should know exactly what a computer comprises. They should use the terminology correctly and know how each part works. They also need to know the elements of programming and should learn how to program simple functions. From there, they should be helped to extrapolate to sophisticated systems and to be able to describe in general terms how these perform. This knowledge is essential as a basis from which to assess and analyse the functions and impacts of computers in every walk of life. People everywhere should not be talking about 'black boxes' when they discuss the issues.

Current uses of computers
Obviously this aspect of basic computer knowledge changes rapidly from year to year and will vary from one country to another. Learners need to see computers at work in their own area or, more generally, in their own country so that they can comprehend what and how computers contribute. This will give an understanding of the all-pervasiveness of computers and their contribution to decisions which are made about the governance and economy of every country. Learners also need to see the scope and complexity of computer applications in professional settings.

Future computer applications
Learners need to know enough about computer applications that they can envision likely possibilities for the future and can make decisions about their own future or help suggest directions which their profession or occupation might take. Heppell (1994) has worked with children in the United Kingdom in a learning centre where they play computer games and investigate educational multimedia. He suggests that the current child in a developed country has great powers of concentration, evidenced by the ability to 'channel hop' rapidly and keep track of a number of television programs simultaneously. He also notes that children are autonomous viewers who want control of their learning experiences (e.g. control of navigation through a multimedia program) and who have '...broader forms of literacy and new media grammars which they bring as real assets into their learning environment.' (page 201). These confident children are computer users now. Adults need to envision future uses which can enable those children to have a productive adulthood.

Social impacts and issues
Grémy and Bonnin (1995) also looked at the impact which a poorly-designed information system had upon the functioning of a large hospital, and outlined the problems caused by the designers' ignorance of users' needs. They suggest that the designers of any information system should develop a social sense of what goes on in the organization for which the system is intended in order to prevent it causing chaos in the workplace.

One of the biggest impacts on the employment situation in many countries has been the effect of marketplace decisions made by international corporations.

Suddenly large numbers of people have been dismissed from their places of employment because their jobs have disappeared. Computerized applications have taken over some aspects of their work. There is a huge social problem around the fact of so many unemployed people in so many countries. As Armstrong and Armstrong (1990) note: 'What has been called work...is that which is done for pay or profit in the market...Unpaid work done in the market has frequently been excluded, as has all unpaid and some paid work done in the home or on the streets.' (page 13). People who become long-term unemployed lose recognition as contributors to society's concept of their national economy.

Ohmae (1995) discusses a 'civil minimum' which he calls a 'very moody tiger' which national governments climb on when they succumb to many strong interest groups among their citizens. They are unable to satisfy every group sufficiently to stifle the demands and so must devise a minimum level of service, whether it is in telecommunications or health care, such that people recognize that it is the level that the country as a whole can have. Ohmae suggests that, as the costs of providing services continue to rise, governments and their citizens must think creatively about ways to pay for them. If the time-honoured method of raising taxes is used, it will simply drive away the businesses which currently support the economy, or those businesses will invest more capital in machines and automation.

Issues such as these (unemployment and the civil minimum) should not be confined to philosophy or political studies. They belong in the core informatics curriculum where the learners who intend to design and use computers, can examine the many social aspects which will be impacted.

In addition, informatics should be taught across the curriculum to help learners develop their critical faculties with regard to information delivered by the computer. There is a tremendous range of offerings already, from educational multimedia programs developed for specific target groups (e.g. *A.D.A.M.* for learners of human anatomy and physiology) to CD-ROM 'books' like the Encyclopedia Britannica through to 'edutainment' and 'infotainment', offerings which attract varied groups of viewers. Learners need to develop abilities to critique them, so that the educational content, if any, can be distinguished from the media 'push' (Kelly and Wolf, 1997). One way to develop these abilities is for learners to engage in the production of multimedia themselves; they can critique other presentations since they understand the technologies used and biases involved in choosing one element over another.

4 THE PRESENTATION

Visual memories

Good visual presentations seem to provide strong memory traces. Children tend to remember what they have seen on television better than material they have read, even when the topic is the same. Spinney (1997) reports that children who have grown up with television, have recognition skills associated with the visual medium which are better developed than those they have acquired for reading with understanding. While it may be true that 'a picture is worth a thousand words', and that many people remember something they have seen better than something they have read, it is also true that pictures can be constructed of clever visual effects. Visual presentations, e.g. television and film, are ephemeral, yet their impact may be so strong that learners may wish to take what they see is 'true'. Thus, even children need a knowledge of informatics to inform their visual perceptions.

Discussion of perceptions

Conversation Theory (Pask and Boyd, 1987) shows how the computer can help people understand each other by analysing the words they use in discussing a concept and showing the areas in which their discussion is congruent. For example, negotiators trying to find common ground among opposing parties and in education learners who want to discover what it means to 'be' a member of a discipline, such as being an engineer or a medical doctor. Grémy and Bonnin (1995) suggest that conversation must occur around any mooted technical innovation so that it can fit with the needs of those who will use it. Because, for example, an automated health information system (AIS) may aid, simulate or duplicate human intellectual activities, the authors suggest that: '...all such AIS should be evaluated with special reference to the concepts and methods of sociology, psychosociology, and organizational sciences.' These authors think that an active ongoing conversation about the innovation among the users is very important.

Microworlds

Eklund (1995) gives an example of teaching electronically using 'micro-worlds'. He described commercial software which helped students investigate particular phenomena. Others have used custom software to develop the microworld concept. The techniques allow learners of any age or background to enter 'worlds' in which they can explore and experiment without serious consequences. If they are active in that field of knowledge, they can also input findings from their own work and manipulate them within the 'world'. Authors of microworld software report great user enthusiasm for the 'game' aspect of the software while also providing evidence of deep learning.

Across the curriculum

As mentioned above, valuable learning experiences can be provided by perceptions gained from visual media in an explorative guided discussion of ideas engendered both by personal social knowledge and knowledge discovered in microworlds. Heppell's (1994) reference to children having '...broader forms of literacy...' shows that, more than ever before, teaching must accommodate many different approaches to knowledge. Teaching informatics across the curriculum is fast reaching a high degree of necessity. The teaching methods, as well as supporting theories, must allow a wide range of approaches and accept as valid a variety of outcomes.

Making meaning

There is a debate in the teaching field around the merits of instructivism and constructivisim. Instructivism requires a statement of goals and objectives set by the developer of the content. Good instructivist teaching is evidenced when the learner demonstrates certain behaviour as a result of that interaction (Rieber, 1992). Constructivism requires learners to make sense from their experiences, mental structures and beliefs and to use these constructions to interpret happenings and objects in the world. Khoo and Lou (1996) state that: a '..constructivistic environment..naturally promotes self-directed learning', but then offer a caveat that high achievers tend to do better in a constructvist environment compared with low achievers. Mezirow thinks that it is a characteristic of adult learning that allows a learner to construct a meaning which is: '..more inclusive, discriminating, integrative and permeable (open)..' He does not suggest that a learner needs to be a high achiever, but posits that it is a function of adult development. Khoo and Lou (1996) studied primary school teachers as novice multi-media developers and found that some of their learners were afraid of the technologies they were invited to use and constrained themselves from being exploratory and innovative. Norman's Schemata theory says that the way in which a learner interprets new knowledge is unique and is based on schemata already in place from prior learning. If the framework is skimpy and perhaps even misconceived, the learner will interpret new knowledge very differently than would someone who has a better basic framework at the beginning.

There appears to be room here for all three views of learning. Instructivist teaching can help learners build a useful framework through which to develop deeper understandings as they explore and 'construct' a subject area more fully. Mature reasoning and reflection will help learners place ensuing discoveries in context.

The gap

As Khoo and Lou (1996) have shown with primary school teachers, there is a huge gap in the knowledge and skills regarding informatics in those who must help the current body of learners build their frameworks. While there are arguments for face-to-face teaching, it is probably appropriate that an informatics subject (or the informatics part of another subject) should be taught electronically. The teaching can reach a global audience, if necessary, and can help bring an enormous number of would-be practitioners into the knowledge area quickly. On-line subjects are being taught successfully and the tools for on-line work by individuals and groups of students are readily available and easy to use. O'Neill (1997), in looking at some of the offerings on the Internet, suggests that the best uses of the Internet are made by educators and researchers. Writing for Australian newspaper readers, she finds that a poll of 'netizens' showed that, although 21% use the Internet primarily for entertainment, 15% use it for e-mail and 12% for general research (O'Neill, 1997). She notes that all learners can be helped through discussion in a medium such as e-mail to acquire the skills needed to critique information at the thinking level they have reached and can then research the Internet capably.

Addressing the gap

Collis provides examples of good ways to use the Internet for teaching through her publications which include a URL:
http://www.to.twente.nl/ism/online96/week/week1/followu.htm
for the outline of an on-line subject she taught in 1996. She models good on-line teaching: She lists things to do and gives the reasons for doing them. She provides workspace for all her learners to access, see others' contributions and input their own, and she sets up information/discussion/ feedback areas so that the learners are updated, can engage in discussion, and receive feedback on their input. E-mail pages and biographical materials for each learner are readily available, so that participants can see something about each other and can chat. She ensures that the materials the learners should work with are available at certain Web sites or she gives advice on ways to do their own searches and the steps they should take once they find what appears to be appropriate material. She keeps everyone on target, on-line and participating in the work by using a variety of tools and methods; she values each contributor's participation. Whether or not she so intends, Collis utilises the ROPES+ framework espoused by Hannafin and Rieber (1989) which emphasizes: '..relationships among external capabilities of technologies, task, and performance requirements, known causal relationships in learning, and the processing capabilities of individual learners.'. This framework may be the best for the design of courses which will bring adults (especially professionals) into that state of cognitive awareness in which they understand computers, the capabilities and can predict likely future applications. Then those who are teachers will be equipped well to teach their confident, button-pressing students.

5 REFERENCES

Armstrong, P. and Armstrong, H. (1990) *Theorizing women's work.* Garamond Press, Toronto, 13.

Eklund, J. (1995) A project approach to teaching and learning with technology: A case study with Microworlds Project Builder, in *Learning with technology, ASCILITE conference proceedings* (eds. J. Pearce and A. Ellis), The Science Multimedia Teaching Unit, University of Melbourne, Melbourne, Australia, 126-130.

Grémy, F. and Bonnin, M. (1995) Evaluation of automatic health information systems: What and how?, in *Assessment and Evaluation of Information Technologies* (eds. E.M.S.J van Gennip and J.L. Talman), IOS Press, Oxford, 9-34.

Hannafin, M.J. and Rieber, L.P. (1989) Psychological foundations of instructional design for emerging computer-based instructional technologies: Part II. *Educational Technology Research and Development*, **37** (2), 102-114.

Heppell, S. (1994) Learning and the children of the information age, in *Proceedings of the Second Multimedia Symposium*, Perth, Australia, 200-203.

Kelly, K. and Wolf, G. (1997) We interrupt this magazine for a special bulletin -- PUSH! *Wired,* **5** (2), 12-23.

Khoo, C.C. and Lou, C.T. (1996) From virtual novices to real interactive multimedia producers: a research study, in *From virtual to reality, Apple University Conference*, The University of Queensland. See also: http://www.uow.edu.au/auc/Conf96/Papers/KhooCC.html.

Mezirow, J. (1978). Perspective transformation. *Adult Education,* **28** (2), 100-110.

Nunn, J., Else, D., Pitt, J. and Carroll, P. (1995) Computing, communicating and contracting: A first-year experience in lifelong learning, in *Learning with technology, ASCILITE conference proceedings* (eds. J. Pearce and A.Ellis), The Science Multimedia Teaching Unit, University of Melbourne, Melbourne, Australia, 432-440.

Ohmae, K. (1995) *The end of the nation state. The rise of regional economies.* The Free Press, New York, 46-57.

O'Neill, H. (1997) The Internet backlash. *The Weekend Australian*, 15-16 March 1997, 1 (Syte section).

Pask, G. and Boyd, G. (1987) Conversation Theory as basis for instructional design, in *Interactive media: Working methods and practical applications* (ed. D. Laurillard), Holstead Press (Div. John Wiley & Sons Ltd.), New York, 91-96.

Rieber, L.P. (1992) Computer-based micro-worlds: A bridge between constructivism and direct instruction. *Educational Technology, Research and Development*, **40** (1), 93-105.

Spinney, L. (1997) Square eyes and strong memories. *New Scientist,* **153** (2073), 5.

6 BIOGRAPHY

Helen Geissinger is an educational developer interested in the effects of the use of various media in adult learning. She has worked with a number of universities in the development of study programs which have used multiple media and has then researched the learning outcomes of the student groups. She is currently researching the effects of innovative teaching in Australian tertiary institutions which use computer media.

Peter Ho has a degree in computer science (Honours) from The University of New South Wales (UNSW), Australia. He has nine years industry experience as a software engineer and as a consultant. He joined the School of Computer Science and Engineering at UNSW in 1991, where he initiated and worked on a number of projects related to distance learning, multimedia tools for use in education, home computing and software engineering.

Ken Robinson is a senior lecturer and head of the Department of Software Engineering in the School of Computer Science and Engineering at the University of New South Wales (UNSW). He has a long record of teaching computer science and software engineering with a special interest in rigorous software development methods, and in the recognition of computing as an engineering discipline. He played a leading role in the introduction of a new computer engineering course in 1989 and a new software engineering course in 1997 at UNSW.

8

Teaching introductory computer science as science of information

Gopal K. Gupta
Department of Computer Science, James Cook University
Townsville, Qld 4811, Australia, e-mail: gopal@cs.jcu.edu.au

Abstract

Since the development of first computer science programs in the early 1960's, introductory computer science teaching continues to be problematic with many departments reporting high drop-out and high failure rates in their introductory courses. The present approach to teaching introductory computer science as teaching procedural programming using an apprenticeship approach needs to change. We suggest an alternate approach which is based on information, its processing, presentation and communication. Programming continues to be an important part of the proposed curriculum, but it does not occupy the central place which it currently does.

Keywords

Informatics, information systems, informatics majors, curriculum (general), curriculum (start)

1 INTRODUCTORY COMPUTER SCIENCE COURSES

The computer science curriculum has been a topic of intense discussion since the birth of the discipline in the early 1960's, as is for example reflected by the debate in Denning (1989). A number of model curricula, including Curriculum 68, Curriculum 78 and Curriculum 91, have been developed by ACM and have been widely used as basis for curriculum design. Other computing societies have developed their own recommendations. Introductory computer science courses appear to have evolved only slowly over the last thirty years. Curriculum 68 noted that the first course (Course B1: Introduction to Computing) was designed to

Informatics in Higher Education F. Mulder & T. van Weerts (Eds.)

provide the student with the basic knowledge and experience necessary to use computers effectively in the solution of problems and suggested that the course could be used both for majors as well as nonmajors.

More recently, Koffman, Miller and Wardle (1984) presented a model curriculum for an introductory course CS1 with the following objectives:

- to introduce a disciplined approach to problem-solving methods and algorithm development;
- to introduce procedural and data abstraction;
- to teach program design, coding, debugging, testing and documentation using good programming style;
- to teach a block-structured high-level programming language;
- to provide a familiarity with the evolution of computer hardware and software technology;
- to provide a foundation for further studies in computer science.

Although most introductory computer science courses, we suspect, have objectives similar to those listed above, the debate about curriculum for the introductory course continues unabated. For example, there has been considerable discussion in the literature whether an introductory course should focus narrowly on some aspect of computer science (often programming) and ignore breadth of coverage, or be a breadth-first course which gives up some of the narrow programming emphasis. Often though the first one or two courses are dominated by programming. Scragg, Baldwin and Kooment (1994), and Doran and Langan (1995) present what in their view are symptoms of the problems with introductory computer science courses. These are high drop-out rates in the undergraduate programs, in particular in the introductory courses, complaints by the employers that the graduates are not able to apply what they have learned and high drop-out rates from computer science Ph.D. programs (which presumably reflects the poor preparation). Furthermore, anecdotal evidence suggests that computer science students completing an introductory course sometimes do not even know how to use a spreadsheet effectively. Although these symptoms are by no means found in all computer science programs, these are common enough to be familiar to most computer science academics. Bagert, Marcy and Calloni (1995) give an extreme example of drop-out and failure rates in which a first year class of 216 students was reduced to only five graduates four years later. A number of solutions has been proposed to solve these problems. Some suggest, for example, that an introductory course should include a study of good examples of software systems, modify and combine programs as well as creating them and present theory and models in the context of practice. Baldwin *et al.* (1994) and Scragg *et al.*(1994) state that the central mission of their introductory sequence is to teach design, theory and empirical analysis. Doran and Langan (1995) take a very different approach. They refer to the six levels of learning in the educational process: knowledge, comprehension, application, analysis, synthesis and judgement. They comment that the introductory courses should try to primarily teach the first three levels, since the other three (analysis, synthesis and judgement) require a good mastery of the first three and maturity gained by extended usage.

Most conventional introductory courses expect students to complete programming assignments without a great deal of assistance, but this is quite unrealistic since programming is a complex cognitive task. The apprenticeship approach, although suitable for learning a trade or technical skills, is perhaps not suitable for learning conceptual material and in any case is often ineffective due to lack of staff resources. It results in average students constantly battling with programming assignments and thus having no time to consider the conceptual basis of the discipline. The concept of closed laboratories, which has not been common in computer science teaching in North America, but has been the normal practice in Australia for many years, helps, but does not overcome the problems. Given the conventional curriculum many students think that computer science is just programming; that is what we tell the students in our introductory courses as noted by Denning *et al.* (1989): 'The emphasis on programming arises from our long-standing belief that programming languages are excellent vehicles for gaining access to the rest of the field, a belief that limits our ability to speak about the discipline in terms that reveal its full breadth and richness. ..Clearly programming is part of the standard practices of the discipline and every computing major should achieve competence in it. This does not, however, imply that the curriculum should be based on programming or that the introductory courses should be programming courses'.

Furthermore, the conventional introductory curriculum is too dependent on changes in technology which an introductory course ought not to be. The curriculum discussions in computer science departments are thus often dominated by whether the programming language being used needs to be changed to the latest one to the neglect of more important issues. Such language discussions have been known to turn into religious wars which can do serious damage to the fabric of a department.

To summarize, we believe that current introductory computer science courses suffer from the following problems.

- The courses focus on programming and algorithmic computation and do not present a broad picture of computer science.
- The courses require too much programming in too early a stage which is often intimidating for at least a significant minority of students, perhaps more so for the female students.
- The courses use an apprenticeship approach which is often very time consuming for most students given the lack of staff resources.
- The pass rates in most current introductory courses are often low and the drop-out rates high; retention of less than 50% after the first course appears common but is in our view unacceptable.
- Although the programming assignments can be time-consuming, the courses convey few intellectual challenges to some of the brightest students.

Current trends in curriculum design appear to indicate that new developments are unlikely to solve the problems listed above. Nearly the only concern in designing new introductory curricula presently appears to be object-oriented programming, although it is clear that use of object-oriented programming is not going to solve the problems identified above.

2 NEW APPROACH

We believe that a different approach to teaching computer science is needed, not only because the present approach suffers from significant difficulties, but also because computing and the computing industry have changed dramatically over the last four decades. The primary concern in computing now appears to be shifting to information storage, retrieval, display and presentation. As a result the information technology industry now offers many opportunities for people with a variety of skills (e.g. networking, Web applications as well as programming; see Keaton and Hamilton, 1996). We therefore need a new curriculum which recognizes that not all students studying computer science are going to (or need to) become programmers or software developers. Some may also not be capable of and/or interested in acquiring such skills beyond basic programming. We should not deny such people an opportunity to develop computing knowledge and expertise in areas other than software development. In some ways the computer science academic community faces a real choice now: We may design computer science curricula to be inclusive, so that students from many different backgrounds may pursue computer science studies, or we may design curricula to be exclusively focused on producing first-rate software developers. The exclusive option is not the one we recommend and in our view exclusive curricula proposals like those of Dijkstra (Denning, 1989) and Parnas (1990) are not worth considering since they propose solutions which are likely to lead to a serious decline of the discipline. We propose that a very broad view of information be the basis of the computer science curriculum and we agree with Denning (1995) that a computer science program should be taught as the science of information. However, what we propose is very different from most 'information systems' and 'information science' curricula. Information systems curricula often only consider a limited view of information, in particular the role of information in decision making. Information science curricula on the other hand often are closely related to 'library science'. Our proposed curriculum takes a very broad view of information as the basis of computer science and focuses on the concept of information and the manipulation, communication and display of its representations, rather than on algorithmic computation. Following this approach the introductory computer science course, as well as the courses which follow, are significantly different from what we teach today. As an example we propose that an introductory course consists of the following topics.

The concept of information

- the concept of information and its many forms, the question 'what is information?', definition and characteristics of information;
- non-temporal information:
  - > linear and non-linear **text**:
    - ~ linear text without form, sequence of characters, how many different characters, ASCII, ISO character sets, character sets for LOTE (Languages other than English); text with form, need to store content and form both, storing form by using mark-up languages (Troff, Latex, SGML, ODA), storing form by specifying form in a WYSIWIG-editor, presentation, fonts, device independent fonts, storage and printing of fonts, geometric descriptions of fonts, kerning, PostScript;
    - ~ non-linear form of text: hypertext, representation of hypertext, Web;
    - ~ operations on text: retrieval, character and string operations, editing, formatting, pattern matching and searching, spell checking, style checking, compression, encryption;
  - > **images**:
    - ~ images as a two-dimensional array of pixels, monochrome, grey and colour images; colour models, representation of images;
    - ~ operations on images: editing, point operations, filtering, compositing, geometric transformations, conversions, compression;
  - > **graphics**:
    - ~ difference between graphics and image data, representation of graphics data, geometric modelling (GKS, PHIGS, etc.), solid models, other models;
    - ~ operations on graphics data: editing, shading, mapping, lighting, viewing, rendering;
- temporal information:
  - > video:
    - ~ video as sequence of images or frames, analogue video and digital video, analogue representation and major formats (NTSC, PAL, SECAM, etc.), video storage, digital representation, data rates, digital video storage;
    - ~ operations on video: video sources and sinks, video mixer, retrieval, editing, compression of digital video, MPEG, JPEG, etc.;
  - > audio:
    - ~ digital and analogue audio representation, speech, encoding, audio formats (CD, DAT, etc.);
    - ~ operations on audio: storage, retrieval, editing and filtering;
  - > music:
    - ~ difference between music and audio, representing music (MIDI, SMDL);
    - ~ operations on music: playback, synthesis, editing, composition;
  - > animation:

  - ~ animation as sequence of synthetic image frames, animation versus video, animation models;
  - ~ operations on animation: motion and parameter control, rendering;
- information transformation:
  - > transforming text to audio, speech to text, music to audio, animation to video, etc.;
- optional:
  - > what is knowledge? representing knowledge e.g. plans, games, rules, etc.;
  - > natural language representation and understanding.

Information storage and retrieval

Information storage and retrieval, value of information, need for many different types of manipulation, etc. Storage and retrieval of large amounts of information on paper; books, chapters, table of contents, index, telephone directory, organisation of books in library, files and filing cabinets in a office, inventories, archiving, introduction of terms like sequential, index sequential, trees; analogies between manual information handling and information handling by computers. Information as a commodity and its unique properties, needs of graphical display of information, computing aggregate values, and other manipulations.

Computers as machines

Computers as (simple) machines which manipulate information; simple introduction to computer organization. Conceptual model of a computer, computer examples: computer games, ATM, a computer in a washing machine or a car, large mainframes, desktop, laptop and mobile computers. Concept of instructing computers; analogies between instructing a computer and instructing a human worker.

Input and output

The need to input information to computers and to output information from computers; many different types of inputs and outputs. Input to computers via keyboard, scanners, cameras, speech, instruments, touch screens, pen, mouse, joystick, etc.; conceptual understanding of how these devices work, devices like scanners and fax and their working; importance of user-friendly information input. Output from computers via monitors, printers of different types, speech, music, graphical output, control signals, etc.; conceptual understanding of how these devices work, importance of user-friendly information output.

Information storage

The need to store information in computers, techniques for storing and retrieving information; introduction to storage devices: core memory, disks, CD-ROMS, tapes etc.; introduction to data structures (sequential, indexed sequential, trees, hashing), concept of relational database and a simple retrieval language.

Ownership

The concept of ownership, availability and fair use of information; issues of copyright, personal privacy, information rich and information poor, ethics; who owns information, access to information held by public and private organisations, intellectual property rights, concept of information privacy, information privacy principles, information society, concept of information rich and poor societies, ethics for information processing professionals.

Communication

The need to communicate information from an input device to a computer, from a computer to an output device and from one computer to another. Computer communications, e-mail, Internet, World Wide Web, networks, mobile computing, conceptual understanding of how they work.

Manipulation

The need to manipulate information (mathematical computations, symbolic computations, intelligence), techniques for simple and complex information manipulation; information manipulation via available packages, word processing, spreadsheets, graphics packages, mathematical packages, expert systems; examples where a package will not do the job.

Instructions

The need to instruct the machine to manipulate information; introduction to one procedural language; examples of algorithms and their implementations using the language, debugging, testing and documentation; procedural and non-procedural languages, machine code, assembler, components of a procedural language, introduction to one procedural language, examples of algorithms, simple programs implementing those algorithms, extension of those algorithms and programs, the importance of debugging, testing, and documenting software.

3 CONCLUSION

The dramatic changes in computing and the computing industry in the last thirty years require that we look at computer science curricula afresh. In this paper we have considered the introductory computer science curriculum and have presented a curriculum which is significantly different from any proposal we know. In our view the proposed curriculum is exciting, since it approaches computer science from an information point of view which enables a much broader approach to computer science in the first course. The new approach has a number of other advantages. Major programming is deferred to and isolated in the design and implementation group project courses which should follow the introductory course (for details see Gupta, 1996a). The primary focus here is on implementation and we believe that sufficient staff resources ought to be provided to guide the students to good implementations. The new approach is believed to reduce the frustration and workload in the first course allowing the student to focus on the conceptual basis of the discipline.

4 ACKNOWLEDGEMENTS

A number of people have helped me in putting these ideas together. It is a pleasure to thank Reinhart Gillner, Shyam Kapur, Bruce Litow, Tony Sloane, Rodney Topor, Chris Wallace, and David Wessels. An earlier version of this paper was presented at CSI96 conference in Banglore, India (Gupta, 1996b).

5 REFERENCES

Bagert, D., Marcy, W.M. and Calloni, B.A. (1995) A Successful Five-Year Experiment with a Breadth-First Introductory Course. *SIGCSE Bulletin*, **27** (1), 116-120.

Baldwin, D., Scragg, G. and Kooment, H. (1994) A Three-Fold Introduction to Computer Science. *SIGCSE Bulletin*, **26** (1), 290-294.

Denning, P.J. [ed.] (1989) Teaching Computer Science. *Communications of the ACM*, **32** (12), 1397-1414.

Denning, P.J., Comer, D.E., Gries, D., Mulder, M.C., Tucker, A.B., Turner, A.J. and Young, P.R. (1989) Computing as a Discipline. *Communications of the ACM*, **32** (1), 9-23.

Denning, P.J. (1995) Can There be a Science of Information? *ACM Computing Surveys*, **27** (1), 23-25.

Doran, M.V. and Langan, D.D. (1995) A Cognitive-Based Approach to Introductory Computer Science Courses: Lessons Learned. *SIGCSE Bulletin*, **27** (1), 218-222.

Gupta, G.K. (1996a) *Teaching Computer Science as the Science of Information.* Internal report TR11, Dept of Computer Science, James Cook University.

Gupta, G.K. (1996b) *Teaching Introductory Computer Science: Past, Present and Future*. Proceedings of CSI96, Tata McGraw Hill, 95-102.

Keaton, J. and Hamilton S. (1996) Employment 2005: Boom or Bust for Computer Professionals. IEEE Computer, **29** (5), 87-98.

Koffman, E.P., Miller, P.L. and Wardle, C.E. (1984) Recommended Curriculum for CS1: 1984 a report of the ACM Curriculum task force for CS1. *Communications of the ACM*, **27** (10), 998-1001.

Parnas, D.L. (1990) Education for Computing Professionals. *IEEE Computer*, Jan 1990, 17-22.

Scragg, G., Baldwin, D. and Kooment, H. (1994) Computer Science Needs an Insight-Based Curriculum. *SIGCSE Bulletin*, **26** (1), 150-154.

6 BIOGRAPHY

Gopal Gupta is professor and head of the Department of Computer Science at James Cook University since 1986. He graduated in 1965 from the University of Roorkee (India) and received in 1968 a Masters degree in engineering from the University of Manitoba (Canada). After working at Bristol Aerospace in Winnipeg he took up a studies in computer science and completed a Masters degree at the University of Waterloo (Canada). From 1971 he spent 14 years at the Monash University (Australia). In 1976 he received his Ph.D. from this university. His last position at the Monash University was senior lecturer and deputy chairman of the Computer Science Department. During the Monash period he has been on leave at the University of Illinois (1 year) and at the Asian Institute of Technology in Bangkok (2 years). His research interests are: data structures, database systems and computer science education.

Marketing programming to nonprogrammers

Peter Juliff
School of Management Information Systems
Faculty of Business and Law, Deakin University, Burwood VIC 3125 Australia, e-mail: pjuliff@deakin.edu.au

Abstract

Based on a case study this paper looks at the problems associated with stimulating the involvement of noninformatics students in academic units related to software development. It provides advice, drawn from experience, on the means by which such students can be attracted to programming, can achieve a professional level of competence and can be encouraged to pursue further information technology studies.

Keywords

Programming languages, information bases, interaction and presentation, economics and business administration, noninformatics majors, curriculum (start), curriculum (core)

1 CASE STUDY AS BACKGROUND

Context

This paper draws on the lessons learned in the running of the Bachelor of Commerce (Business Computing) programme at Deakin University. Deakin is situated in the state of Victoria in Australia and has an undergraduate enrolment of some 26.000 students, half of whom are studying in distance education mode. The Bachelor of Commerce is the generic degree offered by the Faculty of Business and Law and has an enrolment of approximately 6000 students distributed over three campuses. Five years ago Deakin amalgamated with Victoria College. This was one

Informatics in Higher Education F. Mulder & T. van Weerts (Eds.)

in a series of such amalgamations in which Colleges/Institutes of Advanced Education (polytechnics) were combined with existing universities to form larger institutions and eliminate the so-called 'binary' education system which had existed up to that time.

Deakin IT studies and subjects

At Deakin, prior to this amalgamation, business (and any other noncomputing) students who wished to take information technology (IT) studies were obliged to do so by enrolling in subjects offered by the Department of Computing and Mathematics. The Commerce degree had a compulsory 'Introduction to computing' subject which was, of course, taught by the computer scientists. The Computing department offered a small number of IT subjects, including programming, which it hoped would attract commerce students beyond their compulsory first year subject. The enrolment in these units was negligible. When asked about the reasons for the reluctance to progress to further IT studies, the commerce students gave answers such as:

- 'it all sounds like rocket science';
- 'they put us in with the computer science students and then only lecture to them';
- 'we can't see any reason to have to study programming when we are going into a business career'.

Victoria College IT stream

At Victoria College, prior to the amalgamation, there was a viable computing stream in the Bachelor of Business degree which had a reputation for producing excellent commercial IT graduates in the traditional areas of systems analysis and design, software development and database management. These studies ran through the three years of the degree and attracted a large number of noncomputing students into the mainstream computing subjects as well as specialist units designed with such students in mind.

Contrasting scenarios

The amalgamation of the two institutions brought these two contrasting scenarios into conflict. The first act of the computer scientists was to contend that all computing studies of any kind within the amalgamated institution should be taught by their department. In this they failed and two separate IT academic departments were established: the School of Computing and Mathematics in the Faculty of Science and Technology and the School of Management Information Systems in the Faculty of Management - later renamed the Faculty of Business and Law. Having lost the first round the computer scientists then claimed that the teaching of programming was the exclusive province of computer scientists. This they won. By executive fiat the university decided that the School of Management Information Systems was to discontinue its Software Development major programme and that, henceforth, any commerce student wishing to study software must be taught within computer science subjects. This meant a reversion to the prior Deakin model which had demonstrably been a dismal failure over the years prior to amalgamation.

This paper is the story of how, two years later, the School of Management Information Systems has more students enrolled in software development units than the School of Computing and Mathematics and attracts a large number of computer science students who follow the same units. The School of MIS does this without having a single 'programming' unit in its curriculum.

2 WHY TEACH PROGRAMMING TO NONINFORMATICS STUDENTS?

There are several reasons why students who do not necessarily see themselves as being computer scientists or as someone in a similar technical role, should seriously consider pursuing some IT studies. Not the least reason is that graduates often gravitate to positions which they never even contemplated during the tenure of their studies. Business graduates may well find themselves more involved in the technology of their occupation than in its commerce. Redmond-Pyle (1996) draws attention to changes in skill requirements of system developers and to the growing distinction between component builders, likely to remain computer science graduates, and solution providers who must understand the application domain. In this context of producing solution providers some of the major reasons for the teaching of software development skills are listed below.

To understand the nature of the operations of IT systems

By necessity the development of programs brings students into contact with all of the components of a computer system. It forces them to appreciate the tasks performed by operating systems and other of the more arcane components of a typical production system, such as utility programs, configuration control procedures, the functioning of internal memory and the nature of different data types and structures. All of these can be covered at a conceptual level in other subject areas, but the process of actually implementing a software system requires them to be dealt with at an operational level and, therefore, makes them harder to ignore.

To inject reality into other areas of the IT curriculum

One of the main problems with teaching the modus operandi of IT systems in subjects which are of the nature of analysis and design, is its presentation as a body of theoretical knowledge and skills which produces a blueprint from which an IT system will subsequently be implemented. Many of the problems in the design of any IT system, in the classroom or in the profession, only emerge in the process of the system's implementation. If students are required to take a design document and to actually bring the design to fruition as an operational system, they have the opportunity to appreciate many of the problems which are unforeseen at design time.

The inherent nature of the task itself
I would direct readers to Fred Brooks' (1972) seminal work 'The Mythical Man-Month' in which he extols 'The Joys of the Craft' as being:

- 'the sheer joy of making things';
- 'the pleasure of making things which are useful to other people';
- 'the fascination of fashioning complex objects ... and watching them work';
- 'the joy of always learning';
- 'the delight in working in such a tractable medium'.

Brooks' statement that 'programming is fun because it gratifies creative longings built deep within us and delights sensibilities we have in common with all men' is as valid today as it was twenty-five years ago when the book was written.

To acquire skills in project management
Another of the most significant long-term problems in the implementation of IT systems is that of project management: the consequent difficulties in estimating the time for a software project and then monitoring the progress of that project. As always, these topics can be covered at a conceptual and descriptive level, but are much more readily appreciated and understood after the students have themselves been required to produce a software system in a specified time and with limited resources. This aspect of software development is best learned by having the students working in teams and reporting to a supervisor in an environment as close as possible to a working situation.

Even if the students do not themselves go on to be software developers, this aspect of their studies will equip them with an insight into the processes involved and better enable them to operate in a supervisory capacity if required.

The inherent training in problem solving
One of the most pervasive themes running through all IT studies is that of problem solving. Nowhere is this more essential that in the design and implementation of software. There are few other areas of human endeavour which are more insistent in their emphasis on the skills of problem analysis, the subsequent decomposition of large problems into their constituent smaller components and the rigorous specification of the interaction between those components. The skills acquired in the activity of algorithm design are transferable to almost all other facets of graduates' subsequent employment.

The computer is also a harsh mistress. There is a correct answer to a problem and the software either arrives at that solution or it does not. The program is therefore demonstrably right or wrong. In a descriptive discipline a student may be required to produce an 'acceptable' solution. In programming the student must produce a 'correct' solution.

The importance of integrating IT studies with non-IT disciplines
Given the all-pervasive nature of information technology in today's society it is difficult to imagine a career pursued by a graduate which does not involve a daily interaction with some aspect of IT within the working environment. The corollary to this is that the more comfortable graduates are with IT systems as a result of their undergraduate studies, the more opportunities will be open to them in their working life. If the study of software development can be made attractive to noncomputing as well as computing students, it provides an excellent vehicle to give all undergraduates a feeling for all of the design and implementation aspects of the type of software systems with which they will interact.

An appreciation of the complexities of human-computer interaction
An old proverb runs: 'I hear and I forget; I see and I remember; I do and I understand'. Given the availability of system development products such as Visual Basic and Delphi, it is not a difficult matter to have students put together a (simple) software system and to experiment with a variety of methods of presenting information on a screen and a variety of methods of soliciting interaction with a user. Despite lengthy lectures on the principles of graphical user interface (GUI) design, nothing brings home the problems of a clumsy human-computer interaction model like having to use it and demonstrate its operation to peers and supervisors.

3 WHAT IS THE BEST WAY TO TEACH PROGRAMMING?

There is an advertisement on Australian television for a breakfast cereal which has as one of its thematic lines: 'If you don't tell them that it's good for them, they'll eat it by the boxfull'. I have come to believe that this is the essential theme for marketing programming to noninformatics students. The surest way to alienate students who are not primarily enrolled for computer science curricula (and even some of those who are), from software subjects is to devise and describe a subject in the following style:

> **Computer Programming 101**
> A detailed study of algorithm design; multi-level decomposition; data typing and scope rules; logic constructs enabling structured programming and information hiding; abstract data structures and recursive processing techniques.

All but the committed student read these words and immediately think 'this is rocket science'.

Thirty years ago most of us who were teaching programming, were starting at the level of machine code or assembler language. When the students had mastered the intricacies of instruction addressing modes, indirect addresses, the binary representation of mantissas and exponents, the fetch-decode-execute cycle and the conversion of relative to absolute addresses, we would allow them to move to a compiler language such as Algol, FORTRAN, COBOL or PL/I. While we may harbour a belief that this is still the way it should be done, the students do not believe us and they will not enrol for the subjects. The major factors in attracting noninformatics students to software development subjects are listed below.

Make the syllabus sound relevant, interesting and, above all, achievable
Compare the following unit description with the one above:

> **Systems Implementation 101**
> The aim of this subject is to develop computer based information systems which run in a Windows environment and have the same professional look and feel as other contemporary applications. You will become familiar with the techniques needed to design screens which interact with their users, including the use of the mouse, drop-down menus, message boxes and command buttons. At the end of this subject you will have a fully executing commercial computer application which will run on any PC and which may be demonstrated to a potential user (or employer).

Note that the subject is not called 'programming', although students will be learning to write programs. It makes no mention of logic constructs or data typing and scope rules, yet students will learn all of these. It emphasizes the point that the outcome is the production of software products similar to those in daily use in the business environment.

Provide students with instant gratification
The scenario of thirty years ago which was mentioned above, also included compilation turnaround times measured in hours, if not days. It was not uncommon to have a week elapse between tests of an executable program. With the current PC environment students can develop a system producing a procedure at a time with instantaneous compilation or interpretation, and testing. At the end of a two-hour tutorial a student can emerge with a small yet complete software application which may then be expanded and enhanced into an impressive product. At the end of a day at kindergarten, youngsters like to have a painting to take home to show the family and to have it displayed on the door of the refrigerator. What makes us think that undergraduates are any different?

Do not destroy the students' spontaneity
We are all aware that there are rules to follow in writing quality software. There are two ends of a continuum in the methods used in teaching programming to students. At one end there is the approach which, allowing students to write sloppy code, instils bad habits that may never be eradicated. This approach dictates that every program, no matter how trivial, must be written with the same attention to the precepts of good software design as a major safety-critical application. Time has led me to believe that this is a mistake. Students are so terrified of incurring the

lecturer's wrath over poor style that all of the enjoyment of just solving the problem is destroyed.

The other end of the continuum is a 'laissez faire' approach to the writing of small programs. A 'Nike methodology': just do it! Concentrate on the problem and the excitement of arriving at a working solution. When the students then realize that this is achievable, they can be convinced that a lack of discipline which was not overly important in a 20 line program would be a disaster in a 200 or 2000 line program. When they realize that programming is something with which they can cope and which they can enjoy, they will be prepared to learn how to do it properly.

Produce software with user interaction and a professional look and feel

How many software assignments have we generated for students which involved the construction and manipulation of complex internal data structures and involved little or no user interaction? While we may be convinced of the inherent value of being able to update a number of complex master files with a transaction string which needs conversion from variable to fixed field format using a state transition table to direct the logic, or the implementation of a depth-first search of a tree structure, the problem is that the students write a lot of code and see almost nothing happening for their efforts. We expect them to achieve their gratification from the knowledge that the job was done correctly.

This is not the type of motivation likely to appeal to noninformatics students. Such students need to feel that they are constructing software which is like the application software which they will encounter in their chosen discipline. They are not interested in the internals so much as the interaction with the professional user. The internal operations must be communicated subliminally. If we can attract them with the promise of relevance, we have the chance of extending their horizons to further, perhaps less inherently interesting areas once they realize that they can achieve in this field of endeavour.

4 WHAT TO USE AS A VEHICLE FOR SOFTWARE DEVELOPMENT?

First programming language

An issue which is guaranteed to generate a debate among teachers of programming, is that of the first programming language. Over the past thirty years I have used as an introductory language: machine code, Ecole, assembler languages, FORTRAN, BASIC, Pascal, COBOL, Scheme and, most recently, Visual Basic. I can name other institutions which are using Turing, Modula 2, Miranda, C or Delphi for this introduction. The majority of academic institutions in recent years have used Pascal or C as reported by Redmond-Pyle (1996), Jones and Pearson (1993), Morton and Norgaard (1993) and Furber (1992).

Does it matter?

Is it any more important than which car you first learn to drive? I believe that the answer is that it does matter, particularly to noninformatics students. Regardless of the merits of various models of cars I do not believe that any of us would advocate using a semi-trailer or a formula-one racing car to teach a youngster to drive. These vehicles - like some of the introductory programming languages used - require too much expertise even for the simplest of operations and are not representative of what 90% of the exercise is about. For those advocating the use of object-oriented languages as initial learning tools, Lee and Pennington (1994) point out the difficulty normally experienced by novices in coming to grips with O-O techniques and the likely resultant clouding of the experience of learning to program.

Visual Basic and beyond

Cox and Clark (1992) argue convincingly for Visual Basic as a first language due to its ability to be application oriented rather than syntax-driven. The choice to use Visual Basic as the introductory programming language in Deakin's business computing degree has resulted in an increase of software development enrolments from a total of around 100 two years ago to approximately 500 in 1997. And equally important, this increase is resulting in a commensurate flow-on of students into other information systems units. It is also attracting a large number of computer science students who are looking to increase their skills and exposure to GUI/Windows programming.

Having introduced students to software development via Visual Basic, they are led on to database design by writing applications which require them to interact with and update Access databases, and to further programming using COBOL for the batch processing of files which the students have created using their Visual Basic applications as the medium for data input.

At the end of this two semester unit software sequence, the students have developed and implemented applications which:

- use Windows GUI-applications and require an understanding of the methodology of designing event-driven software;
- use logic/procedure-driven software requiring a structured design methodology;
- manipulate relational databases;
- update commercially oriented files of indexed and random organizations;
- create a hybrid system using mutually acceptable file and data structures to communicate between programs originally written in different languages;
- are developed in teams using professional documentation standards and project management practices;
- have a professional look-and-feel similar to marketplace software likely to be encountered in the students' working environment.

It must also be remembered that most of the students would not consider themselves primarily as 'computing' students.

The attraction of Visual Basic is that:

- much of the activity in an application can be achieved by writing very few lines of code;
- the syntax is simple and intuitive while still enabling the teaching of rigorous software style;
- the programming environment is easy to use and enables the rapid development of applications which contain all the features of contemporary applications;
- it provides a bridge to other Microsoft products, providing students with a transportable skill;
- not the least importantly: it is a recognized skill in the employment market.

5 CONCLUSION

The essential aspects of marketing programming to nonprogrammers lie in making the task enjoyable, obviously achievable and professionally relevant. To this end those of us who are pursuing this goal must choose a delivery vehicle and applications which achieve a balance. On the one hand encouraging a sufficiently rigorous approach to software development so as to satisfy our own professional standards. And on the other hand allowing students some spontaneity in the exercise and their recognition that what they are acquiring are useful knowledge and skills which will be relevant to their chosen, noncomputing career.

6 REFERENCES

Brooks, F.P. Jr (1972) *The Mythical Man-Month.* Addison-Wesley, Reading, Massachusetts.

Cox, K. and Clark, D. (1994) Computing modules that empower students. *Computers and Education*, **23** (4), 277-284.

Furber, D. (1992) A survey of teaching programming to computing undergraduates in UK universities and polytechnics. *Computer Journal*, **35**, 550-553.

Jones, J. and Pearson, E. (1993) An informal survey of initial teaching languages in UK university departments of computer science. *University Computing*, **15**, 54-57.

Lee, A. and Pennington, N. (1994) The effects of paradigm on cognitive activities in design. *International Journal of Human-Computer Studies*, **40**, 577-601.

Morton, L. and Norgaard, N. (1993) A survey of programming languages in CS programs. *SIGCSE Bulletin*, **25** (2), 9-11.

Redmond-Pyle, D. (1996) Software development methods and tools: some trends and issues. *Software Engineering Journal*, March 1996, 99-103.

7 BIOGRAPHY

Peter Juliff is professor of management information systems at Deakin University, Australia. Immediately prior to this, he was head of the Department of Software Development at Monash University and has held several other senior academic appointments. He has spent over 30 years as an IT academic and practitioner, is the author of several books on computer science and software design and has conducted IT programs in Singapore, Malaysia and China. He is a Fellow of the Australian Computer Society and its chief examiner. He is the chair of IFIP Working Group 3.4 on vocational and professional IT education.

10

Meeting the needs of industry: a bold new curriculum in information science

Doris K. Lidtke
Computer and Information Sciences, Towson State University Baltimore, Maryland 21252, USA, e-mail: lidtke@towson.edu

Michael C. Mulder
College of Information Science and Technology University of Nebraska at Omaha, Omaha, Nebraska 68182, USA, e-mail: mmulder@csalpha.uno.edu

Abstract

This paper describes the development of a new curriculum to prepare the next generation of information specialists. The project is unique in that half of the task force developing the curriculum is from business and industry. The curriculum is designed to produce a graduate who possesses the skills described in the 'profile of the graduate' which was developed by the representatives from industry. The curriculum is information centric and integrates communication skills, ethics and teamwork from the beginning. Student learning is top-down: from the broad perspective to the technical details. To accomplish this the pedagogy employed has been changed.

Keywords

Informatics, information systems, context of informatics, university education, informatics majors, curriculum (general), levels of competence, business and industry requirements, professional profiles

Informatics in Higher Education F. Mulder & T. van Weerts (Eds.)

1 INTRODUCTION

The rapid evolution of computing technology and the escalating need for business information systems have exposed a severe, overall weakness in the education of information specialists. Current curricula and supporting pedagogy are out-of-date and possibly out-of-touch with the needs of the workplace. Additionally, no clear methodology exists to deal with large grain, complex information systems design and development. To address this weakness in the education process and to explore solutions to the large information systems dilemma a group of industry and academic professionals was formed to develop a new curriculum with funding from the National Science Foundation. With the co-principal investigators of this grant this experienced task force of five industry and five academic colleagues are producing recommendations as to how to educate the next generation of information specialists. This paper focuses on the current status of the task force's curricular recommendations.

To be certain that the curriculum meets the needs of business the first task of the members from industry was to develop a detailed 'profile of the graduate', describing the characteristics and abilities that industry wants a newly graduated person to possess. In addition the level of knowledge needed for each characteristic or ability was specified.

Industry members of the task force represent a wide spectrum of enterprises and interestingly have very strong agreement on what they want in a newly hired person. They express a strong desire for people who can work in teams, can communicate well, have high professional and ethical standards, are concerned about quality and understand computing within an enterprise environment. Generally, they are pleased with the education students are receiving in the technical areas of computing at many institutions, but unanimously agree that students are lacking in many of the personal and interpersonal skills. This new curriculum meets the needs of industry and employs a new approach to student learning in information science.

With the 'profile of the graduate' as the specification the curriculum was designed and reviewed. For each course or unit in the curriculum the pre-competencies or lack thereof are indicated and the post-competencies which are expected upon completion are specified.

In designing the curriculum the 'profile of the graduate' is the specification for designing the course work for the students. The curriculum is information centric. From the very first course students learn about the role, use, importance, handling, etc. of information in enterprise environments. Ethical and professional behaviour is emphasized from the first course through the last course. Working in collaborative groups is stressed throughout the curriculum. In all the course work the students will work with others, initially working in small groups, then working in larger groups in their later courses and finally participating as team members of a real industrial project with other team members from both industry and academia. Written, oral and listening skills will be emphasized throughout the curriculum.

Students will learn with and from their instructors, their peers and their contacts in business and industry.

2 PROFILE OF THE GRADUATE

One of the unique attributes of this effort in curriculum development is that it began with a profile of a new graduate produced by the industry members of our task force. The members, representing a broad range of information usage, were able to reach consensus on the following attributes.

Technical skills

The technical skills in the graduate's profile are:

- enterprise computing architectures and delivery systems;
- information abstraction, representation and organization;
- concepts of information and systems distribution;
- human behaviour and human-computer interface;
- dynamics of change;
- process management and systems development;
- some domain knowledge.

Personal skills

The personal skills in the graduate's profile are:

- systemic thinking skills;
- problem solving skills;
- critical thinking skills;
- risk taking skills;
- personal discipline;
- persistence;
- curiosity;
- quality awareness.

Interpersonal skills

The interpersonal skills in the graduate's profile are:

- collaborative skills;
- communications skills (oral, written, listening, and group);
- conflict resolution skills.

3 THE PROCESS OF CURRICULUM DEVELOPMENT

This curriculum development effort used as its stated set of requirements the graduate's profile as described briefly above. The approach which we have used, then focused on the relationships between academic processes and industry processes and resulted in a clear view as to how students are expected to learn (that is, be transformed). Also a pedagogy to support the proposed curriculum was identified.

Process relationships

To assist in understanding the role of a curriculum in relation to the business processes in which student knowledge and skills will eventually be used, our task force described this relationship (see Figure 1). This figure helps to translate between the different 'languages' of academia and industry.

Clearly the customer of the company involved is the ultimate recipient of the products developed. Our graduates must understand the industry processes, the support processes and the steps (as seen by industry) in developing information systems. These are the same processes as the ones students should learn to understand and gain experience with, as they progress in their undergraduate program. On the other side those in industry must understand the nature of the academic environment which is also depicted in Figure 1.

Student knowledge/skills: the transformation process

To understand how best to educate information specialists the task force looked carefully at each step of the educational process and developed a model as depicted in Figure 2.

Each course or module in this transformation process represents a stage through which each student must successfully pass; it has a set of inputs and produces a set of outcomes. The inputs consist of the knowledge and skills needed to enter a course or module, or alternatively the skills which are deemed to be lacking thus far. The composite of these outcomes is a graduate who possesses the attributes described in the industry 'profile of the graduate'. Most of the entities in Figure 2 refer roughly to a course in the proposed curriculum, with the collection of courses and modules comprising the collection of required knowledge and skills. This transformation of the student is essential to develop the desired graduate.

Pedagogy

A most significant observation early in our endeavour was that too much material needs to be mastered by the student in a nominal four year program. It became obvious that for the students to reach the level needed to go into industry, both

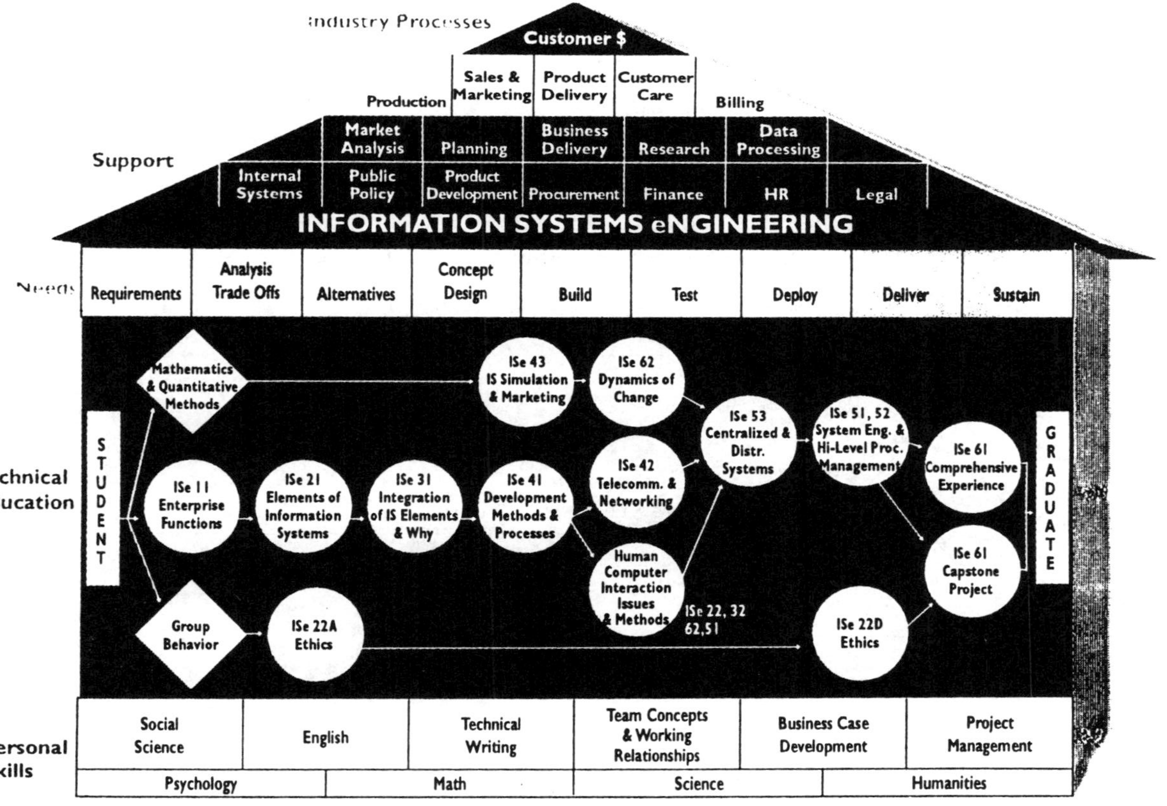

Figure 1 Process relationships.

Figure 2 Student transformation process.

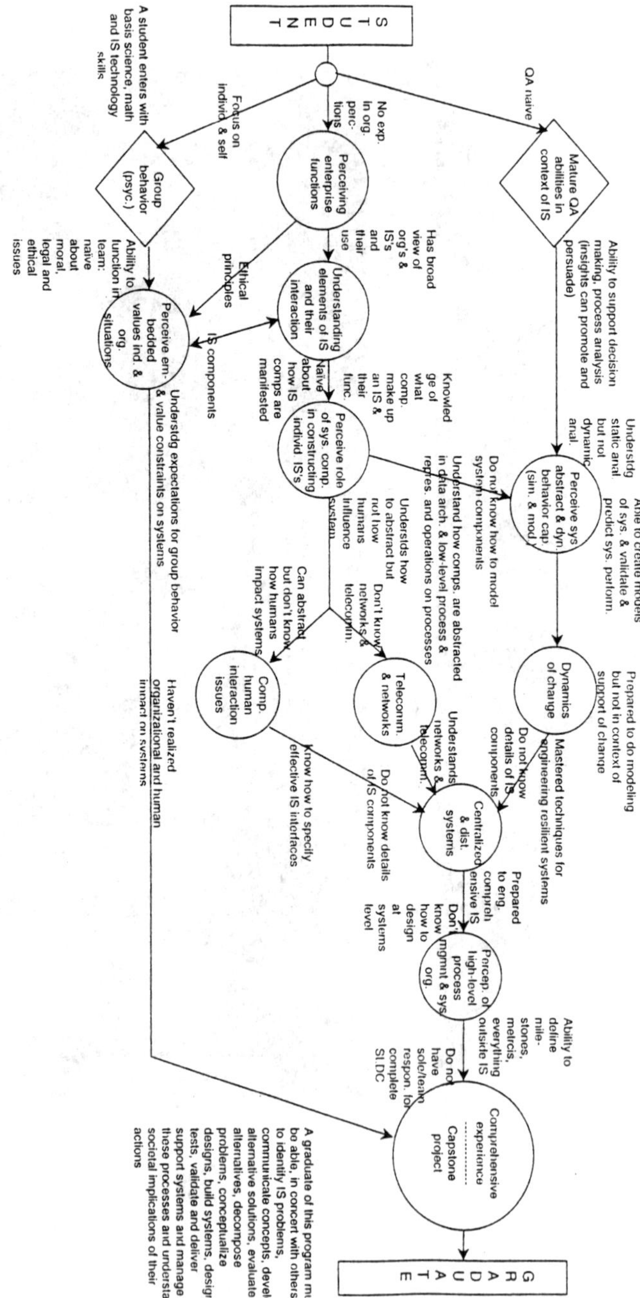

learning and teaching pedagogy would have to change. This lead to the following curriculum recommendations:

- less lecture time, more hands-on practical experience;
- students working in groups of varying sizes, less working alone;
- early exposure to case studies and system modelling, less initial deep details;
- industry involvement in teaching/learning;
- 'capstone' group design project with industry;
- students will assemble a portfolio showing progress, breadth and excellence of work;
- students will develop and practise communications skills;
- students will understand the ethics of the professional;
- students will learn the importance of curiosity, persistence and quality.

4 THE PROPOSED CURRICULUM

The curriculum comprises required courses, possible electives and additional subjects.

Required courses

The following courses are compulsory:

- Information systems in enterprises;
- Information systems architecture I;
- Ethics (integrated into the entire curriculum);
- Information systems architecture II;
- Human behaviour and human-computer interface;
- Data, information, transaction processing;
- Telecommunication and networking;
- Modelling and simulation;
- Application development;
- Process management and system engineering;
- Distributed systems;
- Capstone;
- Dynamics of change.

See the appendix in section 9 for brief sample course outlines.

Possible electives

The following courses can be elected:

- Data warehousing and mining;
- Artificial intelligence;
- Virtuality.

Additional subjects
In addition to the technical courses in the discipline students need courses in the following subjects:

- Psychology of the family or groups;
- Probability and statistics;
- Quantitative methods;
- Psychology;
- English;
- Technical writing;
- Social science;
- Humanities.

5 IMPLEMENTATION CONSIDERATIONS

This curriculum will not necessarily be appropriate, adaptable or feasible for all institutions. It is not the typical computer science program, nor is it the typical information systems program. Implementators must be aware that the courses described require considerable additional work when compared to most current courses in computing. Presently there are no texts to support many of the courses. The pedagogy is new and requires considerable faculty effort to change from the typical lecture methods which are widely used.

However, we are firmly convinced that materials to support this new curriculum will be developed and that there will be adequate materials from which to draw. Students will learn from their instructor, from their peers and from their contacts in industry. Students will develop new ways to learn, such as using the Internet and the Web, and students will 'learn to learn'. Industry will provide speakers and tours of their facilities. Many industries are happy to work with institutions to develop better prepared information specialists. Industrial experiences will provide advantages to the students by motivating them in their studies, providing them with hands-on industry experience and often providing them with their initial job. Faculty members will become more attuned to the needs of industry because they will be working as team members in student, industry and faculty teams in the capstone courses and because there will be an exchange of faculty and industry personnel. Strong ties between business, industry, government and educational institutions can be formed to the advantage of all.

6 CONCLUSION

This is a new approach to developing a curriculum to meet the needs of industry. Industry has been involved and the curriculum is different from current curricula. Students are introduced at the beginning to information and its place in enterprises, to the ethics of computing, to working in collaboration with others and to developing and practising communications skills. Active learning is emphasized, with students working in groups and the instructors providing mini-lectures as needed. Industry is involved in the curriculum. In the early stages by providing tours and talks about information, its uses, handling and importance in the enterprise. At later stages by participating as adjunct or exchange faculty, or providing projects and team members for the capstone course. Two pilots of the capstone course have been extremely successful. Currently other courses are being developed and tested.

7 ACKNOWLEDGEMENTS

This work is supported by the National Science Foundation (NSF/DUE 9455450) 'Educating the Next Generation of Information Specialists in Collaboration with Industry'. The task force members are: James Blair (USWEST), Della Bonnette (Univ. of SW Louisiana), Jimmie Haines (Boeing), Liz Kaufman (Citicorp), David Feinstein (Univ. of S. Alabama), Forouzan Golshani (Arizona State Univ), Tom Howell (Bull Info. Systems and NSF), Norman Kerth (Elite System), Anita LaSalle (American University) and Gordon Stokes (Brigham Young Univ.). Co-principal investigators are the paper's authors. National visiting committee: Gordon Davis (Univ. of Minnesota), Jimmie Haines (Boeing), A. Joe Turner (Clemson Univ.).

8 REFERENCES

Bruffee, K.A. (1993) *Collaborative learning: higher education, independence, and the authority of knowledge*. Johns Hopkins Press, Baltimore, MD.

Gibbs, W.W. (1994) Software's chronic crisis. *Scientific American*, September, 1994, 86-95.

McDonald, G. and McDonald, M. (1995) Active learning using closed laboratories: an alternative paradigm for computer science. *The Journal of computing in Small Colleges*, **10** (5).

Mulder, M.C. (1994) *Educating the next generation of information specialists: a framework for academic programs in informatics*. Report of NSF Sponsored Task Force [NSF/DUE 9354944], University of Southwestern Louisiana Press.

Mulder, M.C., Stokes, G.E. and Lidtke, D.K. (1997) Enterprise enhanced education: an information technology enabled extension of traditional learning environments. *SIGCSE Bulletin*, **29** (1), 355-59.

National society of Professional Engineers (1992) *Report on surveys of opinions of engineering deans and employers of engineering graduates on the first professional degree*. Report No. 3059, Washington, DC.

Pulham, C. (1996) Boeing helps students prepare for life in the real world. *Boeing News,* April 19, 1996, 5.

Williams, K.A. (1997) Educating the next generation of information specialists: industry and university collaborative learning pilot project. *SIGCSE Bulletin,* **29** (1), 350-54.

9 APPENDIX

Samples of brief course outlines

ISe 11 Information systems in enterprises
1.0 Enterprise information systems
2.0 Information resources in organizations
3.0 Enterprise information architectures
4.0 Current enabling tools
5.0 IS project cycles

ISe 21 Information systems architecture I
1.0 Introduction to information systems engineering
2.0 Introduction to IS communication and networking
3.0 Introduction to distributed IS platform technology
4.0 Project life cycles
5.0 IS external interfaces
6.0 Elements of an information system architecture - tying it together

ISe 22 Ethics [distributed throughout the curriculum]
1.0 Philosophical foundations of ethics
2.0 Professional ethics
3.0 Property rights for software
4.0 Privacy
5.0 Computer crime, abuse, hackers
6.0 Responsibility and liability
7.0 The future

ISe 31 Information systems architecture II
1.0 An introduction to information abstraction
2.0 Basic information elements
3.0 Hardware elements of an information system
4.0 Case studies of the role of information abstraction (with practical exercises)

ISe 32 Human behaviour and HCI
1.0 Nature of human interaction, overview and theoretical framework of HCI topics
2.0 Human as an interacting social being
3.0 Types of application areas individual vs. group, paced vs. unpaced
4.0 Human-machine fit and adaption
5.0 Human information processing
6.0 Language, communication and interaction
7.0 Ergonomics

8.0 Computer systems and interface architecture
9.0 Dev. process and design
10.0Usability tests
11.0Social organization and work
12.0 Conceptual psychology
13.0View of human behaviour
14.0Cognitive psychology
15.0Ethnography
16.0Research methods including development of conceptual models
17.0Quantitative research methods
18.0Group behaviour

ISe 41 Data, information, transaction processing
1.0 Information modelling (external view)
2.0 Internet information structures
3.0 Database design, data dependencies and integrity constraints - project
4.0 Data retrieval and query languages - project
5.0 Database operations - project
6.0 Embedded databases

ISe 42 Telecommunications and networking
1.0 Data communication and open systems standards
2.0 Data transmission
3.0 Data link protocols
4.0 Local area networks
5.0 High speed LANs
6.0 Wide area networks
7.0 Inter networking
8.0 Intranets
9.0 Systems view
10.0Network management
11.0Security
12.0Client server

ISe 51 Application development
1.0 Overview
2.0 Information organization
3.0 Multi-database environments
4.0 Decision support systems (project)
5.0 Project
6.0 Real-time control systems (project)

ISe 52 Process management and system engineering
1.0 Software engineering as an agent of change and enforcer of ethical standards

2.0 Critical success factors
3.0 Software engineeing methodologies and tools
4.0 Teaming: JAD, cleanroom, inspections
5.0 Information and data gathering and organization
6.0 Translating info. into systems architecture
7.0 Feasibility analysis and budgeting
8.0 Analysis and design (process-orientation, data-orientation, object-orientation)
9.0 Design partitioning (implementation models and evaluation)
10.0Software security issues
11.0Human interface design
12.0Software quality assurance
13.0Metrics
14.0Software testing and evaluation
15.0Procurement
16.0Delivery and maintenance

ISe 53 Distributed systems
1.0 Organizational issues
1.1 Enterprise wide information study
1.2 Enterprise distributed system policies
1.3 Enterprise distributed information system standards
1.4 Enterprise distributed system management structures
2.0 Distributed system issues
2.1 Connectivity
2.2 Directories
2.3 Transaction management
2.4 Backup
2.5 System security
2.6 Performance
3.0 Meeting the users needs

ISe 62 Dynamics of change
1.0 Dynamics and omplexity
2.0 Design for change
3.0 Experimentation as a means of capturing dynamics
4.0 Modelling process and systems

10 BIOGRAPHY

Doris Keefe Lidtke is professor of computer and information sciences at Towson State University in Baltimore, Maryland (USA) and serves currently as chairperson of the ACM SIG Board, on the ACM Council, the ACM Education Board and is president of the Computing Sciences Accreditation Board. She is the principal investigator for three National Science Foundation grants, in the field of curriculum development and implementation. ACM recognized her contributions by awarding her its 1996 Distinguished Service Award. She is a member of several ACM SIGs and a Golden Core member of the IEEE Computer Society.

Michael C. Mulder is dean of the College of Information Science and Technology at The University of Nebraska at Omaha, and co-dean of the Omaha Institute. He is an elected member of the Board of Directors of the Institute of Electrical and Electronic Engineers (IEEE), a member of the Board of Governors of the IEEE Computer Society, a commissioner of the Computing Sciences Accreditation Commission (CSAC), and an advisor to the National Science Foundation (NSF). He has a broad and varied background in computing, including leadership roles in academe, industry, and government. He remains an active researcher in complex information systems and educational teaching/learning pedagogy. He has received $3.7M in external funding from the NSF (8) and industry (17) grants and awards. He is a senior consultant with The Boeing Company for many years. He has published with 14 journal/transactions and 97 other peer reviewed technical and educational papers. He has received 10 awards and recognitions of his many contributions to the profession. He is a senior member of the IEEE and is a registered professional engineer.

11

Specifying and comparing informatics curricula through UCSI®

Fred Mulder
Faculty of Engineering (Informatics), Open University, PO Box 2960 6401 DL Heerlen, The Netherlands, e-mail: fred.mulder@ouh.nl

Anneke E.N. Hacquebard
Consultancy for Informatics and Education Hacquebard bv Keppelseweg 48, 6999 AR Hummelo, The Netherlands e-mail: hacque@pi.net

Abstract

UCSI is a classification system primarily aiming at informatics education and training. Since its conception in 1992 it has been used in various pilot projects in different educational sectors in the Netherlands. In this paper we discuss the origin, the scope and possible applications of UCSI. Also some results are presented of a study in which curricula of four Dutch educational programmes for informatics engineers were compared. These results both exemplify the approach and give indications for other relevant curriculum studies, especially in an international context.

Keywords

Informatics, other disciplines, curriculum (general), taxonomies, levels of competence, educational profiles

Informatics in Higher Education F. Mulder & T. van Weerts (Eds.)

1 INTRODUCTION

Not satisfied with the continuing struggle on terminology in our field the Unified Classification Scheme for Informatics (UCSI) was introduced in 1992 as a new classification system for the discipline 'informatics' (Mulder, 1992; Mulder *et al.*, 1992). Another reason for its introduction was the fact that the various available systems, although of reputation and certainly adequate on their own, were too specific in their approach of the discipline and therefore virtually incompatible.

In the beginning of the nineties we were running a project to characterize and compare in a quantitative manner higher informatics education in the Netherlands. However, the needed overall 'measuring instruments' were lacking. Of course the more familiar qualitative descriptive method could have been followed, but that implied drawbacks such as the impossibility to achieve objectivity, reproducibility, accuracy and depth. UCSI was introduced to avoid these drawbacks.

2 UCSI: MERGE OF EXISTING SYSTEMS

UCSI has been developed on the basis of a number of recognized, specific source systems or schemes and merges them into one overall and broader system.

2.1 Six sources, three approaches

UCSI is based on six sources:

- **Computing Reviews 1991,**
  the well-known and very detailed taxonomy for the classification of literature of the journal Computing Reviews, which is a four level system (we have used the version presented in Coulter (1991));
- **Computer Abstracts 1990,**
  the global system for the classification of literature of the journal Computer Abstracts, which exists since 1957 and is a one page, two level system (we have used the substantially updated 1990 version, see Computer Abstracts (1990));
- **DPMA 1991,**
  the three level knowledge tree, which is the basis of DPMA's model curriculum for 'information systems' (see Longenecker and Feinstein (1991); DPMA stands for the Data Processing Management Association from the USA);
- **ACM and IEEE-CS 1991,**
  the matrix with knowledge elements on the basis of which a whole spectrum of model curricula varying between 'computer science' and 'computer engineering' has been developed by ACM and IEEE-CS (see ACM/IEEE-CS (1991); ACM = Association for Computing Machinery, and IEEE-CS = Institute of Electrical and Electronics Engineers Computer Society, both from the USA);

- **IEEE-CS 1983,**
  the older, comprehensive modular domain description of 'computer science and engineering' of IEEE-CS, which was the starting-point for various educational programmes (IEEE-CS, 1983);
- **IFIP 1987,**
  the older, modular curriculum for 'information systems', developed by BCS and adopted by IFIP (see Buckingham *et al.* (1987); BCS = British Computer Society, and IFIP = International Federation for Information Processing).

In selecting the sources, we have taken care of finding a fair balance between the three 'classical' and originally rather separate approaches of the discipline in the USA:

- computer science;
- computer (science and) engineering;
- information systems.

An interesting source is the fourth one, ACM/IEEE-CS (1991), which represents a successful common effort to bring together the first two of the three approaches, building on the influential paper by Denning *et al.* defining 'computing' as a discipline. A similar joint activity of ACM, DPMA (which now is called AITP = Association of Information Technology Professionals) and AIS (= Association for Information Systems) has explored the third approach or field of 'information systems' (IS) and has been reported on recently (Davis *et al.*, 1997). The resulting model curriculum IS'97 is based on an IS body of knowledge which still has to be added as a seventh, new source underlying UCSI. A first quick study, however, shows a large similarity with the earlier approach of DPMA (1991), so that there is no need to change UCSI in its latest three level release (as presented in Figure 1).

2.2 Design process, outcome and maintenance

UCSI has resulted from an iterative process of going through the six source schemes and their related terminologies (which sometimes differ substantially). In order to manage the rather extensive information contained in the descriptions of the existing schemes as well as in the new scheme UCSI, a database has been designed.

In each iteration step a particular level of UCSI was specified by refinement into the next level. Input for each step was a carefully chosen set of UCSI descriptors; sometimes the terms used are similar to existing ones, sometimes not. Other input consisted of the items collected from the various source schemes. Allocation of these items to the UCSI descriptors yields a comprehensive specification for each descriptor. The next iteration step then starts with the conversion of these descriptor specifications into a limited number of new UCSI descriptors, one level deeper.

The final outcome of the process is a specification of the discipline 'informatics' in a four level knowledge domain tree. Figure 1 shows four (numbered) main domains at the highest UCSI level. Each main domain - apart from 'miscellaneous' - is further specified by at most five domains, which in turn are specified by not more than four subdomains. The subdomains are specified at the fourth level (not shown in Figure 1) by sets of selected descriptors. Except for the fourth level, it is easy to show the relations between UCSI and the source schemes, thanks to the use of the database mentioned.

1 Computer systems	**2 Software systems**
1.1 Hardware structures and digital systems	*2.1 Programming languages and environments*
1.1.1 Digital components	2.1.1 Language constructs
1.1.2 Circuits and structures	2.1.2 Specific languages and environments
1.1.3 Digital systems	2.1.3 Language processors
1.1.4 Integrated circuits	2.1.4 Language concepts
1.1.9 Miscellaneous	2.1.9 Miscellaneous
1.2 Computer architecture	*2.2 Software architecture*
1.2.1 Memory systems	2.2.1 Data structures
1.2.2 Processor architectures	2.2.2. Algorithms
1.2.3 Instruction sets and data representation	2.2.3 Programming techniques and strategies
1.2.4 Assembly languages	
1.2.9 Miscellaneous	2.2.9 Miscellaneous
1.3 Interfacing and peripherals	*2.3 Software engineering (SE)*
1.3.1 Interfacing technology	2.3.1 Software requirements and specification
1.3.2 Input/output systems	2.3.2 Software development process
1.3.3 Storage systems	2.3.3 Software exploitation
1.3.4 Peripheral devices	2.3.4 SE methods, techniques and tools
1.3.9 Miscellaneous	2.3.9 Miscellaneous
1.4 Communication and networks	*2.4 Artificial intelligence (AI)*
1.4.1 Communication technology	2.4.1 AI fields
1.4.2 Network architectures	2.4.2 AI methods, techniques and tools
1.4.3 Network protocols	2.4.3 AI concepts
1.4.4 Network management	
1.4.9 Miscellaneous	2.4.9 Miscellaneous
1.5 Operating systems and system software	*2.5 Theory of computing*
1.5.1 File and device management	2.5.1 Formal languages and automata
1.5.2 Process management	2.5.2 Computability and complexity
1.5.3 System management	2.5.3 Semantics of programs
1.5.4 System software	2.5.4 Information and coding theory
1.5.9 Miscellaneous	2.5.9 Miscellaneous
1.9 Miscellaneous	*2.9 Miscellaneous*

Figure 1 (First half) Three level specification of the discipline 'informatics' according to UCSI

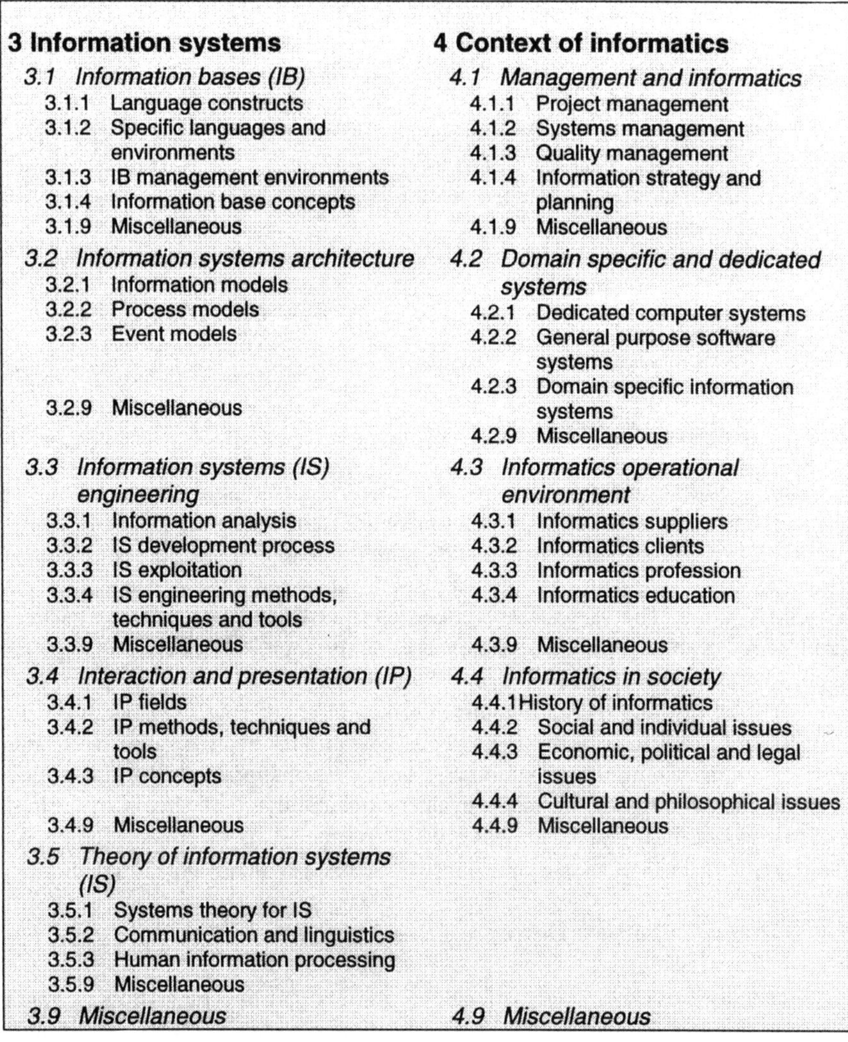

Figure 1 (Second half) Three level specification of the discipline 'informatics' according to UCSI (release 1.2, 1997); there is a detailed fourth level which is not shown.

Once created, maintenance of the system is a simple task. This paper describes UCSI in release 1.2 which implies a minor update on the first three levels:

- a number of descriptors has been changed;
- some subdomains were combined into one subdomain or were swapped;
- 'miscellaneous' is indicated now by a '9' instead of an 'm'.

At the fourth level changes are substantial: for example, to be more complete and precise, descriptors have been added from new sources. A rather high degree of dynamics is however acceptable at this level, since - contrary to the three upper levels - the fourth level does not provide classifying items.

Summarizing: UCSI has been designed to offer a more balanced and broader view of 'informatics' than each of its individual sources. The main advantage of UCSI is that it 'unifies' a number of more specific approaches of the discipline 'informatics'.

3 CURRICULUM SPECIFICATION AND COMPARISON: INGREDIENTS

3.1 Mapping curriculum information

Comparing educational programmes can be done at different moments (for one and the same institute) or between different institutes (at the same moment). In the first case one can use the approach and terminology of that institute and obtain - dependent on the quality of the data - a comparison of the curriculum over successive years. The second case is complicated by the fact that approach and terminology at the various institutes are rarely identical. Such a comparison requires an instrument based on accepted standards.

For each institute the curriculum information about courses, laboratories and projects (referring to aspects as contents, educational goals, examination, study load, position within the programme) should be mapped onto a standardized scheme. On the basis of the mapped data a quantitative comparison of curricula across different institutes is straightforward. As far as the informatics contents is concerned UCSI offers an adequate unified scheme. But that is not sufficient.

3.2 Other disciplines: Dewey

Generally informatics educational programmes also contain noninformatics subjects. This may not be the case for short, specific courses and training components, but always holds for full programmes extending over a number of years. As a consequence another ingredient is needed for specification of this noninformatics component.

This has been found in the well-known general library classification system of Dewey/Mitchell *et al.*, 1996 (for an impression see Figure 2). This system was designed and introduced in 1876 by Melvil Dewey (size: 44 pages) and was in 1996 in its 21st edition (various printed volumes, but also online available). Dewey's system is multi-level and covers all disciplines in detail; it includes informatics, but in our opinion not in an adequate way. Therefore UCSI is used for informatics and Dewey's system for the other disciplines, but only in a global and very selective way.

3.3 A taxonomy of views

Any classification scheme should take account of the nature, depth or level of the components of the curriculum. For instance, it obviously matters what students do with a subject as 'operating systems' (UCSI domain 1.5): do they merely receive hands-on Windows user experience, or skills to design new operating systems, or theoretical insight in the concepts behind operating systems? The additional ingredient therefore has to be some taxonomy.

000 Generalities
- 010 Bibliography
- 020 Library & information sciences
- 030 General encyclopedic works
- .
- 090 Manuscripts & rare books

100 Philosophy & psychology
- 110 Metaphysics
- 120 Epistemology, causation, humankind
- 130 Paranormal phenomena
- 140 Specific philosophical schools
- 150 Psychology
- .
- .
- .
- .
- .
- 190 Modern western philosophy

200 Religion
- 210 Philosophy & theory of religion
- .
- 290 Comparative religion & other religions

500 Natural sciences & mathematics
- 510 Mathematics
- 520 Astronomy & allied sciences
- 530 Physics
- .
- 590 Animals

600 Technology (Applied sciences)
- 610 Medical sciences Medicine
- 620 Engineering & allied operations
- 630 Agriculture & related technologies
- 640 Home economics & family living
- 650 Management & auxiliary services
- .
- 690 Buildings

700 The arts Fine and decorative arts
- 710 Civic & landscape art
- .
- 790 Recreational & performing arts

Figure 2 Fragments from the Dewey Decimal Classification (part 2).

300 Social sciences

310	Collections of general statistics
320	Political science
330	Economics
340	Law
350	Public administration & military science
360	Social problems & services; associations
370	Education
380	Commerce, communications, transportation
.	
.	
390	Customs, etiquette, folklore

400 Language

410	Linguistics
420	English & Old English
.	
.	
490	Other languages

800 Literature & rhetoric

810	American literature in English
820	English & Old English literatures
830	Literatures of Germanic languages
840	Literatures of Romance languages
850	Italian, Romanian, Rhaeto-Romanic
860	Spanish & Portugese literatures
870	Italic literatures Latin
880	Hellenic literatures Classical Greek
890	Literatures of other languages

900 Geography & history

910	Geography & travel
920	Biography, genealogy, insignia
.	
990	General history of other areas

Figure 2 Fragments from the Dewey Decimal Classification (part 2).

The experience from the pilot projects is that an educational goal taxonomy like Bloom's (Bloom *et al.*, 1956) is not appropriate. In such a taxonomy one is forced to descend to micro level to be able to assign educational goals to small units. Apart from the fact that the programme information does in general not offer enough detail, it also seems pointless to go into so much detail.

Here a global taxonomy is used in which we distinguish six so-called 'views', the view of:

1. **concept,**
   which emphasizes the mastering of theoretical concepts and abstract problems;
2. **model,**
   in which models are developed for concrete problems and situations;
3. **application,**
   which accentuates the application of theories and models to obtain practical results;
4. **design,**
   in which systems are designed from scratch to realization;
5. **use,**
   which concentrates on working with ready for use systems (both generic and specific);

6. **knowledge,**
   which deals with bare knowledge and insight in a specific subject.

Originally a set of five views was proposed (Mulder, 1992); here one of these views has been split into two new ones: 'application' (3) and 'use' (5). Views 1, 2 and 4 are more or less similar to the three so-called 'basic processes' or 'paradigms' in Denning *et al.* (1989), along which the discipline 'computing' can be considered, namely:

- theory, rooted in mathematics;
- abstraction , rooted in science (the experimental method);
- design, rooted in engineering.

4 EXAMPLES OF UCSI-BASED CURRICULUM COMPARISON

With UCSI we have compared the curricula of all informatics engineer's programmes that exist in the Netherlands; they run at the three Technical Universities (TU's) of Delft, Eindhoven and Twente and at the Open University (OU). The institutes' information on the programmes for students served as input in order to specify the various curriculum components on the basis of UCSI and Dewey. At the TU's we took all the courses of the first two years, whereas at the OU we took the compulsory part. Accidentally these have the same size in terms of study load: 84 so-called study points (each point the equivalent of 40 hours of study) or 3360 hours of study load in total which equals 50% of the full programmes.

For each course of the individual curricula the following data were assembled in a database:

- name, code, position in the curriculum, educational setting (class, lab, etc.) and study load (institute's data);
- the UCSI or Dewey specification, dividing the programme components - when necessary - over various domains (we decided on a global specification, not deeper than UCSI level 2);
- the corresponding views, choosing from the six types as described in subsection 3.3.

On the basis of these data all kinds of reports may be produced answering questions with respect to the curricula, both for a particular institute and comparatively across the institutes. Let us give two examples.

4.1 Different streams at one institute

In Table 1 we analyse the OU curriculum with respect to the four specializations or 'streams' that can be chosen by students. Course data have been totalled over the various UCSI (main) domains. For the noninformatics subjects the basis is the

Dewey classification, but collected in four main disciplines, as shown in Table 2. The remaining part of the curriculum, elective courses (60 study points) and a substantial final project (24 study points), is more difficult to specify, being student dependent. No unique specification can be made for this component.

Other than is the case with just a list of subjects or courses, the data from Table 1 'speak for themselves'. The variance in emphasis on the four different streams is clearly visible in the study load data of the compulsory component. It would be both possible and useful to draw conclusions from the table's data, but in this paper we confine ourselves to the mere presentation of 'numeric prints' of the educational programme of one institute in its various appearances.

Table 1

UCSI specification of the informatics engineer's programme of the Dutch Open University: version 1994/1995, compulsory part (50% of the full programme), four streams: CS = computer systems, SS = software systems, IS = information systems, I&M = informatics and management

	UCSI main domain and domain	*Study load (in hours) per stream*			
Code	*Descriptor*	*CS*	*SS*	*IS*	*I&M*
1	*Computer systems*	*1044*	*564*	*288*	*564*
1.1	Hardware structures and digital systems	204	84	84	84
1.2	Computer architecture	216	180	36	180
1.3	Interfacing and peripherals	120	36	24	36
1.4	Communication and networks	144	144	144	144
1.5	Operating systems and system software	120	120	–	120
1.9	Miscellaneous	240	–	–	–
2	*Software systems*	*786*	*1266*	*462*	*666*
2.1	Programming languages and environments	276	468	192	276
2.2	Software architecture	240	276	120	240
2.3	Software engineering	120	120	120	120
2.4	Artificial intelligence	30	42	30	30
2.5	Theory of computing	120	120	–	–
2.9	Miscellaneous	–	240	–	–
3	*Information systems*	*522*	*750*	*990*	*522*
3.1	Information bases	168	228	228	168
3.2	Information systems architecture	120	180	180	120
3.3	Information systems engineering	114	222	222	114
3.4	Interaction and presentation	120	120	120	120
3.5	Theory of information systems	–	–	–	–
3.9	Miscellaneous	–	–	240	–

Table 1 (continued)

4	*Context of informatics*	*48*	*60*	*252*	*288*
4.1	Management and informatics	–	12	204	–
4.2	Domain specific and dedicated systems	–	–	–	–
4.3	Informatics operational environment	24	24	24	24
4.4	Informatics in society	24	24	24	24
4.9	Miscellaneous	–	–	–	240
	Informatics (total)	**2400**	**2640**	**1992**	**2040**
–	*Systems*	120	–	12	–
–	*Mathematics*	600	720	840	630
–	*Engineering*	240	–	–	–
–	*Management*	–	–	516	690
	Other disciplines (total)	**960**	**720**	**1368**	**1320**
	Total	**3360**	**3360**	**3360**	**3360**

4.2 Curricula at different institutes

Another example is presented in Table 2 where we compare the different informatics engineer's programmes in The Netherlands. Again it is not within the scope of this paper to draw conclusions, still the large differences between the institutional profiles are noteworthy.

Table 2
UCSI specification of the informatics engineer's programmes of the three Dutch Technical Universities (TU1, TU2 and TU3) and the Open University (OU): versions 1994/1995, 50% of the full programme (compulsory); for the OU two of the four streams are shown (see also Table 1)

UCSI main domain		*Component (%) per educational programme*				
Code	*Descriptor*	*TU1*	*TU2*	*TU3*	*OU/SS*	*OU/I&M*
1	Computer systems	21.2	9.0	13.5	16.8	16.8
2	Software systems	21.2	40.1	28.8	37.7	19.8
3	Information systems	10.6	2.1	9.8	22.3	15.5
4	Context of informatics	5.9	4.8	13.1	1.8	8.6
–	Informatics, not assigned (elective)	7.0	–	2.3	–	–
	Informatics (total)	**65.9**	**56.0**	**67.5**	**78.6**	**60.7**
–	Mathematics	23.5	43.0	27.1	21.4	18.8
–	Other disciplines (mainly Management)	10.6	1.0	5.4	–	20.5
	Other disciplines (total)	**34.1**	**44.0**	**32.5**	**21.4**	**39.3**

Table 2 is presented in terms of the UCSI main domains, but could just as easily be presented at any UCSI level of detail since the data are available in the database. From the data in Table 2 not only a comparison of different programmes can be made, but other questions can be answered as well, for example with respect to the relative use of the six views within the programmes and to the development throughout the years of a programme within one institute.

5 CONCLUSION

UCSI is a useful instrument for 'measuring' informatics educational programmes, as shown in the examples in this paper. The results of this kind of study are important for beginning students as well as for industry and government who take in graduates. The various informatics educational programmes can be mapped on 'numeric prints', showing the similarities and the differences. Similar comparative studies can be done at an international level, for example comparing the two curricula on computing science (ACM/IEEE-CS, 1991) and information systems (IS'97, see Davis *et al.*, 1997).

6 ACKNOWLEDGEMENTS

The authors would like to thank Deny Smeets and Tinie Veenstra-Strijland for their valuable help in running a pilot project in which UCSI was developed.

7 REFERENCES

ACM/IEEE-CS (1991) *Computing curricula 1991*, Report of the ACM/ IEEE-CS Joint Curriculum Task Force. ACM, New York; IEEE-CS, Los Angeles.

Bloom, B.S. [ed.] (1956) *Taxonomy of educational objectives, Handbook 1: Cognitive domain*. David McKay, New York.

Buckingham, R.A., Hirschheim, R.A., Land, F.F.and Tully, C.J. (1987) Information systems curriculum: a basis for course design, in *Information systems education: recommendations and implementation* (eds. R.A. Buckingham, R.A. Hirschheim, F.F. Land and C.J. Tully), BCS Monograph in Informatics. Cambridge University Press, Cambridge, 14-133.

Computer Abstracts (1990) Classification scheme. *Computer Abstracts,* **34**, table of contents in each volume number.

Coulter, N.S. [ed.] (1991) Update to the Computing Reviews Classification System. *Computing Reviews,* **32** (1), 5-50.

Davis, G.B., Gorgone, J.T., Couger, J.D., Feinstein, D.L. and Longenecker Jr, H.E. (1997) IS'97: Model Curriculum and Guidelines for Undergraduate Degree Programs in Information Systems. *Data Base*, **28** (1), 1-94.

Denning, P.J., Comer, D.E., Gries, D., Mulder, M.C., Tucker, A.B., Turner, A.J. and Young, P.R. (1989) Computing as a discipline. *Communications of the ACM,* **32** (1), 9-23.

Dewey, M. [devisor] / Mitchell, J.S. [ed.] (1996) *Summaries DDC 21: Dewey Decimal Classification,* edition 21. Forest Press, New York. Online version: http://www.oclc.org/fp/.

Hacquebard, A.E.N., Mulder, F., Smeets, D. and Veenstra-Strijland, T. (1992) Wat doet een opleiding aan informatica? Onderzoek het met UCSIE!. *TINFON,* **1** (3-4), 96-99 [in Dutch].

IEEE-CS (1983) *The 1983 IEEE Computer Society model program in computer science and engineerin.* Report of the Model Program Committee of the Educational Activities Board. IEEE, Los Angeles.

Longenecker Jr, H.E. and Feinstein, D.L. [eds.] (1991) *Information systems. The DPMA model curriculum for a four year undergraduate degree.* Report of the DPMA Curriculum Task Force 1990s. DPMA, Park Ridge IL.

Mulder, F. (1992) *Identiteit van informatica-onderwijs.* Inauguration. Open universiteit, Heerlen [in Dutch].

Mulder, F., Hacquebard, A.E.N., Smeets, D. and Veenstra-Strijland, T. (1992) Database technology for curriculum comparison as applied to informatics education, in *European Conference on Educational Research. Book of summaries, Vol. 1* (eds. Tj. Plomp, J.M. Pieters and A. Feteris), University of Twente, Enschede, 165-167.

8 BIOGRAPHY

Fred Mulder is working at the Dutch Open University from its start in 1983 and is full professor in informatics education since 1991. From 1993 till 1996 he was dean of the Faculty of Engineering. He holds degrees in chemical engineering (Bachelor), applied mathematics (Engineer) and theoretical chemistry (Ph.D.). After a postdoc research project in Canada, he went to teach informatics and mathematics in higher professional education, prior to his OU career. He has served on various national committees, such as the quality audit committees for informatics programmes at universities as well as higher professional institutes and committees for informatics at secondary schools. He is representing The Netherlands in the education committee TC3 of IFIP.

Anneke E.N. Hacquebard is a consultant for informatics and education since 1986. Her main fields of interest and professional activities are informatics curricula in higher professional education, the introduction of informatics curricula in secondary schools at a national level and the introduction of the European

Computer Driving Licence in the Netherlands. She chairs the education department of the Dutch Computer Society. From 1970 till 1986 she has taught mathematics, operational research and informatics and was a staff member at an institute for higher professional education. She holds a degree in mathematics from Leiden University and a qualification for teaching informatics at the higher professional level.

12

Computer science education in Japanese universities

Hajime Ohiwa
Department of Environmental Information, Keio University
5322 Endo, Fujisawa-shi, Kanagawa 252, Japan
e-mail: ohiwa@sfc.keio.ac.jp

Nobumasa Takahashi
Department of Computer Science, Takushoku University
815-1 Tatemachi, Hachioji-shi, Tokyo 193, Japan
e-mail: takahashi@cs.takushoku-u.ac.jp

Tsurayuki Kado
Information Systems Group, Hitachi Ltd.
6-27-18 Minami-Oi, Shinagawa-ku, Tokyo 140, Japan
e-mail: t-kado@comp.hitachi.co.jp

Abstract

In this paper the early research with respect to computers in Japan is briefly described. Then it is reported how computer science education was started under the name 'information engineering' or 'information science' in most universities in Japan. The situation was not ideal, as is illustrated by the fact that electrical engineering with FORTRAN programming could also be grouped under these headings. Some efforts of the Information Processing Society of Japan to overcome this situation are discussed. Also the results of a discussion about general informatics education for noninformatics majors are reported.

Keywords

Informatics, university education, informatics majors, noninformatics majors, curriculum (general), academic requirements

Informatics in Higher Education F. Mulder & T. van Weerts (Eds.)

1 EARLY COMPUTER RESEARCH IN JAPAN

Research on computers started in the late 1950's in several universities, such as the University of Tokyo, Kyoto University and Osaka University. Research was also started by the electrotechnical laboratory of the Ministry of International Trade and Industry, the Musashino Electro-Communication Laboratory of Nippon Telegraph and Telephone(NTT) Company and other research laboratories of electronics companies.

Unique to Japan among these research activities is the invention of Parametron by E. Goto of the University of Tokyo. Parametron uses parameterized excitation of a magnetic core and works as a majority logic element. The Parametron was so reliable and cheap that several of the early commercial computers are constructed on the basis of this element and many computer engineers were educated in this technology. However, because Parametron has an inherent limitation of processing speed, it was superseded by semi-conductor technology.

In 1965 a computer centre was established in the University of Tokyo and a large scale transistor computer HITAC 5020 of Hitachi was installed. Hitachi had won the order in severe competition with American computer manufacturers. An operating system was developed for this system by one of the authors of this paper (Nobumasa Takahashi); the resulting computer system was used by all academic researchers in Japan.

At the same time, research on software was started in Japanese universities. For example, a research group supervised by professor Yamanouchi of Keio University did research on language processors together with computer manufacturers. A group led by aforementioned professor Takahashi of the University of Tokyo developed a time sharing system with virtual memory on the Hitac 5020 of the computer centre in collaboration with the research group headed by another of the authors (Nobumasa Takahashi) of Hitachi Central Research Laboratories.

These early research activities were very sound, but they were interrupted in October 1971 by the national decision by the Ministry of International Trade and Industry together with computer manufactures. They decided to follow the IBM architecture; enormous profits have come out from this decision. This meant that, at least in industry, no substantial research other than on the IBM architecture was allowed.

2 COMPUTER SCIENCE EDUCATION IN JAPANESE UNIVERSITIES

In 1970 formal computer science education started at five universities in Japan, although in several universities research on computer science already dated from the late 1950's. The name computer science was used as a department name in new universities, namely, Yamanashi University and the University of Electro-

Communications. However, the name Department of Information Engineering was adopted by Kyoto University and Osaka University. The name Department of Information Science was adopted by the Tokyo Institute of Technology. In these old universities the combination of the terms computer and science could not be understood by fellow professors, because they believed that a computer was just a tool.

The notion of computer science, as described in Curriculum '68 of ACM (ACM, 1968), was correctly understood in all five universities. However, in most of the departments of information engineering in other universities later following the five, computer science was understood as electrical engineering with a FORTRAN option.

Upon establishing a new department in national universities, the Ministry of Education usually offers four chairs for each department, where a chair is composed of a professor, an associate professor and a research associate. The university must propose qualified faculty members to fill these chairs. Professors must be over forty years of age and must have written a considerable numbers of academic papers. Because of this restriction almost no computer scientist could become a professor at the departments founded after the first five. Persons in computer related fields or even with no experience with computers became professors of information engineering at these new departments. The name of information engineering allowed this, because almost any field relates to information.

Although such an implementation of information engineering departments is deplorable from the viewpoint of computer science, it should be noted here that from the viewpoint of Japanese society in general it really was very effective for overcoming the shortage of human resources in electronics industry. Further details of engineering education and its relationship to Japanese industry can be found in Takahashi (1992).

In the late 1980's the Ministry of Education tried to reform the engineering departments of national universities in such a way that several departments were brought together in a large department with an enlarged chair of several professors, associate professors and research associates. For example, a department of information engineering, a department of electronics and a department of applied physics became one department of electronics and information engineering. The number of students who did something with computers automatically tripled, but no substantial increase was made for the faculty as a whole. As a consequence the quality of computer science education was degraded.

Depreciation of computer science is also often seen in Japanese industry. The discipline in which the management of computer industries has been educated is mostly electrical engineering. Many of these managers have no real experience with computers, because when these senior engineers were the students, no computer science existed. They do not like to discuss technical details with their engineers and prefer to employ university graduates with little computer science background.

One of the reasons for this depreciation of computer science both in industry and academia may arise from the fact that in Japan very competent engineers graduate from very good engineering educational institutions. In the field of computer applications to engineering problems, the difficulties lie in the problem itself and not in programming. These engineers can do their jobs without professional training in computer science. In fact, after a two or three month course in a programming language, engineers start their professional jobs. This is true not only for electrical or mechanical engineers but also for software engineers.

3 COMPUTER SCIENCE CURRICULUM J90

Some computer scientists in Japan deplored the depreciation of computer science and started to establish a computer science curriculum for Japanese universities. In 1987 a committee was established in the Information Processing Society of Japan (IPSJ). The next year, the Ministry of Education asked the committee to propose a standard curriculum for the information engineering departments. In 1990 the results were reported as Curriculum J90 from the IPSJ. Since then this curriculum has been used for establishing new departments in computer related fields by the University Establishment Council which is organized by the Ministry of Education.

Curriculum J90 of the IPSJ is based on Curriculum '78 of ACM (ACM, 1978) with some extensions on Japanese language processing and with some modifications being made according to 'The report of the ACM task force on the core of computer science' (Denning *et al.*, 1989). The report of J90 contains examples of laboratory work and test problems to be addressed by students in computer science.

The core of Curriculum J90 consists of the following modules:

- JCS1 Introduction to programming;
- JCS2 Program design and its implementation;
- JCS3 Introduction to computer systems;
- JCS4 Fundamentals of computer hardware;
- JCS5 Information structure and algorithm analysis;
- JCS6 Operating systems and architecture I;
- JCS7 Structure of programming languages.

In addition to this core half the number of the following modules is recommended for study by computer science major students:

- JCS8 Operating systems and architecture II;
- JCS9 File and database systems;
- JCS10 Artificial intelligence;
- JCS11 Human interface;
- JCS12 Models of computations and algorithms;
- JCS13 Software design and development;
- JCS14 Theory and practice of programming languages;

- JCS15 Theory and practice of numerical nomputations.

This curriculum is now under revision by the professors of computer science who graduated from Japanese information engineering departments. The revised curriculum, Curriculum J97, is expected to be published soon.

4 COMPUTER SCIENCE CURRICULUM J97

Curriculum J90 was revised because of the changing position of universities in Japanese society. In 1991 the Ministry of Education changed its policy and removed the difference between general and specialized subjects in undergraduate university education; the emphasis was put on graduate education. Entrance qualifications were lowered so that the number of students making the transfer from junior colleges and technical colleges to university was increased. Also the need for recurrent education for engineers currently working is increasing in Japanese society. Because of these social pressures the Japanese universities are now reforming themselves.

The curriculum revision committee decided that in view of the wide variety of knowledge and abilities of the students the curriculum should cover the width of computer science, rather than address the essential elements, the clarification of which was the important objective of the J90 curriculum. Although width was pursued in the curriculum, also the central notions of computer science had to be addressed.

These were expressed as follows.

- Computer science deals with the logical concept of information in the physical world in such a way that the proposed ideas must be verified in the real physical world.
- The levels of abstraction in information processing must be carefully incorporated into the curriculum.

The notion of abstraction is central in computer science, but this notion may allow a black box solution thereby possibly hiding the real issues in the problem. To avoid this, computer science education must give the students systematic knowledge of the various abstraction levels, flexible views on computation and ability to cope with real world problems for which no single solution exists.

Currently the following subjects are proposed. Changes may however occur after the review process by the members of the Information Processing Society of Japan. In the proposal a model syllabus is given for each subject.

Computer literacy

L-1 Introduction to computer science

L-2 Introduction to programming

Mathematics for informatics

M-1 Information algebra and coding theory
M-2 Discrete mathematics
M-3 Computation theory
M-4 Probability and information theory
M-5 Mathematical programming
M-6 Mathematical logic

Undergraduate education subjects

U-1 Logic circuits
U-2 Formal languages and automata
U-3 Data structures and algorithms
U-4 Computer architecture
U-5 Introduction to programming languages
U-6 Logic design
U-7 Operating systems
U-8 Compilers
U-9 Digital communications
U-10 Databases
U-11 Artificial intelligence
U-12 Information network
U-13 Design and construction of programs
U-14 Numerical computations
U-15 Integrated circuits
U-16 Signal processing
U-17 Image processing
U-18 Pattern recognition
U-19 Human interface
U-20 Computer graphics
U-21 Natural language processing

Advanced subjects for graduate students

A-1 Advanced logic circuits
A-2 Advanced computer architecture
A-3 Advanced operating systems
A-4 Advanced databases
A-5 Advanced image processing
A-6 Advanced computer graphics
A-7 Advanced signal processing

Other subjects for graduate students

G-1 Algorithms for hardware
G-2 Logic design and CAD
G-3 Semantics of programs

G-4 Network architecture
G-5 Distributed systems
G-6 Software engineering
G-7 Functional programming
G-8 Object-oriented programming
G-9 Voice signal processing
G-10 Information security

5 GENERAL INFORMATICS EDUCATION

In 1991 the Ministry of Education asked the Information Processing Society of Japan to develop a curriculum for general informatics education of noninformatics majors students. A committee of 21 members was formed for this purpose and discussions lasted two years. The members of the committee were computer scientists, computer users and company engineers chaired by one of the authors (Hajime Ohiwa).

The results of the discussions were:

- clarification of the philosophy of general informatics education;
- the contents of such an education;
- guidelines as to how to carry out such education.

As to the philosophy, the committee concluded that general informatics education should make the students understand the notions of computers and information and should develop the ability to utilize these notions for the benefits of society. The philosophy also stressed that the foundation of this general education should be computer science. As to the contents, computer literacy, 'programming', and concepts of the computer and information were proposed. Here, computer literacy covers topics from keyboard training to word processing and communication through computer networks.

Generally speaking, programming education for noninformatics majors did not work well in Japan until then. This was because students were only taught programming language rules and were not taught how to write a program. The committee recommended that 'programming' education should be a problem solving activity. Starting from the definition of the problem a design process should follow. Then implementation and its evaluation should be done. The whole process must be reviewed and re-definition of the problem or re-design may come afterwards. As for the concepts of the computer and information, it was stressed that the important concepts of computer science should not be directly taught, but in the form of concrete examples.

It should be noted that most of the contents of computer literacy education should be taught at elementary and secondary level. However, computer education for this level is at the moment virtually non-existent in Japan and for those students entering universities computer literacy education must for the moment be done at university level.

Finally, the committee stressed that the education should be performed by instructors who have sound knowledge and experience in computer science and that not only lecturing, but also hands-on experiences with computers are essential for this education.

6 REFERENCES

ACM Curriculum Committee on Computer Science(1968) Curriculum 68. *Communications of the ACM*, **11** (3), 151-197.

ACM Curriculum Committee on Computer Science(1978) Curriculum 78. *Communications of the ACM*, **22** (3), 147-166.

Denning, P., *et al.*(1989) Computing as a Discipline. *Communications of the ACM*, **32** (1), 9-23.

Takahashi, N. (1992) Engineering Education in Japan. *IEEE COMMUNICATION MAGAZINE*, **30** (11), 28-36.

7 BIOGRAPHY

Hajime Ohiwa received his BSc, MSc and DSc in physics from the Faculty of Science, University of Tokyo in 1965, 1967 and 1971, respectively. He became a research associate of the Faculty of Science, University of Tokyo. He joined the foundation of Toyohashi University of Technology as a lecturer in 1978 and became associate professor and professor of computer engineering in 1980 and 1985, respectively. In 1992, he became professor of environmental information, Keio University. He was a British Council Scholar visiting the Cavendish Laboratory, University of Cambridge from 1974 to 1976. He also was a visiting associate professor of Applied Physics, Cornell University in 1980.

Nobumasa Takahashi received his BSc degree in mathematics and PhD in operating systems research in 1957 and 1975, respectively. After graduation he worked in the Central Research Laboratory of Hitachi Ltd. Mr.Takahashi was the first digital computer programmer at Hitachi. In 1977 he became professor in the newly established Department of Computer Science at the Tokyo University of Agriculture and Technology. In 1997 he moved to his current post at Takusyoku University. He is now a vice-president of the Information Processing Society of Japan.

Tsurayuki Kado currently holds the unique position of chief instructor at Hitachi Ltd. He graduated at the Department of Science, Gakushuin University in 1964 and immediately started work with Hitachi. Since then, he has worked in the information systems field during thirty three years. Ten of these years were spent as a designer of hardware and software, twelve as a systems engineer. Since 1986, he is in charge of education and training.

13

Computer science education at the crossroads

Ken Robinson
Department of Software Engineering, School of Computer Science and Engineering, University of New South Wales, Sydney NSW 2052 Australia, e-mail: K.Robinson@unsw.edu.au

Abstract
Computer science has been the dominant discipline for computing education over more than four decades. This paper examines some current changes and suggests that computer science education - as it is currently presented - may be entering a period of decline as new demands assume a more prominent role. The intention of the paper is to provoke discussion on the future directions of computing education.

Keywords
Informatics, software systems, software engineering, natural sciences and engineering, informatics majors, curriculum (general), educational profiles

1 COMPUTER SCIENCE

Throughout this paper 'computer science' and 'informatics' are assumed to be interchangeable terms. Computer science is the term used most commonly in Australia, the United Kingdom, the United States of America and Canada, while the term informatics is commonly used in Europe. This paper will use the term computer science.

Since around 1960 computer training has been carried out under the umbrella of computer science. It is widely agreed that the term is more wishful thinking than grounded in any reality. Computer science courses have been generalist computing courses from which graduates entered various computing occupations and professions. At the same time it was common for electrical engineering courses to contain substantial computing content and it was common for those who wished to

Informatics in Higher Education F. Mulder & T. van Weerts (Eds.)

have significant computer hardware expertise, to undertake an electrical engineering degree combined with computer science.

Much of the discussion in this paper is drawn from experiences and initiatives at the University of New South Wales. This is done because the author is close to those experiences
and initiatives. Similar initiatives are seen to be occurring in many other universities and it is presumed that the experiences might be analogous to ours. The assumption is that what we are seeing locally might be part of a global change.

2 RECENT DEBATE: ENGINEERING VERSUS SCIENCE

In Wegner and Israel (1995) there is a discussion of the nature of computer science. In this discussion Belady (1995), Brassard (1995), Denning (1995), Freeman (1995), Hartmanis (1995a), Loui (1995), Plaice (1995), Savage (1995), Stewart (1995), Ullman (1995) and Wegner (1995) take part, prompted by the 1994 Turing Award Lecture by Hartmanis (1995b). This debate touched on the question of whether computing is an engineering or a science discipline - irrespective of what you call it. The significance of this discussion is not that it reached a particular consensus, but rather that the discussion was occurring - in the particular forum where it was occurring - at all. This discussion probably would not have happened ten years ago.

The 'engineering versus science' discussion is much older and goes back to the time when the phrase 'software engineering' was invented and coined in 1968, nearly four decades ago. While certainly not unanimously accepting the proposition that computing is an engineering discipline, the cited discussion is evidence of a gradual awareness, if not acceptance, of the notion of computing as a genuine engineering discipline. This discussion of the nature of the computing discipline is clearly related to, but is not the same as, the goals of computing education.

3 LOCAL EXPERIENCE

The strongest local evidence for a change comes from our own School of Computer Science and Engineering. This School came into being as a school in 1991, having previously been a Department in the School of Electrical Engineering since 1964. In 1989 we introduced a four-year computer engineering course, administered jointly with the School of Electrical Engineering. The objective of this course was to educate design engineers who could work on computer systems - possibly embedded - that consist of either hardware or software, or both. The new course was additional to an existing three-year computer science course.

The computer engineering course immediately established itself as one of the highest entry level computing or engineering courses in Australia and it has maintained that position. Entry into University of New South Wales courses is based on a Tertiary Entrance Ranking - score (TER - score) which is computed from the New South Wales Higher School Certificate (NSW HSC). The HSC is a state of New South Wales public examination. A student who obtains a TER of 95 is in the top 5% in the state. The computer engineering course commenced with a minimum TER of about 97 for 60 students. In 1997 the course took in about 150 students with a minimum TER of about 92.

This year, 1997, we introduced a new four-year software engineering course administered jointly with the School of Information Systems. The software engineering course commenced with an intake of 25 students with a minimum TER of 97.

Since 1989 the computer science course has moved from being our major computing course - in terms of numbers of students - to being second to computer engineering. Over the same period the minimum entrance requirement has fallen to a TER of 78 in 1997.

Anecdotal evidence from other Australian universities suggests that interest in and entrance levels for computer science courses have been falling in recent years. Anecdotal evidence from the United Kingdom and other countries suggests that there are similar experiences in those countries.

4 WHAT IS IN A NAME?

Computer engineering and software engineering form a continuum from the electrical and computing hardware interface through software to the application interface. These courses are intended to satisfy a demand from society and industry for system developers, whether the systems are implemented in software or hardware. If the courses are well targeted and successful - it is too early to judge in the case of software engineering - then they will be satisfying a need previously supplied by computer science. We would expect to see both of the engineering courses having large numbers of very good students and presumably a much smaller number of students doing computer science.

There is a serious question raised by the above expectation. If the new engineering courses become the preferred source of graduates for industry and commerce, why would anyone want to study a computer science course? That is not intended to be a rhetorical question. It is expected that there may be cogent reasons, but that they are not likely to include many of the dominant reasons that have enticed students to computer science in the past.

It could be thought that the move from computer science to engineering courses is merely a change of name. Has anything of substance occurred? It is true that the new courses share a substantial number of subjects in common with the computer science course. Indeed it is almost the case that the new courses contain the computer science course. But there are new subjects and there is a different emphasis. The engineering courses have a much greater concern for the development of systems: hardware systems, software systems and combined hardware and software systems.

Characteristics of computer science courses

The characteristics that appear to distinguish the objectives of computer science courses are as follows.

- Computer science is devoted to developing 'computing in the small'.
- Despite a significant level of theory in computer science courses, that theory does not address design and implementation. This is partly another manifestation of the 'computing in the small' characteristic, but it also derives from a concentration on algorithms and data structures, and a lack of concern with systems.
- Computer science courses do not develop a strong concern for reliability and quality. Indeed it might be claimed that computer science tends to perpetuate the hacker approach to system development.
- Computer science courses seem to have no particular focus.

Characteristics of engineering courses

As a counterpoint to the above an engineering course has to produce graduates who know how to develop (potentially large) systems. This requires:

- an appreciation of the problems which occur in developing systems;
- methods for aiding the design and implementation of systems;
- an understanding of the process of system development;
- a concern for reliability and quality, which entails a sense of professional responsibility that is characteristic for the engineering professions.

While emphasizing the above aspects of an engineering education, it is desirable that innovation - a strong characteristic of computer science - is not lost. It is also important to emphasize that the above engineering requirements should not be achieved by mixing common computer science subjects with qualitative subjects. There is a need to answer the requirements with a course that is as strongly based on sound principles and as rigorous as possible.

5 INVERTING THE CURRICULUM

Evidence of 'computing in the small' can be seen in traditional computer science course sequences: the course will commence with programming in the small, proceed to intermediate data structures and algorithms, and then move on to various application or problem domains.

There is an argument for effectively inverting this sequence. The discussion of algorithms and data structures is not well motivated, since the need for particular data structures or algorithms is driven by particular requirements, and hence is problem and implementation dependent. It would be much more supportive of developing an understanding of systems to start with nontrivial systems for which students developed components, starting from simple components and working towards complete modules. Particular requirements would provide an opportunity to discuss alternative data structures and algorithms. Something like this approach is advocated in various object-oriented design subjects. It certainly fits in well with a comprehensive software engineering approach to the development of systems.

A trivial, but significant, example of the consequence of the 'programming in the small' attitude can be seen in the selection of the first programming examples. A tradition has developed in which the canonical first program is a program that writes 'hello world' on a text file. The next program probably reads numbers from an input file and writes the value of some expression on output. If these exercises are attempted using a modern object-oriented programming language, the exercise may be not particularly simple, needing knowledge of classes and possibly exceptions.

Based on the assumption that these programs are intrinsically simple and fundamental, this might be used as an argument for not using such programming languages. However, if the first programs are given in the context of a complete system, then maybe the first exercise is a procedure/function/method that receives values as parameters and returns a result - perhaps the circumference of a triangle. Starting from this simple exercise there are many procedures which can be developed for a nontrivial system; for example, a simple simulation of an Automatic Teller Machine (ATM) with all input/output through a supplied graphical interface. Such exercises would develop, from the beginning, an understanding of system requirements and specification.

Examples of such an inverted curriculum - albeit for specific object-oriented programming languages - can be found in Meyer (1993) and Duke (1997).

6 CONSEQUENCES FOR COMPUTER SCIENCE

If we assume that computer and software engineering courses are successful, both in attracting students and in satisfying many of the needs of industry, then we have to concede that computer science courses will lose a significant vocational component from their list of attractions. This will be true at all institutions, whether a particular institution has engineering courses or not. The competition will be both within institutions and between institutions. The serious question then is: 'What happens to computer science?'

One could think of the following possibilities.

1. Computer science could become irrelevant and dwindle to a very small size, perhaps disappearing in some institutions.
2. Computer science could be used mainly in conjunction with major studies in other disciplines.
3. Computer science could fashion itself as a true science of computing for the first time. Computer science would then be concerned with the more

foundational elements of computing and be closely associated with new research directions in fundamental aspects of computing.

All of the above probably represents a significant contraction in the size of computer science. Option 1 is unattractive, and a mixture of 2 and 3 seems most desirable. It is important to appreciate that option 3 will not happen without serious rethinking.

7 CONCLUSION

If local experiences are representative of global ones, then we may be seeing a transition period for computing education. We may be experiencing the emergence of computing from a craft period to an engineering period. At least society may have reached a point where it now requires graduates who are able to develop the complex computing systems on which society is becoming more dependent.

We would argue that conventional computer science courses are not well suited to producing such graduates and that there is a need for courses with a strong engineering orientation. The important point is not the name of such courses, but their objectives and hence their content. Such courses could be named 'computer science', but because of the significant shift in objectives it is likely that such courses will be called 'engineering' courses. This would leave computer science and computer/software engineering operating in parallel, and strongly suggests that the objectives of computer science courses will need to be redefined. Hopefully this paper contributes to that.

8 REFERENCES

Duke, R. (1997) In search of the inverse curriculum, in *The Proceedings of the Second Australasian Conference on Computer Science Education,* July 1997, 65-70.

Hartmanis, J. (1995b) Turing Award Lecture: on computational complexity and the nature of computer science. *ACM Computing Surveys*, **27** (1), 7-16.

Meyer, B. (1993) Towards an object-oriented curriculum. *Journal of Object-Oriented Programming,* May 1993, 76-81.

Wegner, P. and Israel, M. (1995) Computing Surveys symposium on computational complexity and the nature of computer science. *ACM Computing Surveys,* **27** (1), with the following contributions:

- Belady, L.A. (1995) The disappearance of the 'pure' software industry, 17-18.
- Brassard, G. (1995) Time for another paradigm shift, 19-21.
- Denning, P.J. (1995) Can there be a science of information?, 23-24.
- Freeman, P.A. (1995) Effective computer science, 27-29.

- Hartmanis, J. (1995a) Response to the essays 'On computational complexity and the nature of computer science', 59-51.
- Loui, M.C. (1995) Computer science is a new engineering discipline, 31-32.
- Plaice, J. (1995) Computer science is an experimental science, 33.
- Savage, J.E. (1995) Will computer science become irrelevant?, 35-37.
- Stewart, N.F. (1995) Science and computer science, 39-41.
- Ullman, J.D. (1995) The role of theory today, 43-44.
- Wegner, P. (1995) Interaction as a basis for empirical computer science, 45-48.

9 BIOGRAPHY

Ken Robinson is a senior lecturer and head of the Department of Software Engineering in the School of Computer Science and Engineering at the University of New South Wales (UNSW). He has a long record of teaching computer science and software engineering with a special interest in rigorous software development methods, and in the recognition of computing as an engineering discipline. He played a leading role in the introduction of a new computer engineering course in 1989 and a new software engineering course in 1997 at UNSW.

14

Introduction to computing: a course in computer science fundamentals

Russell L. Shackelford
College of Computing, Georgia Institute of Technology
Atlanta, Georgia, 30332, USA, e-mail: russ@cc.gatech.edu

Richard J. LeBlanc, Jr.
College of Computing, Georgia Institute of Technology
Atlanta, Georgia, 30332, USA, e-mail: rich@cc.gatech.edu

Abstract

The traditional approach to introducing students to computer science has been through a course built around the development of programming skills, ignoring the practical reality of increasing powerful application-oriented software packages. In this paper we describe a two course sequence which has been taught to majors in computer science and a variety of other disciplines for the last four years. We emphasize effective use of abstraction and the acquisition of software development skills which are language independent. Our experience with these courses has convinced us that it is possible to introduce the conceptual foundations of computer science to beginning students in a way which both engages them and gives them a basis for learning advanced ways to solve problems using computing.

Keywords

Informatics, university education, curriculum (start)

1 INTRODUCTION

In 1992 Georgia Tech's College of Computing restructured its lower division curriculum to correct historical flaws and to respond better to modern demands. The restructuring was motivated by recognition that computing is no longer an

Informatics in Higher Education F. Mulder & T. van Weerts (Eds.)

arcane technical discipline of interest primarily to computer science (CS) majors. It has become a core element of university-level education for a broad population. We sought to provide an introduction to the conceptual andintellectual foundations of computing, and to relevant computer use skills. We also sought to improve access for non-CS majors to the revolutionary ideas and capabilities which computing offers.

In the next two years introductory course enrollments skyrocketed from ~400 to ~1400 annually and computing became a de facto part of many of Georgia Tech's engineering curricula. This fact was recently formalized: computing is joining the more traditional disciplines as part of the university's core curriculum. In this paper we summarize the rationale and specific goals of our restructured introductory curriculum and report the lessons learned in our four years of experience with it.

2 THE DEMANDS ON MODERN COMPUTING CURRICULA

Computing curricula have received frequent critical attention. About every ten years since the late 1960s, we have seen a new version of recommendations aimed at repairing curricular weaknesses. These weaknesses emerge in part because, over the thirty years of its curricular existence, computing has seen a multitude of changes which dramatically have increased the demands placed on introductory courses. Among these are the following.

Computer science as a discipline

Computer science is a discipline in itself with its own body of knowledge, its own intellectual and conceptual foundations, and its own effective practices. Thus, we would expect that introductory CS courses would introduce students to foundations of both the subject matter and its application.

Computing now affects everybody

Years ago computing affected very few people and 'computing' equalled 'programming'. Since then computing has impacted virtually every discipline and now means quite a bit more than 'just programming.' Thus we would expect introductory computing courses to introduce a wider audience to the ways that people 'do computing' which means both 'effective application use' and 'effective programming'.

Original requirements (mid-1960's)	*Current requirements (through Java)*
1. Assignment	1. Assignment
2. Numerical operations	2. Numerical operations
3. Data types: int, real, char, boolean	3. Data types: int, real, char, boolean
4. Data structures: arrays	4. Data structures: arrays
5. Control stmts: if's and loop's	5. Control stmts: if's and loop's
6. File operations	6. File operations
7. Formatting of I/O	7. Formatting of I/O
8. Procedures and parameters	8. Procedures and parameters
	9. Structured design
	10. Pointers
	11. Linked lists
	12. Trees
	13. Recursion
	14. Interactive debuggers
	15. Interactive programs
	16. Human-computer interface
	17. Graphics
	18. Larger programs
	19. SW Engineering fundamentals
	20. Complexity ('Big Oh')
	21. Fluency in multiple languages
	22. Application software skills
	23. OOP
	24. Applets

Figure 1 Requirements then and now.

Programming has changed in fundamental ways

No longer can we believe that students will need to know only one or two relatively simple languages. When the traditional curricular structure evolved, teaching someone to program usually meant covering the list of topics shown in the left column of Figure 1. Since that time evolution (in both programming languages and the problems which they are deployed to solve) has expanded the list as shown in the right column of Figure 1. Not only is this list longer by a factor of three, most items are more complex than those before them. It is not unreasonable to suggest that the complexity of 'teaching programming' has increased by an order of magnitude. Thus we would expect computing curricula to emphasize basic and universal algorithmic and programming constructs and skills, rather than to focus on 'programming in a given language'.

Everything about computing is more complex

Such things as 'effective abstraction', 'good design', 'effective debugging and verification' and 'good software engineering practices' are clearly more important than these used to be. Therefore we would expect curricula to explicitly focus on establishing a good foundation in precisely these fundamentals.

3 ARCHAIC ASSUMPTIONS

Over the years we find a history of curriculum revisions (most recently to complex languages such as C++ and Java) which imply 'downloading' more and more material to the introductory courses. In our view simple downloading of more material into an introductory sequence of programming courses is no longer an adequate response. Such an approach produces a number of negative consequences. We believe that each is a reflection of a specific assumption which is no longer valid, but which is implicit in the traditional curricular structure itself.

'Computing means programming'

It does not. Introducing students to computing via traditional programming courses ignores the practical reality that standard application programs have become the 'tools of choice' for solving many computing-related problems. One can bring to bear a tremendous amount of computing power on a wide range of problems without ever 'writing a computer program' in the traditional sense of the phrase. Introducing students to computing via a course which emphasizes 'writing programs' effectively bypasses the most direct means of computer-supported problem solving.

'Software applications are not substantive enough to warrant our attention'

They are. As the power of off-the-shelf application programs has grown, so has their complexity. The boundary between 'programming' and 'use of software packages' has become blurred, such that the very same principles which underlie effective program design (e.g. modularity, abstraction, reusability) also underlie the effective use of increasingly complex software tools. Thus reliance on such tools requires an adequate foundation in algorithmic principles. Treating powerful applications as trivial tools deprives students of guidance in their effective use and misses opportunities for teaching important computing principles.

'The best way to teach principles is in the context of a programming course'

We do not think it is. It may have been so years ago, but those days are long gone. The nature of 'programming courses' dictates that student grades are based largely on programs which students submit throughout the term. Regardless of the degree to which we emphasize things such as abstraction and design, as the deadline for each program approaches students quite naturally tend to forget all that and instead focus on getting their programs to 'somehow work.' As a result we find students manipulating an increasingly complex set of language constructs and features without adequate attention to the principles which govern their effective use. While faculty staff may intend that students obtain a foundation in important algorithmic principles, students often focus on the manipulation of the constructs and environments while ignoring as much as possible the principles of design and abstraction which underlie their effective use. The result is that students frequently leave such courses complaining that they 'managed to get their programs to work', but that they do not have the 'big picture' of what they were doing or why they were doing it.

'We have four years of study to get important ideas across'

We do not. Computing is rapidly becoming a mainstream discipline. As with any mainstream discipline we must face the reality that CS majors will constitute a minority of CS students. The majority will come from other disciplines and will be with us for only a course or two. This simple fact means that we must consider wisely the impact we have at the introductory level. To continue to deploy a curricular model which features two years of 'programming' prior to substantive CS course work means that we effectively deny 'most students' access to the important conceptual and intellectual contributions which computing makes to virtually all disciplines.

Summarizing

In short, we find that the traditional approach is obsolete because of changes we find at every level:

- the problems which we use computing to attack;
- the software applications which have evolved into powerful computing tools;
- the programming languages-and-environments which we use to create programs;
- the 'customer population' of students which computing education must serve.

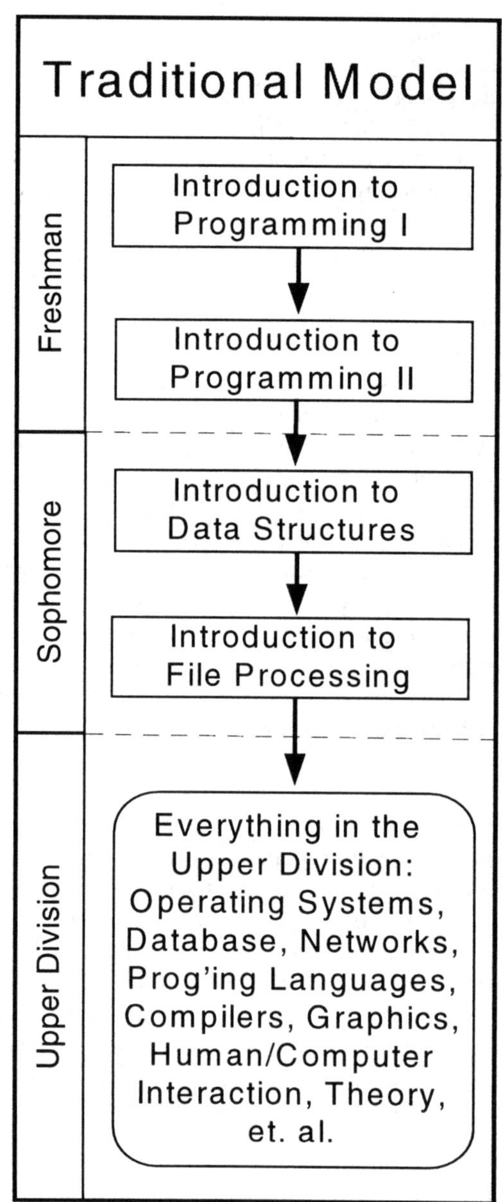

Figure 2 The tall, skinny curriculum tree.

4 THE GEORGIA TECH RESPONSE

Our curricular restructuring was based on the observation that traditional CS curricula are an aberration which lack a basic feature of time-honoured curricular structures. An informal survey of other disciplines reveals a structural pattern:

- introductory courses establish the subject domain and convey fundamental principles and methods;
- other lower division courses provide both breadth and depth in principles, methods and knowledge;
- upper division courses provide greater depth in specific areas of concentration.

In contrast to this pattern, CS curricula have traditionally presented two years of work focused on applied programming skills and constructs, effectively withholding fundamental concepts and knowledge until upper division courses.

This curricular tradition is an organic artefact of a brief history, not the result of explicit design. It is residue of the fact the CS courses originated as 'programming skills add-ons' to mathematics and electrical engineering curricula. As CS matured it simply 'grew upward' in the curriculum, adding more advanced courses 'on top of' the traditional skills-oriented lower division. From this perspective we can see traditional CS curricular structure as something inherited from our ad hoc past, not as the result of any conscious design decision. In recent years numerous efforts have been made to 'repair' the specific courses in the traditional structure without, in our view, adequate consideration of the accidental, historical design flaws of that course structure itself.

Before redesigning our lower division curriculum we surveyed what other institutions were doing in the way of non-traditional introductory courses. Most such offerings seemed to cluster in two categories which might be described as:

- 'Introduction to computing applications', i.e. instruction in using word processors, spreadsheets, etc.;
- 'Introduction to CS as a discipline', i.e. a survey of areas such as databases, networks, compilers.

We rejected both approaches. In our view the former lacks conceptual content and the latter 'misses the point' of what computing is and does. Furthermore neither approach prepares students for further computing study and thus must be followed by traditional programming courses.

We elected to design a common freshman sequence for both CS majors and others. In doing so we partitioned the teaching-and-learning agenda of the traditional two-term introduction to programming into chunks which are more focused and manageable:

- 'Introduction to Computing' which focuses on algorithmic concepts and skills and their application in both writing pseudo-code algorithms and using software tools;

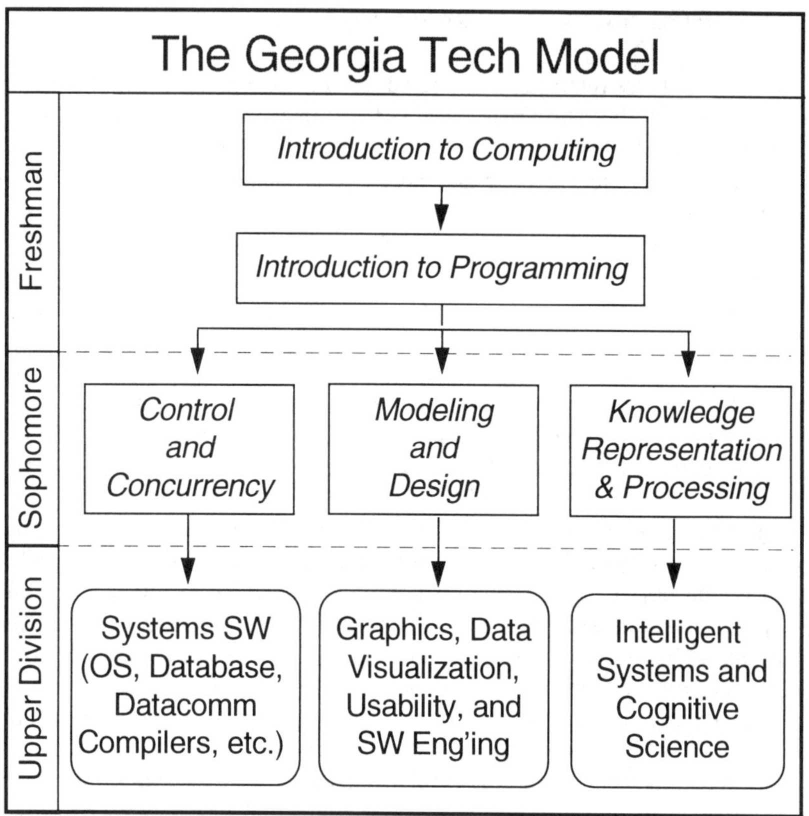

Figure 3 A short, fat curriculum tree.

- 'Introduction to Programming' which focuses on effective practices for algorithm implementation in a complex modern language (after students obtain a conceptual foundation in the previous course).

Following this two-course sequence we offer three sophomore courses, each of which assumes the first two courses as prerequisites and each of which introduces a different programming paradigm, language and set of computing problems. Each of the three serves as a gateway to a cluster of upper division courses, thus allowing non-CS majors access to substantive CS study without a prohibitively long chain of prerequisites. CS majors take all three, in whatever sequence they choose (plus a fourth sophomore course which introduces machine architecture and assembly language programming). We describe particulars of the freshman courses below.

Introduction to computing

The first course has two components, each with its own agenda:

- lecture-and-homework;
- laboratory.

The lecture-and-homework component focuses on basic principles and conceptual tools for creating algorithms, including a pseudo-code based introduction to the complete range of algorithm constructs (subroutines, control structures, data structures, etc.), as well as basic material in algorithm design, analysis and theory. The jury is still out on how successful one can be introducing the object-oriented paradigm without a foundation in the structured paradigm; various points of view have advocates. As a practical matter we must prepare students for a variety of possible futures and, for the present, we find it necessary to introduce both structured and object-oriented design.

With respect to analysis and theory we translate the agenda put forth by Harel (1992) into terms appropriate for freshmen. We introduce the issues of correctness, complexity and computability, with applied problem-solving in the first two. We also articulate the topics of concurrency and parallelism for a freshmen population, then build on them with applied work in determining the limits of parallelism for simple algorithms.

The laboratory component focuses on the use of campus computing resources and standard software applications, including UNIX and Windows, e-mail and news groups, word processors, spreadsheets, databases, equation solvers, graphics editors, use of the World Wide Web and the construction of web pages.

Experience has shown that liberating students from the many annoyances of programming and debugging allows them to focus more effectively on algorithm design and construction. We make sure that they understand and can apply basic concepts in a kinder pseudo-code environment which does not permit compilation. This facilitates both a better grasp and faster conceptual progress.

The laboratory focus on software tools allows us to reinforce conceptual lecture material by showing its relevance to problem solving in high-level software tools. For example, the difference between syntax and semantics can be illustrated using word processor style sheets, just as can the notion of abstraction. Similarly the distinction between procedures and functions is found in spreadsheets, embodied in the form of macros and cell formulae. Abstraction and reusability become key issues when using a graphics editor to construct composite images from graphical components. Modern applications are complex enough for most algorithmic points to be made using them. In addition we find that many students who are new to computing can achieve a sense of success and competence more rapidly than with traditional programming. And in addition it appears that the range of application experience the course provides makes students more immediately attractive to employers.

Introduction to programming

The second course also features a two-part agenda, namely a focus on effective:

- program design, including error prevention and avoidance, reusability, etc.;
- debugging, including skills and strategies.

For the first time we can count on students entering the programming course 'knowing what they are trying to do'. We therefore need not consume lecture time covering the ideas and mechanisms of parameters, modularity, static and dynamic data, recursion, etc., because students are well practised in such things from the prerequisite course. Instead we have the opportunity to focus explicitly on the myriad of important ideas and skills concerning programming. This has led us to recognize that our old curriculum used the wrong title for the introductory course: 'Introduction to programming'. It would have been more accurately described as an 'Introduction to program components in the syntax of language X'. By moving coverage of algorithmic concepts and skills to a non-programming course we enable students to progress with programming at a much faster, thereby for the first time providing a course which is a true 'introduction to programming'.

Course management issues

The fact that the new structure has been accepted across campus presents both good and bad news. The good news is that we are having a much broader impact on many more students, having succeeded in getting computing incorporated into the university's core curriculum. The bad news is that we have got thousands of students to teach each year. This presents many logistical problems, including a heavy demand for student learning support. Rather than use a few graduate students as graders for large numbers of students, we chose to use many undergraduate students as teaching assistants. Because undergraduates are less expensive, we can provide learning support to individual students, not just massive grading. While this strategy was initially viewed as risky, we have found that undergraduates as a group are superior to graduate students in motivation, energy, initiative and caring with respect to a freshmen population. Our undergraduates obtain valuable experience in teaching, public speaking and working with people. Many students report that their teaching assistant job is the only aspect of their entire course of study which allows them to 'do something that's real'.

5 SUMMARY

Our revision of the lower division curriculum was motivated by four goals, i.e. to:

- provide students with an adequate foundation in the important concepts and skills necessary to master the complexities of modern computing;

- have students see algorithms as the focal point of problem solving, with programming language issues secondary;
- introduce students both to programming and to the tremendous power that modern applications provide;
- impact a broad population of students by positioning computing as a mainstream discipline, and by encouraging their participation in whatever computing courses might address their interests.

It appears that our design achieves each and all of these goals. In addition, it has proved to provide three benefits which we did not anticipate.

- The freshman sequence illuminated a 'hidden problem' of long standing: the absence of any course which was a true introduction to programming. Now we have the opportunity to explicitly teach programming knowledge and skills. We hope to have more to say on this in the near future.
- It gives valuable experience for our own undergraduates. Their work as teaching assistants not only enables us to give human-scale support to students in very large classes, it also provides our own students with experience in the very kind of people- and communication skills which have been a traditional weakness of CS graduates.
- Our efforts to open up our curriculum to non-CS majors has had a positive impact on our own undergraduates, as they now find themselves with a range of applied knowledge and skills (both in software applications and in multiple programming paradigms and languages) which make them much more attractive to employers.

As CS educators we have the responsibility of taking our students on a learning journey. We might think of ourselves as the driver, of students as passengers and of our curriculum as the vehicle. Viewed in this light we see that we had been transporting them in a tired old jalopy. The standard curricular structure, like an old worn-out car, did not allow us to travel as rapidly, as safely, as reliably or as far as modern complexities require. As with an old car the time had come when further repair was not sensible. But a new vehicle is costly, and we have been paying that cost, for example through the creation of textbooks (Shackelford, 1997), the invention of new course management practices (Canup and Shackelford, 1998; Schaffer, 1998) and thinking a bit differently about what we do (LeBlanc and Shackeford, 1998; Toothman and Shackelford, 1998). Despite the costs, we are well pleased with our new vehicle. We urge you to get one too.

6 REFERENCES

Canup, M. and Shackelford, R. (1998) Using Software to Solve Problems in Large Computing Classes, submitted to the *Twenty-ninth SIGCSE Symposium on Computer Science Education*, Atlanta, February 1998.

Harel, D. and Rosner, R. (1992) *Algorithmics: The Spirit of Computing,* 2nd edition. Addison-Wesley, Reading, Massachusetts.

LeBlanc, R. and Shackelford, R. (1998) Why Pseudocode Should Be Your Students' First Programming Language, submitted to the *Twenty-ninth SIGCSE Symposium on Computer Science Education*, Atlanta, February 1998.

Schaffer, K. (1998) Doing Something Real: Teaching as Part of the Undergraduate Experience, submitted to the *Twenty-ninth SIGCSE Symposium on Computer Science Education*, Atlanta, February 1998.

Shackelford, R. (1997) *Introduction to Computing and Algorithms.* Addison-Wesley, Reading, Massachusetts.

Toothman, B. and Shackelford, R. (1998) The Effects of Partially-Individualized Assignments on Subsequent Student Performance, submitted to the *Twenty-ninth SIGCSE Symposium on Computer Science Education*, Atlanta, February 1998.

7 BIOGRAPHY

Russell L. Shackelford received his Ph.D. degree in information and computer science in 1989 from the Georgia Institute of Technology, where he now is director of Lower Division Studies in the College of Computing. He came to computer science from a career in clinical psychology, and holds graduate degrees in psychology and in education as well. His research interests include computing curriculum development, the development of computing tools to support teachers and human-science researchers, and the impact of technology on human experience. He thinks computing is almost as interesting as baseball.

Richard J. LeBlanc, Jr. received his Ph.D. degree in computer sciences from the University of Wisconsin - Madison in 1977. He is a professor and the associate dean of the College of Computing at the Georgia Institute of Technology, where he has been a faculty member since January, 1978. His research interests include software engineering and programming language design and implementation. He has published a successful textbook on compiler construction ('Crafting a Compiler' and 'Crafting a Compiler with C') that has been adopted at over 100 colleges and universities. He is currently serving as chair of the ACM Education Board.

15

Representing a body of knowledge for teaching, learning and assessment

Don Sheridan
MSIS Department, School of Business, The University of Auckland Auckland, New Zealand, e-mail: d.sheridan@auckland.ac.nz

David White
MSIS Department, School of Business, The University of Auckland Auckland, New Zealand, e-mail: d.white@auckland.ac.nz

Abstract

As Internet-based professional training becomes universally accepted, national and international standards for professional groups may become a dominant and governing force. Educators and trainers will be expected to demonstrate the relevancy of their programmes in the context of bodies of knowledge which have a wide acceptance. Universities will feel the pressure to meet or exceed the performance of technical institutions and commercial institutes to justify their tuition costs. A university degree in computer science no longer guarantees a job. This paper will discuss the application of a taxonomy in computer science to a computer- supported learning system and its implication for planning and managing one's professional career.

Keywords

Informatics, information systems, economics and business administration, curriculum (general), role of CIT, taxonomies, academic requirements, business and industry requirements

Informatics in Higher Education F. Mulder & T. van Weerts (Eds.)

1 INTRODUCTION

This paper opens with several definitions for the term 'discipline' and from these selects one, the notion of an 'ordered system', as the lead-in to a discussion of several examples of ordered systems or taxonomies of computer science. To maintain and extend the computer science taxonomy or body of knowledge we argue for a computer-supported learning system (CSL)which would represent the status of the universal, as well as the personal body of knowledge (BoK). The CSL not only provides access to the BoK and its knowledge elements, but also to learning materials, assessments and assessment results.

It has been said that 'what gets measured gets maintained'. In this instance, if we know how knowledge elements are assessed, then we have specific examples of the taxonomy in action. In the style of a debate we first consider the resolution.

Resolved
Informatics is a discipline and shares attributes in common with other disciplines and professions.

The word discipline in this statement can be interpreted in many ways.

- **Rules or methods**
  On one level we can think of our discipline in terms of rules or methods which include the early learning of the syntax of programming languages and the application of logic coupled with an understanding of the natural structures of informatics.
- **Mind-set or mode of thinking**
  As we make a greater commitment to our field we develop a mind-set or mode of thinking which arises from the deep understanding of systems theory and its application.
- **Professional code of operation**
  In addition, as a professional we become an active member of an informatics association and recommend and follow the code of ethics of our society. In this sense the discipline of informatics as a profession includes a wider acknowledgement of our role in our environment and governs our general behaviour in subtle but important ways.
- **Body of knowledge**
  Finally, our discipline is a body of knowledge and in teaching our discipline we articulate it as an ordered system of groups or categories, with natural relationships based upon principles and laws which govern its composition and formation.

For the purposes of this paper we wish to discuss informatics as a body of knowledge and also our method of representing the body of knowledge for teaching, learning and assessment. More particularly we wish to describe informatics in the context of an education in management science and information systems.

2 BODY OF KNOWLEDGE (BOK)

A variety of bodies of knowledge (BoKs) for computer science and information systems have been developed over the years, based upon numerous studies by individuals and professional organizations. See for example Couger (1973), IEEE (1980), ACM (1983) and DPMA (1986)). The most substantial of these bodies of knowledge is IS'95 (Longenecker *et al.*, 1995), a model curriculum in information systems (IS), proposed by the Association for Computing Machinery (ACM), the Association for Information Systems (AIS), and the Data Processing Management Association (DPMA). IS'95 details hundreds of knowledge elements and classifies these in several ways including the use of a taxonomy of educational objectives (Bloom,1956). Combinations of the knowledge elements form units which in turn form the basis of courses of study in IS. The curriculum model of the Information Resources Management Association (IRMA, 1996) is another articulation of the information systems field. It takes a more generalized approach by providing a list of recommended papers including the objectives and topics to be covered.

At the University of Auckland, School of Business, we have developed a computer-supported learning (CSL) system with an Internet browser interface delivering active pages generated by Microsoft ASP + COM objects from a database engine mounted on an Windows NT Server (Sequent NUMA-Q 2000).

The CSL data model shown in Figure 1 incorporates the attributes necessary to represent the detail of the IS'95 curriculum model and other BoKs while providing the practical necessities such as: on-line testing in a secure environment, web-based grade book, web pages for guidelines, assignments, news, e-mail, resource booking (computer labs, appointments with tutors) and batch generation and marking of off-line tests.

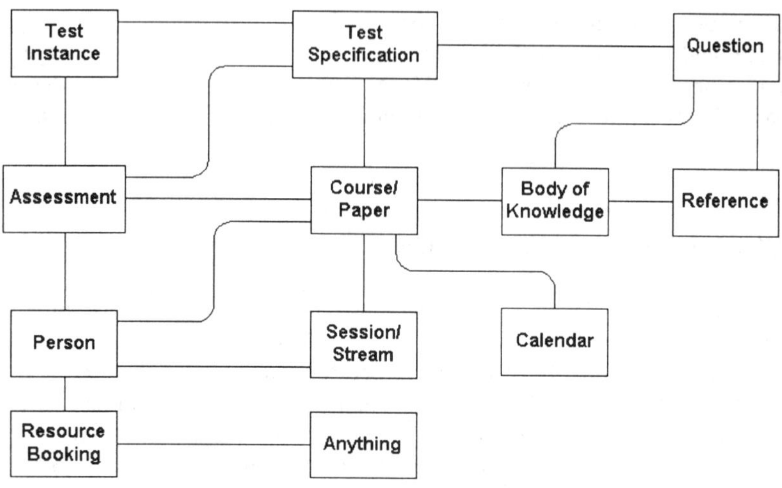

Figure 1 CSL data model.

CSL is used to link the BoK of IS with instances of the BoK knowledge elements as reflected in papers, instructional objectives within papers and assessments (see Figure 2). It is also quite likely that professionals (instructors, consultants, experts) will wish to augment the official BoK with knowledge elements of their own (as presented in Figure 3).

3 USE OF THE COMPUTER-SUPPORTED LEARNING SYSTEM

We have considered various scenarios for the use of the computer-supported learning system.

- Persons may maintain a subcomponent of a BoK on their laptop (for example) and hyper link to their own digital libraries.
- As new knowledge elements are created individuals may wish to add these to the global BoK (following peer review).
- Individuals may wish to put their personal BoK on-line as a networked-personal BoK for others to use or to fill-out or augment their own BoKs (see Figure 3).

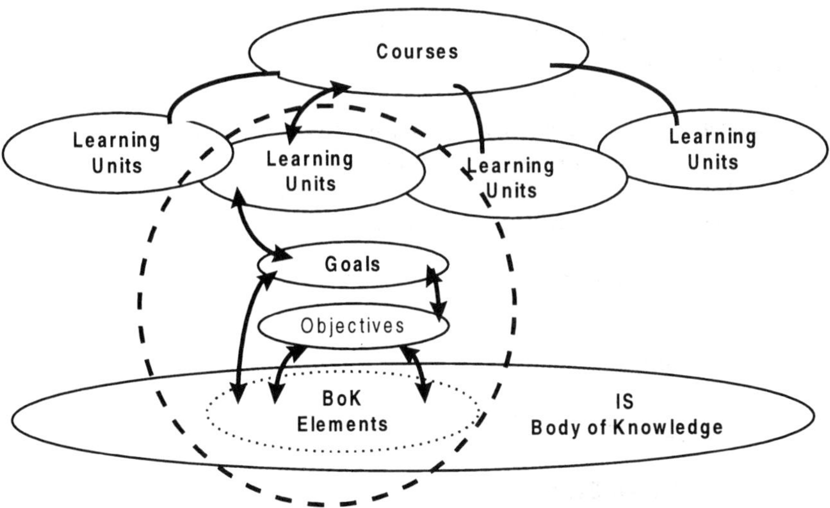

Figure 2 Linking the BoK of IS with instances of the BoK knowledge elements.

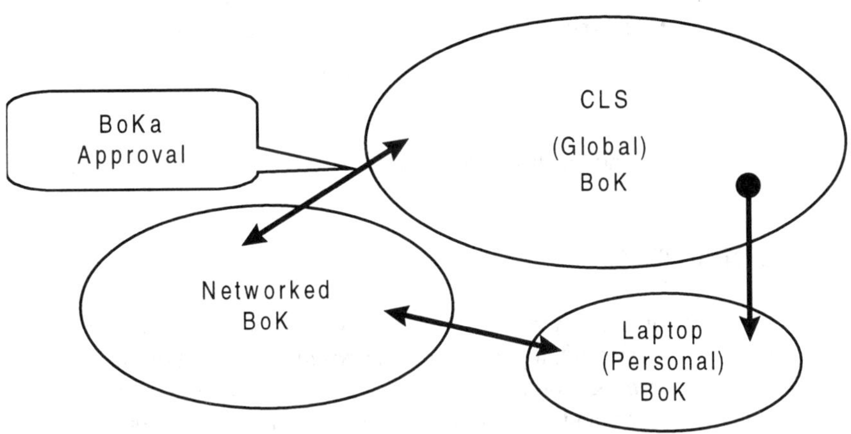

Figure 3 Augmentation of BoK with other professionals' knowledge elements.

We imagine that there may need to be a BoKa, an administrator who determines if and when additions to the professional BoK are warranted.

We intend to use BoKs within CSL to generate a number of educational business options such as certificate and diploma programmes, post-graduate (upgrading) seminars as well as supporting government approved training (NZQA

= New Zealand Qualifications Authority, see Figure 4). All of these services will be provided via the Internet.

Professions such as medicine and engineering require continuous post-graduate education. In computer science and information systems the ACM Code of Ethics, Art. 2.2, requires us to 'acquire and maintain professional competence' (Anderson, 1992). We believe that sophisticated, web-based educational resources will be a common method of meeting our upgrading needs in the future.

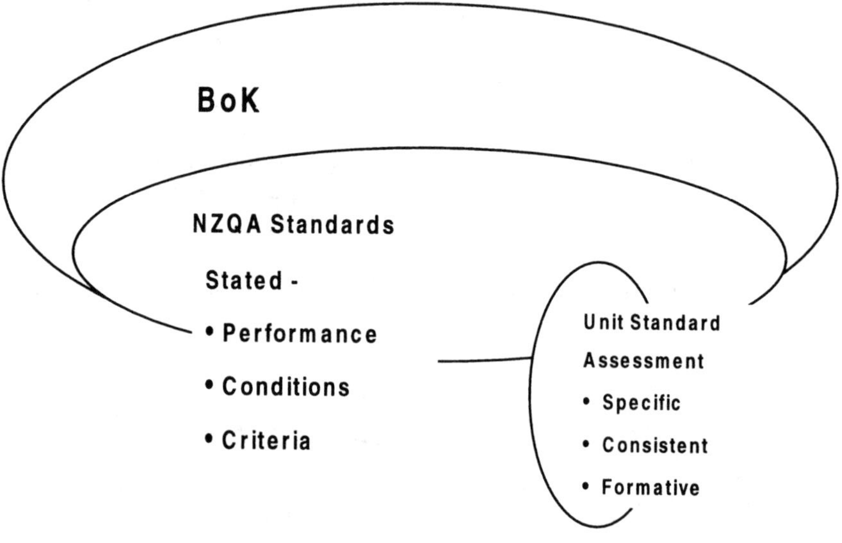

Figure 4 New Zealand Qualifications Authority (NZQA) standards as a BoK.

4 CSL IN ACTION

At the University of Auckland CSL has completed it's third semester with hundreds of students accessing it per day for supervised or external on-line quizzes, grade book queries (marks) or resource bookings. In semester 97B we will be adding more accounting and economics papers, as well as some post-graduate business statistics courses and examples of the national physics examinations. An Intranet accessible version of CSL will be providing still and motion video with audio support to the university-based workstations and lecture theatres during this semester.

Student information is replicated from the university enrolment system daily providing class lists which can then be divided into streams. Departmental staff maintain details of staff assignments to papers which then provides the basis for access security. The staff are then able to:

- specify all details of assessments for the course which are then available to the students via the WWW;

- define the Reference/BoK Network (readings, papers, lab notes, etc. for the course);
- prepare questions, each of which points to at least one reference;
- define test specifications based on the selections of the questions;
- assign a test specification to an assessment;
- make the test which is delivered via the WWW available at a specific time and place.

After the student takes a test, feedback is provided either:

- immediately after each question;
- immediately after the test;
- by e-mail.

This feedback can consist of both or either the correct answers or a pointer to the reference where the answer can be found.

Students are able to access and download all course resources and view their coursework marks via the WWW.

Different instructors are using CSL in many different ways. For instance in one course students take a 15 minute supervised quiz in the week before each lecture, the results of which are then available to the instructor to use to tailor the lecture. In another case large question banks are made available for learning/revision quizzes which the student can take at anytime.

5 CONCLUSION

It has been a challenge to transform a BoK from hard copy to a real-time, interactive learning application. The data model has more than two hundred tables and one thousand attributes. Dynamically linking knowledge elements of a BoK directly to a test item on an assessment and building a course of studies from associated references is an on-going project.

At the beginning of this paper we resolved: 'Informatics is a discipline and shares attributes in common with other disciplines and professions'. We have presented examples of how informatics is an ordered system. We have linked that ordered system, a body of knowledge, to another system which provides professional training (CSL).

The BoK we prefer (IS'95) is composed of attributes of our discipline at a manageable and discrete level. It is not a collection of facts and rules, as in a knowledge base, but rather a reasonably granular description of the various forms of knowledge which need to be possessed to work capably in informatics. We would argue that if science is organized knowledge (Spencer, 1861) then the BoK (IS'95) and its connection to CSL attests to our ability to organize our knowledge and systematically manage its growth.

6 REFERENCES

Anderson, R.E. (1992) ACM code of ethics and professional conduct. *Communications of the ACM*, **35** (5), 94- 99.

ACM (1983) *ACM recommendations for information systems, volume II*. ACM Committee on Computer Curricula of the ACM Education Board, ACM, New York.

Bloom, B.S. [ed.] (1956) *The taxonomy of educational objectives: Classification of educational goals. Handbook I: The cognitive domain*. McKay Press, New York.

Couger, J. [ed.] (1973) Curriculum recommendations for undergraduate programs in information systems. *Communications of the ACM*, **16** (12), 727-749.

DPMA (1986) *DPMA Model Curriculum: 1986*. DPMA, Park Ridge IL.

IRMA (1996) *The information resources management curriculum model (IRMCM): An international curriculum model for a 4 year undergraduate program in IRM*. A joint activity of IRMA and DAMA. IRMA, Harrisburg PA.

IEEE (1980) *Draft report on MSE-80: A graduate program in software engineering*. IEEE Software Engineering Subcommittee of the Computing Society Education Committee, IEEE, Los Alamitos CA.

Longenecker, H.E. Jr., Clark, J.D., Couger, J.D., Feinstein, D.J. and Clark, J.T. (1995) *IS'95: Model curriculum and guidelines for undergraduate degree programs in information systems*. A joint activity of DPMA, ACM, ICIS and AIS. School of CIS, University of South Alabama, Mobile AL.

Spencer, H. (1861) *Education*, Chap. 2. As quoted from *The Columbia dictionary of quotations*, Columbia University Press (1993).

7 BIOGRAPHY

Donald P. Sheridan is associate professor of the MSIS department and director of the Management Teaching Technology Unit, School of Business, University of Auckland. He was an associate professor of MIS and director of the Training Technologies Group, Dalhousie University, Halifax, Nova Scotia, Canada in 1985-1995. From 1980 to 1985 he was officer-in-charge of computer-assisted learning at the Canadian Forces Fleet School in Halifax. He completed his doctoral work at the University of Alberta under the supervision of Drs Steve Hunka and Gene Romaniuk, the pioneers who started it all with an IBM 1500 system and to whom much is owed.

David C. White B.E.(Hons) is a systems engineer who has a wide range of experience with local and multinational corporations since 1969. He is a part-time lecturer in information systems analysis and design at the University of Auckland. He has also taught in the areas of database design and expert systems. Currently he is involved in a project building a computer- supported learning (CSL) system. Primary areas of interest are in modelling and user interface design.

16

Trends in teaching informatics

A. Joe Turner
Department of Computer Science, Clemson University
Clemson, SC 29634-1906, USA, e-mail: turner@cs.clemson.edu

Abstract

Most of the development of informatics curricula has focused almost exclusively on the technical content of the courses in a curriculum. More recently there has been increasing attention paid to pedagogical and nontechnical subject course material. This paper surveys some of the trends in informatics education relative to pedagogical and nontechnical aspects. Some observations are made on current trends and the importance of these aspects relative to more traditional curricular concerns.

Keywords

Informatics, university education, informatics majors, curriculum (general), academic requirements, business and industry requirements

1 INTRODUCTION

Until relatively recently informatics curriculum recommendations and most work in informatics curriculum development have focused almost exclusively on the technical content of the courses and the sequence in which topics should be taught. The 1991 report of the joint ACM/IEEE-CS Curriculum Task Force (Tucker *et al.*, 1991) is the first major informatics curriculum report known to the author which in a significant way addresses important nontechnical content, as well as experiences and capabilities beyond learning of technical content which are important in the education of a student majoring in informatics. More recently there has been an increasing emphasis on pedagogy, nontechnical course content and the development of professional skills in undergraduate informatics programs, as can easily be seen by looking at the proceedings of conferences in computing education during the past five years or so.

Informatics in Higher Education F. Mulder & T. van Weerts (Eds.)

It is not surprising that little attention was paid to the nontechnical aspects of informatics programs. Most informatics faculty members have received intensive education in technical subjects, and many, if not most, are active researchers in technical subareas of informatics. Many faculty members feel that they have inadequate preparation to teach social, ethical andprofessional topics. During most of the time that informatics programs have been in existence there has been a strong demand from industry for graduates of the programs and enrolments have been high, so there has been little incentive to put a lot of effort into the development of effective teaching and learning techniques. The prevalent faculty reward system, which only pays lip service to education and not only rewards research productivity, but often uses it as the sole criterion for tenure and promotion, is also a contributing factor.

The past ten years have seen a significant increase in the emphasis which is placed on nontechnical course content, supporting educational experiences and effective paradigms for teaching and learning in informatics curricula. Some of this increased emphasis has been due to complaints from industry that informatics graduates were too self-centred, lacked communication skills and the ability to work effectively in teams, and were unable to work effectively in problem domains outside core informatics areas. But the changes also reflect a maturing of the discipline and growth in the number of informatics faculty members who have a strong interest in effective teaching and learning.

In the remainder of this paper some of the pedagogical and nontechnical aspects which have been used or proposed for computing programs are surveyed. Some observations about trends in informatics education and the importance of the pedagogical and nontechnical aspects conclude the paper. It is not the intention to assess the effectiveness of the proposed or implemented curricular or pedagogical changes, but only to survey them as examples of the kind of activities which are occurring. Many of the references include assessment information. It should also be noted that the cited references are not necessarily the first or most descriptive for each topic, but mostly they are chosen for their discussion of recent experiences.

The observations and opinions expressed here are mostly based on activities in the USA. These do not necessarily apply to other countries as well, but many similar activities are occurring outside the USA. The terms ‘informatics’ and ‘computing’ are generally interchangeable as used in the paper.

2 SOME TRENDS IN INFORMATICS EDUCATION

We begin by looking at some recent experiences in teaching informatics which do not focus on what informatics topics should be taught. These are partitioned into three groups: teaching and learning paradigms, the professional context and sequencing of the informatics subject material. The last group is included even though attention has been given to topic sequencing issues almost since the beginning of informatics education, because the particular issues which are addressed here, are mostly different from the traditional considerations.

2.1 Teaching and learning paradigms

Four approaches to getting students more involved in their education are:

- discovery learning;
- active learning;
- collaborative learning;
- peer learning.

There is some overlap in these approaches and the general objectives and motivation are similar: Students learn more effectively by doing, rather than by listening.

Discovery learning
Discovery learning (Baldwin, 1996) refers to a process in which students are lead to discover 'knowledge' by working through a series of exercises and problems. Students can work on their own or in groups. The teacher provides guidance when students have questions or difficulties. The objective is to prepare the students to learn on their own, thus making them better prepared for the continuous learning which is required in order to maintain currency in informatics.

Active learning
Active learning (McConnell, 1996) turns class periods away from lecture mode and more toward a laboratory mode in which students work together to solve problems. A class normally begins with a short lecture-discussion giving an overview of a topic. During the middle part of the class students work in teams on problems or questions posed by the teacher. At the end of the class the results from the teams are summarized and discussed, and there can be a general question-answer session on the topics of the day. The motivation for this approach is the belief that understanding and knowledge retention are improved if students learn by doing rather than by listening and passive studying.

Collaborative learning
In collaborative learning (Daigle *et al.*, 1996; Walker, 1997; Williams, 1997) the emphasis is on students working in teams to solve problems, including not only implementation projects, such as software development, but also general problems which illustrate concepts and develop analytical skills The collaboration can be an integral part of the educational process, woven throughout the curriculum. One motivation for collaborative learning is the belief that students often learn better from each other than from a teacher and that students also learn by explaining concepts to each other.

Peer learning
Peer learning (Wills and Finkel, 1994) is a variation on collaborative learning in which students who have completed a course, and perhaps additional courses as well, serve as mentors for students who are currently taking the course. A variation uses, as lab assistants, peers who are a bit further along in the program than the current students, and it has also had good results (Prey, 1996).

2.2 The professional context of informatics

This grouping involves nontechnical knowledge and skills which are needed by informatics graduates in order to function as informatics practitioners in a professional environment. The need for good communication skills has been discussed for some time and much attention has also been given to the need for an understanding of basic social and ethical issues of computing and information technology. Two more recent activities are discussed further here: Some new perspectives on developing team skills and the use of Total Quality Management (TQM) techniques in courses.

Developing team skills
Recent activities in the development of team skills have focused on integrating teamwork throughout the curriculum (Daigle *et al.*, 1996; Prey, 1996). One of the problems in using teams for projects in different classes is that it is easy for some students to 'hide' in positions such as librarian or documenter and therefore experience neither leadership positions nor adequate technical experience. Several recent efforts have attempted to provide coordination among different courses to ensure that students obtain a variety of experiences in team positions during the course of their education. There have also been efforts to demonstrate that the effectiveness of a team project is improved by working with industry practitioners on an actual project (Williams, 1997).

Total Quality Management in courses
Another recent aspect of professional and industrial practice which has been used in classes, is TQM (Null, 1996). At the beginning of a course a student TQM team is formed to coordinate the TQM process. Students formulate, with guidance by the teacher, the goals and objectives for the course. The TQM team then collects feedback from the students throughout the course and the team works with the teacher to evaluate the progress and to effect appropriate changes as needed in the course plan and the objectives. This activity involves students directly in the educational process while introducing them to some techniques which are widely used in industry.

2.3 Sequence of informatics topics

The final grouping includes some recent experiences and proposals regarding the sequence in which topics are covered in an informatics program. Unlike the first two groupings this one is directly involved with the informatics subject content of the courses. But the issues here are not what subject material should be taught, but rather the sequence of the material from a fairly global perspective.

First course with fundamental concepts

Some informatics faculty members have concluded that informatics students often get the wrong impression of the discipline and professional practice from introductory courses which emphasize basic programming and software development. As a result several programs have a first course for informatics majors which has little or no programming, but is designed to introduce students to important fundamental concepts of the discipline without programming (Cook, 1997; Shackelford and LeBlanc, 1998). These are not survey courses, but rather substantive courses which provide motivation for the more specialized courses in programming and other areas which follow.

Inverted curriculum model

Another proposal is to use an inverted curriculum model (Lidtke and Mulder, 1998). The motivation is similar: to provide students with an overview of professional practice in the introductory courses. This is done by having student teams work on 'industrial strength' problems, using available packages, class libraries and other previously-implemented software to develop solutions without first having to spend a substantial amount of time developing the students' software development capabilities. A key part of this approach is just-in-time learning in which new knowledge and concepts needed to solve a problem are not learned until they are needed for solving the problem.

3 OBSERVATIONS ON TRENDS IN INFORMATICS EDUCATION

It is interesting to note that all four of the listings in the teaching and learning paradigms category contain the word 'learning', but none contains the word 'teaching'. This perhaps reflects the trend toward viewing the success of education in terms of outcomes (learning) instead of process (teaching). Of course the learning which takes place in each of these four paradigms is guided and directed by teachers, so teaching is very much a part of the process. A further trend today is away from teacher-centred education, in which the teacher (lecturer) is the purveyor of knowledge and the duty of the students is to learn what is dispensed by the teacher. Instead, the student should be an active participant, with the teacher serving roles as coach and mentor, as well as that of teacher. There are similarities and overlap among the four teaching and learning paradigms, and none is intended to be used exclusively.

The increased emphasis on professional skills is mostly in response to feedback from industry that new hires are seriously lacking in these skills and sometimes even lacking any knowledge of their existence. The increasing public concerns about the societal implications of computing and concerns about safety-critical applications of computing also provide impetus for increased attention to these areas.

The efforts to provide a first course which introduces foundations of the discipline with little or no programming, reflect increasing concerns about the effectiveness of informatics education. The curriculum inversion model also reflects this to some extent, but it is primarily motivated by a desire to do a better job in preparing graduates to become highly productive practitioners in a professional commercial environment quickly after graduation.

Given that there is increasing interest in aspects of informatics curricula other than the technical subject content, it is interesting to speculate on the importance of the pedagogical and nontechnical components relative to the informatics subject content. Given that the objectives of the pedagogical and nontechnical components of a curriculum are to improve the effectiveness of the students' learning and to prepare them more effectively for productive professional practice, it could be argued that these components are at least as important as the specific informatics subject material which is taught.

It has long been the author's opinion that much of the material in most any specific course, could be eliminated from the curriculum without any detrimental effect on the graduates, and that the number of required informatics courses could also be reduced without a detrimental effect. But it is less clear that a similar statement applies to effective pedagogy and to activities which develop professional capabilities. So it might even be argued that the pedagogical and nontechnical components are the most important parts of an informatics program. However care must be taken that we do not fall into the trap of 'form over substance'. Pedagogical and professional skills components of an informatics program are definitely enhancements to the technical informatics subject material, rather than a replacement for a significant portion of this material.

Finally it should be noted that many of the changes which are taking place in the teaching of informatics are also taking place in other disciplines. Thus another factor which stimulates the efforts to improve the pedagogy and relevance for informatics curricula is the general pressure to improve the overall effectiveness of education in general.

4 CONCLUSION

The substantial increase in efforts to develop effective methods to improve student learning and to better prepare students for professional practice are probably due to three factors:

- pressure from industry to prepare graduates to be effective practitioners;
- an increased emphasis on the importance of high-quality education at the university level;

- an increase in the number of informatics faculty members who are interested in effective education.

These factors have stimulated the development of many approaches to improving informatics education which are not directly related to informatics subject material. Effective pedagogical improvements and the development of effective professional skills could well be as important to the success of informatics graduates as the specifics of the informatics subjects which are covered in a curriculum. It will be interesting to see whether this trend leads to informatics programs whose graduates are improved in the eyes of their industrial employers.

5 REFERENCES

Baldwin, D. (1996) Discovery learning in computer science. *SIGCSE bulletin* **28** (1), 222-226.

Cook, C.R. (1997) CS0: computer science orientation course. *SIGCSE bulletin* **29** (1), 87-91.

Daigle, R.J., Doran, M.V. and Pardue, J.H. (1996) Integrating collaborative problem solving throughout the curriculum. *SIGCSE bulletin* **28** (1), 237-241.

Lidtke, D.K. and Mulder, M.C. (1998) Meeting the needs of industry: a bold new curriculum in information science, in *Informatics in higher education: Views on informatics and noninformatics curricula* (eds. F. Mulder and T.J. van Weert), Chapman & Hall, London.

McConnell, J.J. (1996) Active learning and its use in computer science, in *Integrating technology into computer science education*, special issue of *SIGCSE bulletin* **28**, 52-54.

Null, L. (1996) Applying TQM in the computer science classroom. *SIGCSE bulletin* **28** (1), 120-124.

Prey, J.C. (1996) Cooperative learning and closed laboratories in an undergraduate computer science curriculum, in *Integrating technology into computer science education*, special issue of *SIGCSE bulletin* **28**, 23-24.

Shackelford, R.L. and LeBlanc, R.J., Jr (1998) Introduction to computing: a course in computer science fundamentals, in *Informatics in higher education: Views on informatics and noninformatics curricula* (eds. F. Mulder and T.J. van Weert), Chapman & Hall, London.

Tucker, A.B. *et al.* (1991) Computing curricula 1991. *Communications of the ACM* **34** (6), 70-84.

Walker, H.M. (1997) Collaborative learning: a case study for CS1 at Grinnell College and UT-Austin. *SIGCSE bulletin* **29** (1), 209-213.

Williams, K.A. (1997) Educating the next generation of information specialists: industry and university collaborative learning pilot project. *SIGCSE bulletin* **29** (1), 350-354.

Wills, C.E. and Finkel, D. (1994) Experience with peer learning in an introductory computer science course. *Computer science education* **5** (2), 165-187.

6 BIOGRAPHY

Joe Turner is a professor of computer science at Clemson University (USA). He currently serves as treasurer of ACM, as a director of FOCUS (Federation on Computing in the United States), as a member of IFIP TC-3, as vice-chair of IFIP Working Group 3.2, and as a member of the Board of Directors for the Association of Specialized and Professional Accreditors. He has previously served as president of the Computing Sciences Accreditation Board, chairman of the ACM Education Board, as a director of the Computing Research Association, and as a director of the National Educational Computing Association.

17

European Informatics Skills Structure (EISS)

Piet J.T. van der Kamp
Professional Development and Qualifications Task Force
Council of European Professional Informatics Societies
Antonie Duyckstraat 107, 2582 TG Den Haag, The Netherlands
e-mail: piet@vanderkamp.nl

Abstract

This paper introduces two different views of looking at professional development of the informatics professional. A top-down classification results in descriptions of "Skill cells' in the European Informatics Skills Structure. These descriptions detail tasks and attributes, entry requirements and required training, development. A bottom-up description of the informatics professional work area is in terms of 'Tasks', respectively 'Functions'. The granularity of these units of work is designed as to fit into any classification model. The paper shows how organizations can use either of the two approaches, and that even more detailed units of work can be derived through the top-down EISS approach.

Keywords

Informatics, taxonomies, levels of competence, business and industry requirements, professional profiles

1 INTRODUCTION

A Scoping Study, 'Getting Our Act Together', last year identified 43 national bodies involved in the development of Information Systems (IS) skills in the United Kingdom. Despite the work of such bodies there

Informatics in Higher Education F. Mulder & T. van Weerts (Eds.)

> remains widespread shortage in IS skills, coupled with an information shortage of precise labour market intelligence.
> (British Computer Society, 1997.)

What applies to the United Kingdom also applies to all other European countries:

- one can identify many bodies involved in the development of informatics professionals;
- there is a widespread shortage in informatics professionals;
- there are no standard naming systems for IS-skills.

For example, a function which one organization calls a 'systems analyst', differs from what other organizations think it is. However, a good notion of what is to be understood under a certain function name is essential in the informatics area. It is the first step to the solving of the shortage of information technology (IT) professionals and to the proper education of people in the IT-profession, which means an education of people who are needed by organizations.

The European Informatics Skills Structure (EISS) is a European approach to solve these problems. EISS is publicized widely throughout Europe by the Council of European Informatics Societies (CEPIS) with a view to its general implementation and use in public and private sector organizations involved in informatics. The goals of EISS are to:

- provide standards and guidelines for high quality performance by informatics practitioners;
- build frameworks for training in employment;
- improve the planning of professional and career development for practitioners;
- establish, together with international and national bodies which are responsible for education and training policies, statements of academic and professional qualifications to facilitate entry into and career development within informatics (Council of European Professional Informatics Societies, 1992).

This paper outlines the work done by the CEPIS Professional Development and Qualification Task Force on the development of the European Informatics Skills Structure. In this respect it must be noted that organizations can be in stages according to the view they have on IS skills development. EISS and other standards are not always suitable in all stages. The paper gives guidance to organizations which have to make a choice of standard for IS skills development. It also shows ways in which EISS can be of use to organizations in the different stages.

2 THE AREA OF THE INFORMATICS PROFESSIONAL

According to the definition by the Dutch Standards Institute informatics is the domain of both the study of information related to information systems and to the processing, transfer and use of information, principally, although not necessarily, using computers and telecommunications systems (Nederlands Genootschap voor Informatica, 1993).

The field of informatics is classified as follows:

- fundamental informatics;
- applied informatics, a specialization directed at applications areas in which informatics plays an essential and extensive role (business oriented and technical informatics).
  (Some people distinguish yet another category: informatics applications in other professional areas; the areas concerned, and not the informatics components, are the principal factors. For practical reasons we include this category in 'applied informatics'.)

Fundamental informatics may be subsequently classified into:

- hardware oriented informatics;
- core informatics (including, for example, fundamental logic, algorithms and operating systems);
- applications oriented informatics, aimed at general applications (such as network software, program generators and working methods).

Applications oriented informatics, combined with applied business oriented informatics, is regarded as comprising business informatics, the professional area under discussion (see the shaded area in Figure 1).

The view of EISS, although differently formulated, is in correspondence with the above view. EISS is concerned with the activities and capabilities of professional practitioners engaged in:

- applying computing and communications technologies (hardware and software) to build systems for collecting, storing, processing, disseminating and administering information within an organization;
- the processes of identifying, planning, specifying, developing, maintaining and operating such systems, based on the disciplined use of appropriate principles, standards, methods and tools;
- educating, managing and furthering the development of professionals;
- researching and developing the technologies themselves, and the tools (hardware and software-based) and methods for improving the performance of the systems and the practitioners.

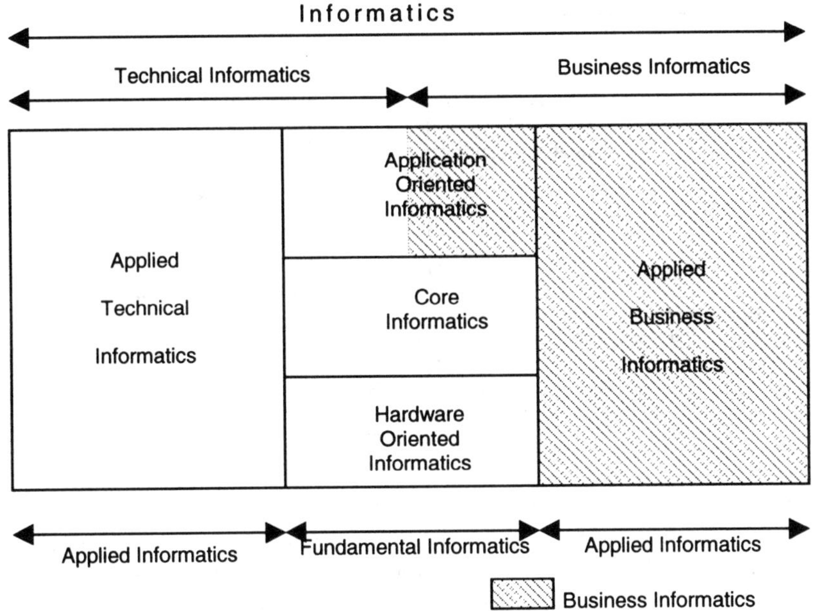

Figure 1 Classification of informatics.

3 OVERLAP OF ACTIVITIES

There exist many models to classify skill areas within informatics. In each model we must distinguish between informatics tasks performed by informatics professionals and those performed by other professionals.

First of all informatics tasks in an organization may be identified. A proportion of these is generally assigned to appropriately schooled professionals who devote the greater part of their working time to these tasks: the informatics professionals who carry out informatics functions. They may be professionals in pure informatics or they may be professionals in applied informatics. The latter are especially active in the boundary area between informatics and other professional areas. The work area of the informatics professional is the hatched area in Figure 2.

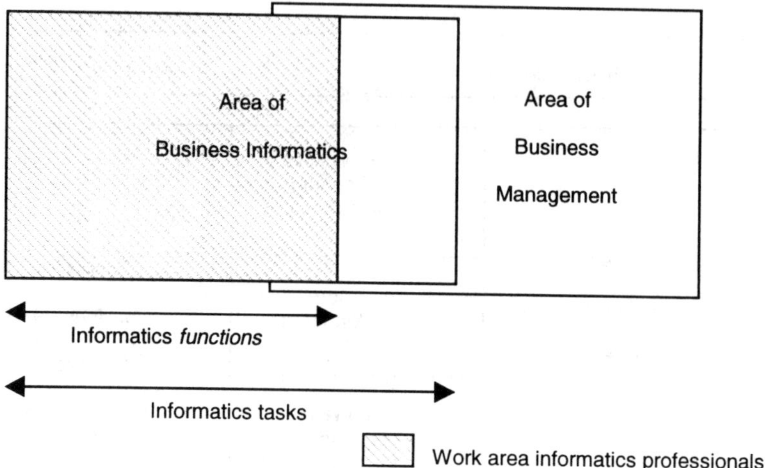

Figure 2 Work area of informatics professionals.

An increasing number of informatics tasks is carried out by people who primarily function in other disciplines. The functions they carry out are not informatics functions and they are not informatics professionals. We usually refer to them as informatics users.

4 TOP-DOWN APPROACH

In the identification of informatics tasks and functions two fundamentally differing approaches can be recognized, the top-down and the bottom-up approach.

The top-down approach (used in EISS) divides informatics into functional areas of activity, called streams. These streams are further subdivided into substreams. Substream activities can be performed on different levels of skill. Therefore in EISS the following matrix model is used: a horizontal axis of streams and substreams of informatics activities is set out against a vertical axis of ten levels. The levels reflect increasing capability from the lowest level of untrained entry up to and including the highest level of management directly responsible for informatics. Where an intersection occurs between a (sub)stream and a level, a skill cell is identified within the matrix and this is allocated a unique reference code, consisting of a (sub)stream code and a level number (see Figure 3). For example BC6 is the reference code for software engineering at level 6.

Figure 3 The EISS matrix

Stream	*Substream*	*Code*	*Levels*
Policy & management	Strategy and planning	AA	678
	Internal quality	AB	345678
	Information resource management	AC	678
	Informatics consultancy	AD	5678
	Informatics consultant analysis	AE	234
	Informatics management	AF	6789
Development	Development management	BA	45678
	Programming	BB	123
	Software engineering	BC	1234567
	Analysis/Programming	BD	123
	Analysis/Design	BE	234
	Business analysis	BF	34567
	Hardware engineering	BG	234567
Service delivery	Service delivery management	CA	678
	Operations routine	CB	0123
	Operations command	CC	456
	Service level management	CD	456
	Help desk	CE	01234
	Customer/User support	CF	12345
	Network support	CG	23456
	Systems programming	CH	123456
	Analysis/Programming	CI	123
	Capacity & Performance	CJ	4567
	Problem management	CK	4567
	Asset control	CL	456
Technical support	Database	DA	34567
	Hardware	DB	34567
	Communications	DC	34567
	Environment	DD	34567
	Security & Contingency planning	DE	34567
	Knowledge engineering	DF	34567
	Human/Computer interface	DG	34567
	Graphics	DH	34567
Audit	Audit specialist	E	678
Research	Research specialist	F	23456
Boundary-spanning	Boundary-spanning management	G	6789
Education & Training	Teaching	HA	23456
	Education & Training management	HB	5678
Technical authorship	Technical authorship	I	1234

Each identified skill cell is supported by a 'cell definition', comprising the following descriptive material:

- tasks/attributes, i.e. the nature of the work to be undertaken and the skill competencies required;
- entry requirements, i.e. relevant experience and level of skill achieved;
- training and development required, i.e. learning activities required to enhance knowledge, skills and experience.

The EISS matrix gives the starting point for a specific classification model for the informatics work area. Classification models however are more or less organization dependent: each organization chooses its own model and sometimes fervent discussions arise.

5 BOTTOM-UP APPROACH

There are two reasons why a bottom-up approach is becoming more feasible. Function classifications and titles appear not to be generally and unconditionally applicable in all situations; this is because the division of labour, and the degree of specialization chosen, are dependent on the organizational context. There are, for instance, differences between large and small organizations. As a result of technological and social developments the penetration of data processing facilities in organizations has substantially increased. New informatics tasks have come into being and existing tasks have changed. Many of the informatics tasks have shifted from the informatics professional to the information user (Nederlands Genootschap voor Informatica, 1993).

Against this background the bottom-up approach aims at supplying building blocks for the compilation of job profiles and training programmes for both informatics professionals and non-informatics professionals. Examples of this new approach are the Dutch report 'Tasks and Functions in Business Informatics' (Nederlands Genootschap voor Informatica, 1993) and the 'Industry Structure Model, Release 3.0' by the British Computer Society (British Computer Society, 1996).

The Dutch report identifies 86 so-called 'task clusters'. An example of a task cluster is 'task cluster 07 - Manage data'.

Task cluster 07 - Manage data

- Activity:ensure the integrity, completeness and authorized use of computerized data sets. Monitor the compliance with procedures for security, authorization and use.
- Result: valid data.
- Clarification: data is preferably recorded at source for multiple use thereafter. Coordination of use and supervision is to be desired.

The report also contains an algorithm with which job descriptions can be defined out of a collection of task clusters and other functional building blocks. With this algorithm each task cluster has to be completed with:

- environmental factors, such as the structure, size and autonomy of the organization, and used methods and techniques;
- the operational level of expertise required, e.g. freedom of thought and action, complexity of the problems and extent of professional influence;
- the role within which the task is to be performed, e.g. operational, advisory or coordinating.

The ISM3 System of the British Computer Society is computerized. It consists of a Windows application allowing for the interrogation of the ISM3 database. ISM3 identifies 59 'functions' which are defined as distinct areas of activity within information systems. Each function can be performed on several levels. The performance of a function on a particular level is called 'role'. Each role is supported by descriptive material such as:

- background (the combination of education, experience, and knowledge and skills needed before starting to perform a particular role);
- tasks within the role;
- knowledge and skills
  (Within ISM3, knowledge & skill appears in two contexts. First, it is used to define the knowledge and skills which the practitioner needs to possess before starting to carry out a particular role or function. Second, it is used to characterize a role by defining the most important knowledge and skills the practitioner will require to achieve proficiency in the role);
- training activities;
- level (a consistent measure of the degree of autonomy, responsibility and accountability).

See Figure 4 for the ISM3 database structure.

Roles can be merged in different and flexible ways to define jobs within the scope of the model. Thus in the British approach it is possible to define jobs very flexible, as a collection of roles.

In both approaches, the Dutch as well as the British one, certain functional models, i.e. subdivisions of the areas of informatics activities, are used for ease of access only. The definition of the task clusters, nor the definition of the functions is influenced by the model chosen. This is central to the flexibility of these approaches. Because of this it is possible to use each task cluster (NGI), as well as each function (BCS) in each conceivable informatics classification model and get a complete coverage. For example the life-cycle model can be completely covered

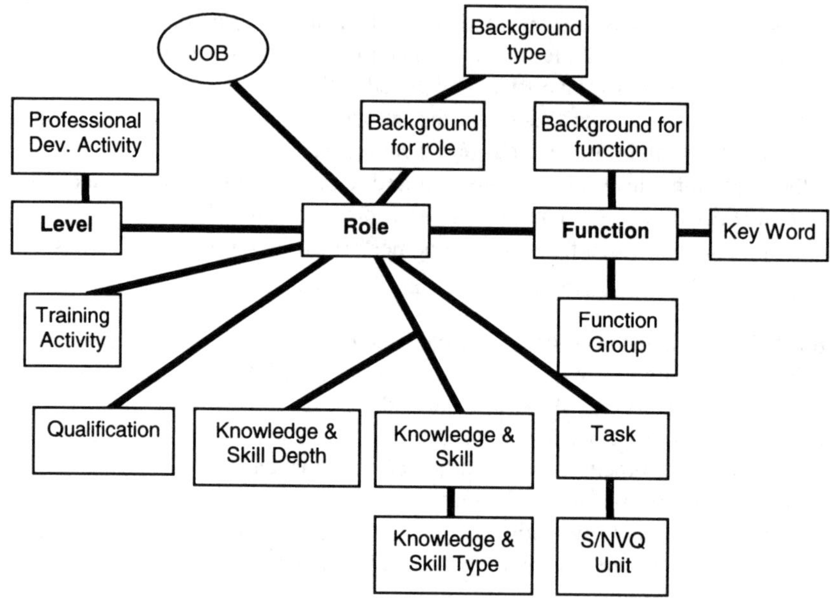

Figure 4 ISM3 structure.

with the activities described in 'task clusters' respectively 'functions' in such a way that:

- the model is completely covered (no gaps left);
- all 'task clusters' respectively 'functions'are used.

6 THE TWO APPROACHES COMPARED

Looking at the development in thinking about functions and tasks in the informatics area over time we see a shift from job oriented thinking to task oriented thinking (see Figure 5)

Nolan in his theory states that each organization must get the opportunity to grow in its own pace. This means that some organizations will still be quite job-oriented in the sense that these organize their work along functional patterns. These organizations may take advantage of the work by CEPIS and we recommend them to use EISS as a top-down framework for the development and qualification of their workers. Other organizations, however, which are more project oriented, and therefore task oriented, are better off using the bottom-up approach, both in determining the skills needed for projects and in performing their overall skills

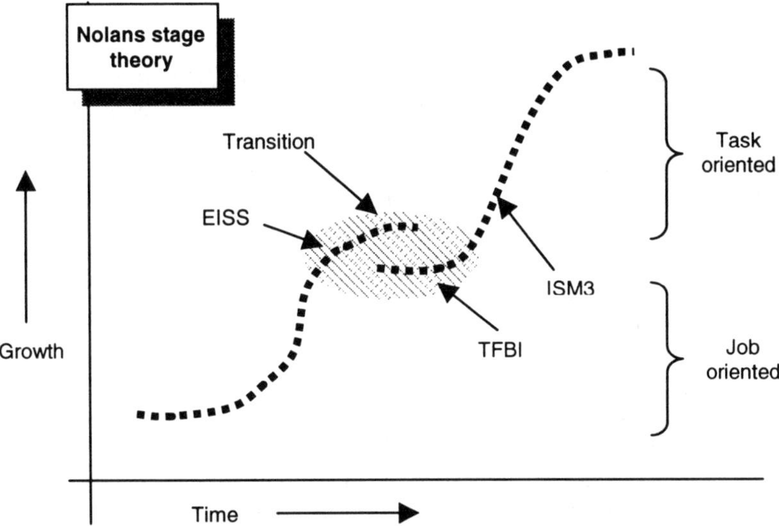

Figure 5 The approaches in the Nolan curves.

management. This above also applies to individual workers in either of the two types of organizations.

An example of the use of EISS is found in the educational profiles for the informatics area (HBO-I, 1997), produced by the 'HBO-I Platform'. (HBO-I is the Dutch Higher Vocational Education Platform for Informatics). These profiles are discussed in another paper in these proceedings (Van Leeuwen and Smeets, 1998). EISS cell descriptions were - amongst others - selected as reference points to describe the learning goals for each of four profiles:

- I/i, Informatics with a specialization in informatics;
- I/ba, Informatics aimed at the business (administration) domain;
- I/t, Informatics aimed at the technology domain;
- I/e&m, Informatics aimed at exploitation and management of information systems.

The learning goals are extracted from the EISS cells and form 'the atoms' of the four profiles. Together the learning goals define the complete field of informatics knowledge and skills. And more importantly, these goals fit into any classification model for informatics, i.e. any activity defined in any classification model can be expressed in one or more 'atomic' goals. This may put a stop to the fervent discussions on classification and by this prove the usefulness of EISS.

7 CONCLUSION

There is on the one hand a clear need to be able to define educational goals in terms of - for example - EISS cell descriptions (the top-down approach). On the other hand there is a wish to describe knowledge and skills (i.e. learning goals) in flexible, task oriented elements (the bottom-up approach).

Many organizations are still organized according to functions: top-down the organizational goals are transformed into functions which are assigned to people. In this type of organization EISS will help in clarifying questions of development and qualification of people. EISS provides a European dictionary of informatics skills which enables employers to properly define a position which they may wish to fill. Potential applicants, regardless of nationality, can describe their skills in matching terms.

Organizations, however, become more and more project and/or product oriented. In order to be able to put together project teams organizations must know which skills are needed within projects. In practice these skills are often defined on the basis of coincidental activities by practitioners in previous projects or on the basis of incidental courses or study in the past. A new bottom-up approach with corresponding methods and techniques has to be developed for the evaluation of these skills. Some examples which provide a good starting point for this approach, are already around.

8 REFERENCES

British Computer Society (1996) *Industry Structure Model Release 3 (ISM3)*, a computerized Windows based application using the BCS ISM3 Database. The British Computer Society, Swindon, UK.

British Computer Society (1997) IS skills gets its act together, *The Computer Bulletin for Information Systems Professionals*, **9** (2), 5.

Council of European Professional Informatics Societies (1992) *European Informatics Skills Structure*. CEPIS, London.

HBO-I Platform (1997*) Opleidingsprofielen HBO-I (Higher Vocational Educational Profiles for Informatics)*. Hogeschool West-Brabant, Breda, The Netherlands [in Dutch].

Nederlands Genootschap voor Informatica [Dutch Computer Society] (1993) *Taken en Functies in de Bestuurlijke Informatica (Tasks and Functions in Business Informatics)*. Kluwer Bedrijfswetenschappen, Deventer, The Netherlands [in Duch].

Van Leeuwen, H. and Smeets, D. (1998) Profiles of informatics graduates as demanded by the market, in: *Informatics in higher education: Views on informatics and noninformatics curricula* (eds. F. Mulder and T. J. van Weert), Chapman & Hall, London.

9 BIOGRAPHY

Piet J.T. van der Kamp is a registered informatician (RI). He served in the Royal Dutch Air Force from 1961 to 1990. When automation started, he became involved in information system development. Currently he is an independant organization and information consultant. He is active in several working groups and committees of the Dutch Computer Society (NGI), amongst which the Committee on Professional Development (COMBO). Since 1996 he is chairman of the Professional Development and Qualification Task Force of the Council of European Professional Informatics Societies.

Profiles of informatics graduates as demanded by the market

Henk van Leeuwen
Hogeschool Enschede, Instituut Informatie- en Communicatietechnologie, PO Box 70 000, 7500 KB Enschede The Netherlands, e-mail: h.vanleeuwen@ict.hen.nl

Deny Smeets
Hogeschool van Arnhem en Nijmegen, Hogere Informatica PO Box 2217, 6802 CE Arnhem, The Netherlands e-mail: smeets@universal.nl

Abstract

The professional field puts demands on the qualifications of informatics graduates. These demands have important consequences for the informatics curriculum in higher education. This should provide a good fit between the qualifications of graduates and the demands of the professional practice. A project group recently has described four profiles for informatics graduates based on both these demands and a view on developments in informatics. These profiles are linked to the domains of business administration, technical work, systems exploitation and management, and software engineering. For each of the profiles the qualifications have been characterized by a level in a (simplified) taxonomy of Bloom.

Keywords

Informatics, economics and business administration, higher vocational education, curriculum (general), levels of competence, business and industry requirements, educational profiles, professional profiles

Informatics in Higher Education F. Mulder & T. van Weerts (Eds.)

1 INTRODUCTION

The Dutch informatics schools in professional higher education (HBO) cooperate in the so-called 'HBO-I platform'. This platform aims to develop a clear description of content and position of the informatics education in these informatics schools. Already in 1992 the demand of industry and other business areas for informatics graduates was investigated as part of a project for quality improvement of informatics education (KIO, 1993b). A subsequent project investigated the profiles of the informatics profession (HBO-I, 1994). And a third project had four goals, namely to:

- design profiles for informatics education following recommendations of the 1994 visitation committee which inspected the quality of professional higher informatics education in all HBO-I schools;
- provide a clear description of education at the HBO-I schools;
- offer a frame of reference for HBO-I schools;
- present a method for implementation and maintenance of the informatics curriculum.

An eventual aim was to:

- realize a general and broad informatics education focused on general (business) information systems, on automation of production and on software as a product or in products;
- realize a business study programme with informatics as a substream (25% of the curriculum).

The project team started in September 1995 and reported (Van Leeuwen *et al.*, 1997) in 1997. This paper describes the project and its consequences.

2 PROFESSIONAL HIGHER EDUCATION IN THE NETHERLANDS

For a better understanding we sketch the situation of the Dutch informatics schools in professional higher education and some developments relevant to the project discussed.

Higher education in The Netherlands consist of two types: HBO (professional higher education) and WO (academic higher education). HBO graduates earn a Bachelor's degree. WO graduates earn a Master's degree. This paper deals with informatics schools at universities for professional education (HBO).

In 1971 the first two informatics schools started in HBO and now there are about 30. Two types have emerged:

- Schools for Higher Informatics (HIO), generally concentrating on software engineering and technical contexts;
- Schools for Business Informatics (BI) aimed at application of informatics in business and economical context.

In 1987 a new type of school emerged, combining HIO and BI in one school for Informatics and Information and integrating education for both types of graduates (HIO and BI).

In the eighties the profession was undergoing profound transformations. Individual schools had to cope with these changes and make their own curriculum choices in which they had much freedom. Cooperation between HIO-schools was weak; BI-schools worked more closely together. A large diversity of curricula resulted. In the nineties it became clear that this lack of cooperation hindered improvement of informatics education. A project, called KIO (KIO, 1993), was started in which all 30 schools (HIO and BI) cooperated and which resulted in the HBO-I platform.

An external stimulus for cooperation followed from the external quality audit of the HBO. All schools of informatics in the HBO were inspected by a so-called visitation committee consisting of experts in the field of informatics, industry and education. Their report 'From isolation to integration' (HBO-Raad, 1994) contained important views, conclusions and recommendations.

3 PROBLEM DESCRIPTION

The problem has been described in the introduction. And from that description the question arise: How can we identify educational profiles? An understanding of the demands of the professional field in the coming years is required. And experiences from earlier projects show that the labour market does not speak with one tongue about these demands. Another question is: What are the tasks our graduates have to perform in the first years after graduation? Important sources for the answer to this question are found in task descriptions published by informatics societies. These may be updated by more recent articles and interviews. And then there is the question of how to select particular task descriptions which can be transformed into qualifications which students have at graduation? How to formulate exit qualifications and how to express the level of expertise? And the last, but by no means the easiest question: How to derive educational profiles from exit qualifications?

4 SOME CLARIFICATION ON TERMS USED IN THIS PAPER

What is meant by the term 'professional profile'?. It is the description of a coherent set of tasks of a HBO-I graduate professional performed a few years after graduation. This profile is not linked to functions, but to tasks. Starting from this set of tasks we can derive qualifications which graduates should have on graduation, as beginning professional. These qualifications are called 'exit qualifications' of a study programme. 'Learning objectives' are intermediate objectives in an educational program leading to the exit qualifications. These are, however, not discussed in this paper.

5 THE RESEARCH

Our first task was to investigate the literature for task descriptions in the informatics. The most complete description was found in the report 'European Informatics Skill Structure' (EISS, 1992) of the Council of European Professional Informatics Societies, CEPIS. This report proved to be of large value because it provides an in-depth and detailed view of knowledge and skills of informatics professionals. Also the Dutch Informatics Society reports in 1989 and 1993 (NGI, 1989; NGI, 1993) were studied. The findings were published in a report (KIO, 1993).

When selecting tasks for identifying exit qualifications we made some restriction and confined ourselves to informatics education. The problem to decide what informatics is was solved by choosing the Unified Classification Scheme of Informatics, UCSI (Mulder, 1992) as a framework. We also excluded tasks as described in EISS in training, hardware engineering, research, boundary spanning management, procurement and contracting, sales and marketing and technical authorship. Some of these subfields were not open for our graduates in the first years of their career, others were not at the right level of professional education or too specific. A second selection concerned task levels. The HBO-I graduates are at the EISS level of trained practitioner (level 3), fully skilled practitioner (level 4) and in some aspects even at a higher level. A last criterion in selecting exit qualifications was time independence: We excluded those qualifications which strongly depend on hypes and questionable 'trends'.

To reformulate task qualifications into exit qualifications requires some guidelines. Every exit qualification has two parts (an operational sentence and a sentence which specifies the object of the operation) and has a skill level in the taxonomy of Bloom (Bloom, 1956). The skill level can be implicitly derived or explicitly mentioned. The operational part of an exit qualification can be formulated as: 'the student knows ...' (k), 'the student can describe ...' (k), 'the student can explain why ...' (u), 'the student can perform ....' (a), 'the student has the skill to ...' (a), 'the student can evaluate ...' (m), 'the student can create new ways for doing ...' (m). The skill level is indicated in parentheses: 'k' stands for knowledge, 'u' for understanding, 'a' for application skill and 'm' stands for 'more': evaluation, analysis and synthesis. For pragmatic reasons we have put the last three levels into one.

To supplement the set of qualifications derived from EISS, other sources were studied resulting in some new exit qualifications reflecting more recent or special topics. Some activity models were helpful: the information systems bi-cycle, the reference model of the Open University course Methodology of information system development (Lemmen, 1993), the I-matrix of an earlier project Profiles for the informatics profession (HBO-I, 1994) and the system management model of Looijen (Looijen, 1995). There are, of course, also exit qualifications which hold for HBO-graduates in general. We have put these in a special category: HBO General.

In the end we got a rather complete set of exit qualifications covering more than can be done in a four year programme. So a choice has to be made. A special property of the set is that not all qualifications cover the same scope: some deal with aspects that are to be learned in short time, others require a long period time. An experiment to formulate qualifications with the same scope failed.

6 EDUCATIONAL PROFILES

6.1 Description of a profile

A profile of a study programme has as characteristics:

- a set of exit qualifications;
- division of the study load over a number of components;
- an overall view.

Exit qualifications are selected on the basis of the study load and the view. In our case the study load of informatics was 50% of the total curriculum, of which 37.5% is common to all profiles and 12.5% can be different. Each profile is further linked to a characteristic domain. The resulting model is shown in Figure 1.

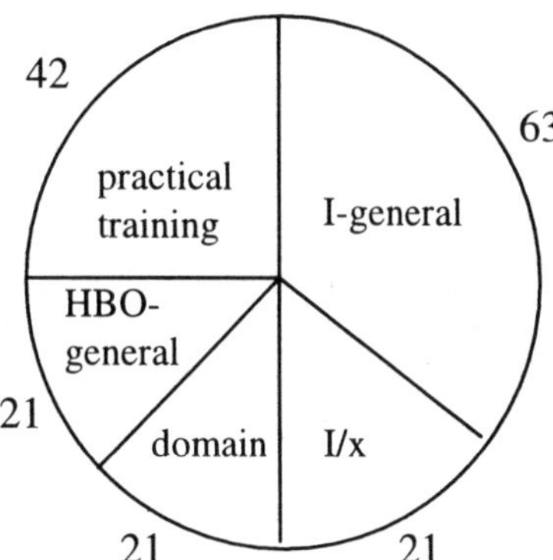

Figure 1 Components of a broad informatics study programme.

The right half of the circle is the informatics part. The half of the circle to the left hand side consists of the practical training, HBO general and the domain. The numbers indicate the number of allocated study points (one study point is 40 hours of study). Each study year consists of 42 study points. Each profile is different in the parts domain and informatics implied by the domain (I/x). In a study programme the notation of the principal field of study is a capital (I for informatics, BA for business administration and X for any other domain). A secondary field in the programme is indicated in lower case, separated from the principal field by a slash. So I/ba is the profile of the informatics study programme which has as its secondary field business administration. I/i is the profile of informatics education specializing in a typical subtopic of informatics.

6.2 Informatics and business administration

All profiles I/x are part of informatics education and all have the characteristic that they are innovative with respect to computer systems, software systems and information systems and their development. The common part of informatics education offers general knowledge of informatics, skills in specification and development of software and information systems, and knowledge of system management. All informatics graduates therefore can fully participate in the development process which is a market demand.

In parallel another task group has developed a profile for the BA/i business administration study programme (BA/i, 1996a and 1996b). The general objective of this programme is to educate experts who can improve business processes applying information and communication technology to that end. The model is shown in Figure 2.

6.3 Identification of profiles

The investigation of exit qualifications had made clear that a big number of applications of informatics is in the business domain. So one of the I-profiles will be in this domain: the I/ba profile. A second important domain is the technical field. This differs substantially from the business administration domain because of the close interaction with technical artefacts and processes. This results in the I/t profile. Information services is a domain strongly emerging. The ever changing, enormous diversity in computer systems, software systems and information systems requires systematic management based on powerful concepts. This is not a skill for scientific profiles, but relevant for HBO-I. The third profile is therefore exploitation and management, I/e&m. Last but not least the problem of designing and realising complex systems for any environment asks for skills in software engineering which surpass the level of the I-general component of the curriculum. This profile is I/i.

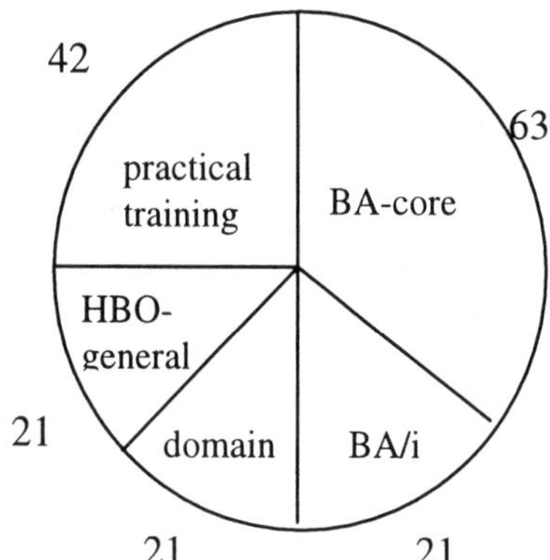

Figure 2 Components of a business administration with informatics study programme.

6.4 Summary of informatics profiles

We distinguish the following informatics profiles (I/x).

I/ba: informatics in the business domain
Graduates of I/ba are able to apply information and communication technology to support business operations and the (re)design of business processes. They are able to play a role in the development of business systems. The analysis of processes and of information is more developed than in the I-general part of the curriculum.

Information policy, change management, quality management and project management are exit qualifications and expand the general I-skills. From business administration topics as business organizations and processes, business economics, information facilities are chosen.

I/t: informatics in technical domains

Information and communication technology is incorporated in technical products and plays an increasing role in production processes. Embedded software is strongly interacting with other parts of the products. There are special requirements for correctness, robustness and ease of use. In most cases special demands are posed upon the use of resources such as memory. In the development of these products the design of hardware and software is concurrent. Another aspect in I/t is the application of informatics in production and process control. Topics of informatics specially related to this profile are process control, real time systems, fault tolerance, robotics, digital signal processing, CAD/CAM and simulations software. And from technical perspective measuring methods, interfacing between technical and computer systems, support of logistics and image processing.

I/e&m: exploitation and management

The installed base of computer systems, software systems and information systems needs application management. From a business point of view this concerns the question of how installed systems function so that they optimally support business processes, operations and organizations. To the I-general part of the curriculum data management, application management, system software, client/server, network management and management of development environments are important in I/e&m. This profile has components of operational management, user service delivery, help desk, system administration. These are in fact special topics of business administration.

I/i: software engineering

The study of problems in designing and implementing large and complex software systems is software engineering. Application of scientific knowledge and methods is supplemented with personal skills. The complexity in software engineering is not the context of the business, but the context of the software and computer systems in which the new software should function. The I-general part of the curriculum is extended with data structures (objects) and algorithms, compiler design, database management systems, artificial intelligence, computer architecture, networks and operating systems. For the software process software quality management is a topic with an increasing attention in the field.

The profiles in tables

The profiles may be described in tables with the following structure (see Figure 3). In the last five columns a letter denotes the skill level of Bloom. No letter means: not required in this part of the curriculum or for this profile.

Code	*Exit qualification*	*I-general*	*I/ba*	*I/i*	*I/t*	*I/e&m*
	knows about ...	k	k	u	u	a
	can apply	a	a	a	m	a
	can explain why ...		u	u		a
	can evaluate and create					

Figure 3 Example of a table describing the profiles
(k = knowledge level; u = understanding level; a = application level; m = more, i.e. a level above application (analysis, synthesis, evaluation)).

7 CONCLUSION

The profiles and exit qualifications described in this paper turn out to be of practical use for informatics education and for the informatics profession. For informatics education they offer a frame of reference and a starting point for further development of curricula. By evaluating the topics in the study programmes with respect to this set of qualifications schools can determine which profiles they want to offer. The total set of qualifications supports schools in selecting their own exit qualifications and intermediate objectives.

It is obvious that the work reported in this paper is not the final solution in curriculum development, but still it offers a good starting point for future work. Also some questions are still open. For instance the question of how to project (subsets of) exit qualifications onto study points. The work reported here is highly time independent, but not totally. So regular updates, at least every three years, are advised.

8 ACKNOWLEDGEMENTS

The authors wish to thank the members of the project team Trudy Berends, Math Dicker, Nico Huffels and Jan Woolderink for their contribution.

9 REFERENCES

Bloom, B.S. [ed.] (1956) *Taxonomy of educational objectives: Cognitive domain.* David McKay, New York.

BK/i (1996a) *Over BK/i: een nieuwe opleiding.* Werkgroep BK/i [in Dutch].

BK/i (1996b). *Eindtermen BK/i.* Werkgroep BK/i [in Dutch].

DOZ (1989) *Doelen formuleren in het onderwijs.* DOZ boek 1, Werkgroep Docenten Onderwijszaken [in Dutch].

EISS (1992) *European Informatics Skills Structure, a set of performance standards covering all functional areas of work carried out by professionals in informatics* Council of European professional Informatics Societies (CEPIS.

HBO-I (1994) *HBO-I op weg naar beroepsprofielen.* Rapportage HBO-I platform 1993 -1994, Deel III, HBO-I-platform [in Dutch].

HBO-Raad (1994) *Van isolement naar integratie.* Eindrapport van de visitatiecommissie informatica-opleidingen, HBO-Raad, Den Haag [in Dutch].

KIO (1993) *HBO-I Informatica.* KIO-rapportage, overzicht, KIO [in Dutch].

KIO (1993b) *KIO, Rapport project Uitstroom.* Onderdeel van de rapportage Kwaliteitsverbetering Informatica Onderwijs [in Dutch].

Lemmen, K.A.M., *et al.* (1993) *Methodologie van informatiesysteemontwikkeling.* Open universiteit, Heerlen [in Dutch].

Looijen, M. (1995) *Beheer van informatiesystemen.* Kluwer Bedrijfswetenschappen, Deventer [in Dutch].

Mulder, F. (1992) *Identiteit van informatica-onderwijs.* Inaugurale rede Open universiteit, Heerlen [in Dutch].

NGI (1989) *Functies in de technische informatica; een voorstel tot ordening van taken en functies op het gebied van de technische informatica.* NGI-commissie beroepsontwikkeling, Kluwer Bedrijfswetenschappen, Deventer [in Dutch].

NGI (1990) *Het organiseren en controleren van het systeembeheer.* Rapport van de werkgroep systeembeheer binnen de sectie EDP-Auditing, NGI, Amsterdam [in Dutch].

NGI (1993) *Taken en functies in de bestuurlijke informatica; een voorstel tot ordening.* NGI-commissie beroepsontwikkeling, Kluwer Bedrijfswetenschappen, Devehter [in Dutch].

Van Leeuwen, H., Berends, T.M., Dicker, L.M.M., Huffels, N., Woolderink, A.J. (1997) *Opleidingsprofielen HBO-I.* HBO-I Platform [in Dutch].

10 BIOGRAPHY

After teaching eleven years at primary and secondary schools, Henk van Leeuwen became a lecturer at the school for Hogere Informatica at Enschede in 1984. He received his Master's degree in mathematics and informatics from the University of Utrecht in 1985. In 1988 he became head of the informatics department at the Hogeschool Enschede. Now he teaches informatics and is coordinator of the IT-stream in a quality project in the Hogeschool Enschede. In 1992 he was chairing a project investigating the demand of industry and other organizations for informatics graduates. He was chairing the project reported here.

Deny Smeets studied electrical engineering at the University of Twente in Enschede. He worked during 2 years for the International Telecommunication Union in Dacca, Bangladesh. After that he has developed during six years informatics courses for distance learning at Dirksen Opleidingen. Since 1985 he is working as lecturer at the Technical Faculty of the Hogeschool van Arnhem en Nijmegen. He is co-author and editor of the book 'Program development in Pascal' and editor of TINFON, a Dutch journal for informatics education. At the moment he is director of the school for Informatics (HIO) at the Hogeschool van Arnhem en Nijmegen. During 1991-1996 he was chairing the HIO-platform and the HBO-I platform.

Use and misuse of taxonomies of learning: integrated educational goals in computer science curricula

Jeroen J.G. van Merriënboer
Graduate School of Teacher Training, Department of Instructional Technology, University of Twente, PO Box 217, 7500 AE Enschede The Netherlands

Elisabeth M.A.G. van Dijk
Department of Computer Science, University of Twente, PO Box 217 7500 AE Enschede, The Netherlands, e-mail: bvdijk@cs.utwente.nl

Abstract

Most systematic design procedures for either curricula or courses start from a description of educational goals. These goals are then decomposed into more specific objectives which are categorized according to some taxonomy of learning. The basic idea is that different categories of goals and objectives correspond with different optimal instructional methods. However, for complex intellectual skills a set of subskills is performed. The ability to perform each of those subskills separately does not guarantee that the skills can be coordinated and integrated in performing real-world tasks. This problem is known as the problem of 'integrated goals' or 'multiple objectives'. This paper argues that educational goals and objectives should be seen and treated as highly integrated and interrelated during the whole educational design process. Approaches to dealing with multiple objectives are discussed.

Keywords

Informatics, curriculum (general), taxonomies, levels of competence, educational profiles

Informatics in Higher Education F. Mulder & T. van Weerts (Eds.)

1 INTRODUCTION

Taxonomies of learning play an important role in the design of curricula, instruction and tests. It is common practice to start with a formulation of educational goals which are subsequentlyspecified into more specific objectives classified according to the desired type of learning. Instructional sequences are designed for each of the objectives and often the objectives also form the basis for development of tests. This paper questions the usefulness and validity of this approach for the design of computer science curricula. In these curricula complex intellectual skills, such as database design, interface design, programming, software engineering or the design of information systems play an important role. The traditional, objectives-based approach to curriculum design yields instruction which is too fragmented and piecemeal. It may block the students' ability to apply their acquired skills and knowledge in the real world.

The structure of this paper is as follows. Section 2 discusses some widely used taxonomies of learning. Section 3 discusses some problems related to the use of taxonomies of learning. Section 4 discusses three approaches for dealing with the problem of multiple objectives: case-based teaching, problem-based learning and integrating schooling with work. The paper ends with a brief summary and conclusion.

2 TAXONOMIES OF LEARNING

Taxonomies of learning have a long history. A rather old taxonomy which is still widely used was introduced by Bloom (1956). While Bloom described three largely independent taxonomies for the cognitive, affective and psychomotor domain, the term 'Taxonomy of Bloom' is typically used to refer to his taxonomy for the cognitive domain. In this particular taxonomy six types of performance are distinguished:

1. **knowledge**,
   referring to remembering or recalling facts or generalities;
2. **comprehension**,
   referring to the ability to process and interpret information and to deduce facts from given information;
3. **application**,
   referring to the autonomous use of generalities, such as the ability to use concepts, procedures and principles;
4. **analysis**,
   referring to the ability to analyse a knowledge domain or product in its elements and in relationships between those elements;
5. **synthesis**,

referring to the ability to build or design a knowledge domain or product from a set of elements;
6. **evaluation**,
   referring to the ability to judge the quality of a knowledge domain or product on the basis of a set of criteria.

It is important to note that this taxonomy is not based on a particular psychological theory of learning. It was developed from a practical viewpoint and the six categories were mainly based on teachers' experiences in the classroom. The main goal was to ask more attention for learning goals related to the 'higher' levels in the taxonomy such as analysis, synthesis and evaluation.

Building on the work of Bloom several authors have stressed different aspects of educational goals, namely:

- their implications for designing curricula and instruction;
- their relationships to subject area profiles;
- their relationships to different types of educational content;
- criteria to their formulation in order to be useful for testing.

2.1 Educational goals and instructional design

From the viewpoint of instructional design, Gagné (1965) made a number of important extensions to the work of Bloom. First, he made clear that specific educational goals can often only be determined on the basis of some kind of 'task analysis'. Complex intellectual skills often consist of a number of subskills or enabling skills; in order to formulate the educational goals for the enabling skills the whole skill must be decomposed. Gagné introduced the 'learning hierarchy' as a means of decomposition: the complex cognitive skill is at the top and enabling skills are lower in the hierarchy. In teaching one starts with the skills lower in the hierarchy and successively works towards the skills higher in the hierarchy.

Gagné also described a taxonomy of learning with clear links to psychological theories of learning. For the cognitive domain the taxonomy makes a distinction between:

1. **verbal information**,
   which category corresponds with Bloom's knowledge category;
2. **intellectual skills**,
   which are at the 'heart' of the taxonomy of Gagné with five subcategories:
   a. discriminations;
   b. concrete concepts;
   c. defined concepts;
   d. rules;
   e. higher-order rules;
3. **cognitive strategies**,
   which are used to integrate and coordinate the performance of intellectual skills.

This taxonomy reflects the fact that some intellectual skills enable the performance of other higher-level skills. For instance, the ability to apply rules or procedures is prerequisite to the use of higher-order rules (i.e. problem solving). And the ability to apply particular intellectual skills is prerequisite to the use of cognitive strategies. In addition, the taxonomy reflects the principle of 'conditions of learning', indicating that particular instructional methods are apt to reach particular educational goals. Thus, analysing an intellectual skill in its enabling skills and then categorizing the enabling skills offers an instructional designer the opportunity to select suitable instructional strategies and tactics.

2.2 Educational goals and subject area profiles

The hierarchical model of Gagné actually introduced only two types of educational goals: performance objectives at the top of a learning hierarchy and enabling objectives or learning objectives lower in this hierarchy. More recent theories of instructional design, for example (Leshin *et al.*, 1992), expand the task-analytical procedures which may be used for the specification of educational goals. A common approach is to define a 'job profile' or 'subject area profile' and an associated 'educational profile'. For instance, a job profile might make a distinction between:

- parts of a job;
- duties which make up a part of the job;
- tasks which make up the duty;
- operations which describe the performance of the task.

The associated educational profile then makes a distinction between:

- terminal objectives which describe the main goals of the whole curriculum;
- course objectives which describe the goals of the separate courses in the curriculum;
- performance objectives which describe the tasks to be taught in a particular course;
- learning objectives which describe what must be learned to master each of the tasks.

As in the Gagné model, the actual development of instruction is still based on the performance objectives and learning objectives.

2.3 Educational goals and content

A second refinement to the use of taxonomies of learning was proposed by Merrill (1983). He argues that not only the level of performance, but also the 'content' of the performance determines the instructional methods which are necessary for reaching a particular educational goal. For the performance dimension he makes a distinction between remember, use and find. For the content dimension he makes a distinction between facts, concepts, procedures and principles. The resulting matrix (see Figure 1) yields a taxonomy of 13 types of objectives (three of the cells are empty because facts can only be memorized).

This taxonomy more-or-less mimics Gagné's taxonomy. For instance, the verbal information in the Gagné model is specified according to the remember levels of performance, the rules in the Gagné model are identical to the use-procedure element in the Merrill model, and so forth. Merrill's Component Display Theory for instructional design specifies instructional methods for reaching each of the 13 types of learning objectives.

	fact	concept	procedure	principle
find		find a concept	find a procedure	find a principle
use		use a concept	use a procedure	use a principle
remember generality		remember definition of concept	remember steps of a procedure	remember relation in principle
remember instance	remember a fact	remember example of concept	remember example of procedure	remember example of principle

Figure 1 Merrill's performance-content matrix.

2.4 Formulating educational goals

Mager (1962) was especially influential with his book 'Preparing Instructional Objectives' stressing the importance of a clear formulation of educational goals and objectives. According to Mager, objectives must:

- describe observable behaviour;
- state the conditions under which the behaviour is shown;
- clearly indicate standards for performance.

The work of Mager heavily influenced the field of educational testing. Essentially, he stated that the mastery of a knowledge domain could be described in terms of reaching specific educational goals or objectives. Each objective should correspond with a test item and a complete test should consist of a set of test items representative for all objectives.

2.5 Summary

Taxonomies of learning invite curriculum designers to decompose educational goals until a level where these can easily be classified according to the categories in the taxonomy. The concrete goals are often called performance objectives (describing desired task performance) or learning objectives (describing what must be learned in order to master the task). It is assumed that particular objectives can best be reached by the application of particular instructional methods (the 'conditions of learning'). In addition the objectives often provide a basis for the development of tests. The basic claim of the models discussed so far is that reaching all the separate objectives ensures that the general educational goal is also met. This claim will be questioned in the next section.

3 PROBLEMS RELATED TO TAXONOMIES OF LEARNING

The use of taxonomies of learning as a basis for instructional design, as discussed in the previous section, is sometimes called a 'part-task' approach, because the student is taught only one or a very limited number of subskills at the same time. New subskills (as specified by the learning objectives) are gradually added to practice and it is not until the end of the instruction that the student has the opportunity to practice the whole cognitive skill (as specified by the performance objective). This approach proved to be very useful for the design of curricula and instruction for relatively simple tasks. However, it also became clear that the approach has severe limitations for curricula in which complex intellectual skills are central to learning. Needless to say, tasks which require such complex skills are very common in computer science curricula. One might think of the design of information systems and software engineering, but also of their constituent skills information analysis and database design, interface design and programming.

3.1 Complex skills and multiple objectives

Many studies contradict the basic claim that a learner is competent in a particular field if all learning objectives for this field have been obtained. The general goal of performing a complex task in the real world is more than the sum of its parts, that is, the sum of its learning objectives. In general, strict part-task approaches only seem to work well for skills which can be mastered in less than 20-40 hours, or for skills which are not characterized by integrated sets of subskills. The approach does not work well for complex intellectual skills in which the performance requires ample coordination of subskills from the learner. This is known as the 'problem of multiple objectives'. Performing a particular subskill in isolation is simply different from performing it in the context of a whole task. It seems to lead to different mental representations (Elio, 1986) and a constituent skill which has been learned in isolation can often not be properly performed in the context of the whole task. The students are not able to develop a holistic vision of the task.

3.2 Fragmentation of the curriculum

The fact that integrated objectives are not easily handled in a traditional, objectives-driven approach to instructional design, is also reflected in the structure of many curricula which are often experienced by students as too fragmented and piecemeal. There is not enough opportunity to integrate and learn to coordinate all subskills necessary for performing meaningful whole tasks. The same problem arises with testing. Tests with items based on separate objectives give an indication of mastery of subskills, but there is no guarantee whatsoever that the student is able to integrate those subskills in real task performance. There is also a risk for a vicious circle: assessment of students is only based on single objectives which can be reliably tested; therefore meaningful task performance characterized by multiple objectives (which can not be reliably tested) is not taken seriously in the curriculum (see Frederiksen, 1984). As a result, students will have great difficulties with integrating the acquired skills in real-world tasks. Current constructivist views on instructional design and authentic testing, such as anchored instruction, cognitive apprenticeship or cognitive flexibility theory acknowledge this problem and stress the use of real-world tasks as the basis for instructional design (for an overview see Duffy & Jonassen, 1992).

4 DEALING WITH INTEGRATED EDUCATIONAL GOALS

In performing meaningful whole tasks the students do not only have the opportunity to practice the isolated subskills related to specific objectives, but also to practice the integration and coordination of these subskills in a meaningful way. This is critical to the acquisition of expertise which is useful in a realistic setting. This is not to say that educational goals and objectives are not important in the instructional design process. However, the individual objectives are not treated as the basis for the design of the curriculum, but as a reference base used to judge the usefulness of the whole tasks presented to the students. Each whole task must be associated with a set of objectives which are related to each other in a meaningful way. The complete set of tasks in the curriculum must be representative and comprehensive for all objectives and educational goals of the curriculum. The rest of this section briefly discusses some examples of such 'whole-task' approaches.

4.1 Case-based curricula

Case-based curricula are popular in fields like medicine and law. In a cased-based curriculum the primary unit is the case or case study. See for example Schank and Cleary, 1995. Well-designed case studies require students to actively participate in actual or hypothetical problem situations in the real world. Often such a case study will describe a spectacular event in order to arouse the students' interest: an accident, a success story, a disputed decision which turned out all right, and so on. A case study in a computer science curriculum might, for example, require students to study a very successful human-computer interface for a particular application. Such a case provides a natural link between multiple objectives which might have to do with the analysis of the task and the user, the interaction styles used (e.g. menu's, dialogue boxes, direct manipulation) and their appropriateness for the user and the task, screen layout, and so on. As a rule case studies contain questions which invite students to think critically about and analyse thoughtfully the relationships illustrated in the case. Sprinkled throughout the description are study questions and study tasks requiring students to examine the ideas, (counter-)evidence and assumptions relevant to the case. These questions help the students to work from what they already know and to stretch their knowledge towards a more general understanding.

4.2 Problem-based curricula

A case-based approach has its limitations for computer science curricula in which especially design tasks are important. Van Merriënboer (1997) describes a problem-based approach in which a distinction is made between projects and tasks. Projects refer to sets of tasks in which meaningful clusters of subskills or multiple objectives are present. For instance, projects in the field of software engineering may refer to tasks requiring students to:

- test and evaluate existing software;
- modify software to changed specifications;
- design, document and implement software systems.

In a sense the projects may be seen as 'parts' of the whole task, but they are chosen in such a way that multiple objectives are easily handled.

In general, each project will encompass a sequence of tasks. All of these represent a meaningful, authentic task, but are sequenced from simple to complex. Often, an elaborate approach to sequencing is useful, meaning that the first task is the simplest task that an expert might encounter in the real world. Subsequent tasks are increasingly more elaborated versions of this task. For instance, if there are particular conditions that might simplify the performance of the task, those conditions might be relaxed one by one when the students acquire more expertise. Other approaches to the sequencing of tasks in problem-based curricula are described by Van Merriënboer (1997). What is critical to the selection and sequencing of both projects and tasks is that they are not directed to obtaining isolated objectives, but that they offer the opportunity to practice multiple objectives in meaningful tasks that an expert might encounter in the real world.

4.3 Integrating schooling and work

Some studies (e.g. Carlson, Khoo and Elliott, 1990) indicate that practice on isolated subskills, related to single learning objectives, may sometimes be helpful to obtaining skill in complex real-world tasks - but only if the learners are able to position this practice in an appropriate cognitive context. In other words, practice related to isolated objectives is only useful if the students have, beforehand, a clear view on how to use this particular subskill in the context of realistic whole-task performance. For this reason the integration of schooling and work may be very useful for facilitating the transition from schooling to work. Here it is important to note that projects to integrate subskills in a realistic context and one or more internships early in the curriculum are probably better for reaching this goal than integrating projects or an internship at the end of the curriculum.

5 CONCLUSION

The main conclusion of this paper is that educational goals and objectives should be seen and treated as highly integrated and interrelated during the whole instructional design process. Goals and objectives are certainly important in the instructional design process, because they determine the content of the curriculum, provide a basis for negotiation about this content, and can be used as a reference base to judge whether the curriculum is comprehensive. But single objectives are not a good basis for the design of instruction for complex intellectual skills. Whole-task approaches provide a way for dealing with multiple objectives. They offer a good alternative to part-task approaches that are driven by single objectives and may facilitate transfer of acquired skills to the post-instructional environment. More and more of such approaches are advocated in the literature. The fact that these approaches are not yet widely used may be due to the situation that no reliable testing procedures for multiple objectives exist (i.e. 'authentic tests'). As long as educational tests are based on items representing single objectives, instead of authentic testing situations representing multiple objectives, it will be hard to implement whole-task approaches in the curriculum. Students will simply refuse to be engaged in rich but demanding learning situations if they receive a traditional multiple-choice test afterwards

6 REFERENCES

Bloom, B.S. [ed.] (1956) *Taxonomy of educational objectives: Cognitive domain.* David McKay, New York.

Carlson, R.A., Khoo, H. and Elliott, R.G. (1990) Component practice and exposure to a problem solving context. *Human Factors*, **32**, 267-286.

Duffy, T.M. and Jonassen, D.H. [eds.] (1992) *Constructivism and the technology of instruction: A conversation.* Lawrence Erlbaum, Hillsdale, NJ.

Elio, R. (1986) Representation of similar well-learned cognitive procedures. *Cognitive Science*, **10**, 41-73.

Frederiksen, N. (1984) The real test bias: influences of testing on teaching and learning. *American Psychologist*, **39** (3), 193-202.

Gagné, R.M. (1965) *The conditions of learning* [1st edition]. Holt, Rinehart and Winston, New York.

Leshin, C.B., Pollock, J. and Reigeluth, C.M. (1992) *Instructional design strategies and tactics.* Educational Technology Publications, Englewood Cliffs, NJ.

Mager, R.F. (1962) *Preparing instructional objectives.* Tearon, Palo Alto.

Merrill, M.D. (1983) Component display theory, in *Instructional design theories and models* (ed. Ch. Reigeluth), Lawrence Erlbaum, Hillsdale, NJ.

Schank, R.C. and Cleary, C. (1995) *Engines for education.* Lawrence Erlbaum, Hillsdale, NJ.

Van Merriënboer, J.J.G. (1997) *Training complex cognitive skills: A four-component instructional design model for technical training.* Educational Technology Publications, Englewood Cliffs, NJ.

7 BIOGRAPHY

Jeroen van Merrienboer specializes in the design of training programs for complex cognitive skills in technical domains. He has a background in experimental psychology and received his Ph.D. in instructional technology from the University of Twente. He has published numerous articles and some books on training computer programming and software engineering, fault management in process industry, statistical analysis, and operating flight management systems. His most recent book (see references) discusses a comprehensive instructional design model for the design of computer-based training systems in vocational settings. From September 1997, he is an associate professor of cognitive and educational psychology at the University of Maastricht (address: Faculty of Psychology, PO Box 616, DRT 10, 6200 MD Maastricht, e-mail: j.vanmerrienboer@psychology.unimaas.nl).

Elisabeth (Betsy) van Dijk is an assistant professor at the Department of Computer Science, University of Twente. She holds a degree in mathematics and has taught mathematics, statistics, and computer science in higher vocational education. She has specialized in teaching methodology in computer science and received in 1996 a Ph.D. in this field from the University of Twente on the subject 'Composing SQL queries: A study on problem-solving strategies in computer science education'. Currently she is involved in the training of teachers for computer science in secondary education. Her research interest also includes human-computer interaction.

20

Informaticians and informatical professionals: a conceptual framework

Tom J. van Weert
School of Informatics, Faculty of Mathematics and Informatics
University of Nijmegen, PO Box 9010, 6500 GL Nijmegen
The Netherlands, e-mail: school@cs.kun.nl

Abstract

What informatics knowledge do noninformatics majors need? To answer this question the relationship between informatics and other disciplines must be clear. This relationship is dependent on which view of the world is taken. Here we take the view that the world of informatics regards systems of interacting processes. From this view follows a relationship between informatics and other disciplines. This relationship allows derivation of competencies needed by noninformatics majors from competencies needed by informatics majors. First a terminology set is presented. Then a conceptual framework is developed which makes a distinction between informatics as a discipline and so-called informatical disciplines as well as between informaticians and so-called informatical professionals. Finally a common core of informatics is identified.

Keywords

Informatics, other disciplines, noninformatics majors, curriculum (core), educational profiles

Informatics in Higher Education F. Mulder & T. van Weerts (Eds.)

1 TERMINOLOGY

The following terminology is used in this paper.

- Science = Discipline:
  a branch of knowledge or study, especially concerned with establishing and systematizing facts, concepts, theories, methods and techniques as by experiments and hypotheses.
- Application oriented science:
  scientific facts, concepts, theories, methods and techniques oriented towards an application domain.
- Technology:
  artefacts as applications of science.
- Professional:
  a graduate of higher education working in a particular discipline.
- Informatics = Computer Science = Computing Science.
- Informatician:
  a professional in informatics (this term can be seen as a direct analogue of the 'mathematician' who is a professional in mathematics).
- Informatical:
  the adjective of 'informatics' (this term can be seen in analogy with 'mathematical' or - as you like - 'physical' or 'economical').

2 INFORMATICS, ITS TECHNOLOGY AND THE WORLD

Technology push

Since the first electronic computer was introduced for performing calculations, a lot has changed. The next step was to develop technology for automation of simple administrative processes. Miniaturization then made computers reach the personal work place supporting processes of work with information processing technology. And now we are moving into a future were Integrated Broadband Communication (IBC) facilities make the computer the gateway to information. And the computer is reaching the home: in the first decade of the next century 50% of the private homes in Europe will have these IBC facilities according to the Commission of the European Union.

But there is more. Computers can change their own programs and therefore can learn. They can for example adapt themselves to their users through software embedded in microwave ovens or television sets. They can also learn to act as personal intelligent agents in a communication network.

Technology pull

The organization of activities in our society is changing (Hammer and Champy, 1993). Because of a growing demand for flexibility and quality, market oriented business units have appeared with a flat organization in which teams of professionals operate supported by participative management. It is a type of organization in which professionals need powerful information processing tools and in which horizontal communication is a must. These organizations exercise a technology pull on integrated and powerful computerized work places which are connected in a network supported by intelligent agent-based groupware.

Interacting processes
Unprecedented applications of informatics emerge from the more familiar areas of calculating or data and information processing. We are moving from a world of information to a world of communication and interaction.

3 DEFINITIONS OF INFORMATICS: VIEWS OF THE WORLD

Definitions of informatics reflect the perceived role of informatics and its technology in the world. They are connected with different views of the world.

3.1 Processing of data and information

An early definition of informatics is found in the 1971 IFIP Guide to concepts and terms in data processing (Gould, 1971). Informatics is described as 'those aspects of science and technology applicable to data processing'.

In later definitions the role of information processing is stressed. The International Bureau for Informatics of UNESCO states that informatics 'concerns the design, the realization, the evaluation, the use and the maintenance of information processing systems; including hardware, software, organizational and human aspects, and the whole of the industrial, commercial, governmental and political implications'. And Denning *et al.* (1989) define the discipline of computing as 'the systematic study of algorithmic processes that describe and transform information: their theory, analysis, design, efficiency, implementation, and application. The fundamental question underlying all of computing is: What can be (efficiently) be automated?'.

3.2 Hardware, software and beyond

The Computing Reviews Classification System (Coulter, 1991) distinguishes 11 areas:

A. General literature;
B. Hardware;
C. Computer systems organization;
D. Software;
E. Data;
F. Theory of computation;
G. Mathematics of computing;

H. Information systems;
I. Computing methodologies;
J. Computer applications;
K. Computing millieux.

This system actually is a very detailed four level tree of (sub)domains of knowledge and is used mainly for the classification of literature. This knowledge domain tree can be seen as a specification of the discipline. The tree is rooted in hardware and then folds out via software to other aspects of what traditionally in the USA is called computer science.

In the Unified Classification Scheme for Informatics (UCSI) which has been developed by Mulder and Hacquebard (1998) a specification of informatics as a discipline is given in a four level knowledge domain tree of which the first level distinguishes four domains:

- computer systems;
- software systems;
- information systems;
- context of informatics.

Although in this system informatics is seen as a broad discipline, it remains a bare hierarchy in which the various knowledge domains are separated. Knowledge domain trees have in common that they represent a typical static view of the world.

3.3 Applications orientation

Reflecting the growing importance of applications of data and information processing the following set of definitions was introduced in 1986 by an advisory group of the Dutch Minister of Education (Commissie Hoger Onderwijs InformaticaPlan, 1986). It includes the concepts of application oriented informatics and so-called 'informatiekunde', a Dutch neologism of which the closest English translation probably is 'information engineering'. The report distinguishes:

- Informatics:
  discipline dealing with data processing systems.
- Application oriented informatics:
  domain of informatics dealing with the development of data processing systems for broad application areas.
- Information engineering:
  field where (application oriented) informatics is integrated into a specific other discipline (for example: business information engineering, medical information engineering, physical information engineering, etc.).

Besides there is the whole range of self-contained other disciplines, not necessarily related to informatics. In these disciplines various applications of informatics are manifest or conceivable.

The interesting point in these definitions is the explicit denotation of a relationship between informatics and the disciplines in which informatics is applied.

3.4 Interacting processes in application areas

In the context of the technological developments outlined in section 2 a set of definitions may be proposed, building on the set of definitions in the previous subsection but now based on the interacting processes paradigm.

- Informatics (as a self-contained discipline):
  discipline dealing with programmed computer systems which embody (generic) systems of interacting processes.
- Application oriented informatics:
  domain of informatics dealing with programmed computer systems which embody specific systems of interacting processes from particular broad application areas.
- Informatical discipline:
  field where (application oriented) informatics is integrated into a specific other discipline (for example: informatical business administration, informatical medicine, informatical physics, etc.).
- Other disciplines:
  disciplines, different from informatics, in which various applications of informatics and its technology can be manifest or conceivable.

In these definitions the adjective 'informatical' is introduced as an analogue to 'mathematical' and 'physical'. An informatical discipline can be considered as a domain of the adopting discipline or eventually as a new hybrid discipline, emerging from the adopting discipline and informatics. Such hybrid disciplines are not new, take for example mathematical physics and physical chemistry. Of course when integrating disciplines, informatics can also be the adopting discipline and then the roles are reversed. An example is mathematical informatics, which is not the same as informatical mathematics.

4 COMPETENCIES OF INFORMATICIANS

We adopt the fourth view in which informatics is seen as a system of interacting processes (Wegner, 1997). From this 'process' view the activities of an informatician can be detailed as in Figure 1, which is an earlier version of the one found in Wupper and Meijer (1998).

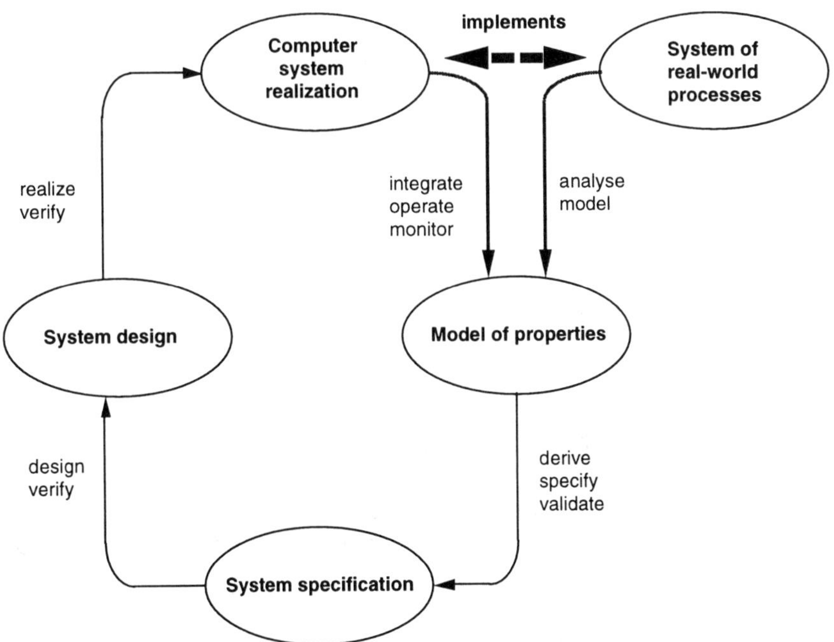

Figure 1 Definition of the activities of an informatician from a 'process' view.

Figure 1 shows the processes in which an (application oriented) informatician should be competent. Each of these competencies can be pursued in a practical sense (applying the competencies) and in a theoretical sense (developing the theory behind these competencies). We specify the required competencies below.

Problem analysis and modelling

- analyse properties of systems of real life processes;
- model properties.

Specification

- derive a specification from model;
- specify nonmodelled properties;
- validate specification.

Design

- derive concrete design from specification;
- verify design.

Realization

- realize design in computer system;
- verify realization.

Integration

- integrate computer system realization into the real world;
- operate computer system realization;
- monitor adequacy of computer system realization.

Not in Figure 1, but important as an overall set of competencies, is the following.

Activity control

- plan and schedule all activities;
- manage the sequence of processes;
- assure the overall quality.

5 INFORMATICS AND OTHER DISCIPLINES

Informatics and other disciplines are related to each other through application areas for which informatics produces computer system realizations of real world application processes.

5.1 Information processing support

Professionals from application areas in other disciplines can solve problems from these areas using information processing tools. Sometimes the technology used is generic (e.g. word processors, spread sheets, data base systems), sometimes application specific (e.g. juridical information systems). Sometimes the technology is 'off the shelf', sometimes it is tailor-made.

5.2 Dynamic modelling

Another type of application is to produce a computer system realization which is a dynamic model of a system of processes in a particular application area. When the relationship between the dynamic model and reality is systematically studied through experiments and hypotheses for establishing and systematizing facts, principles and methods, the modelled processes are part of the other discipline (Figure 2).

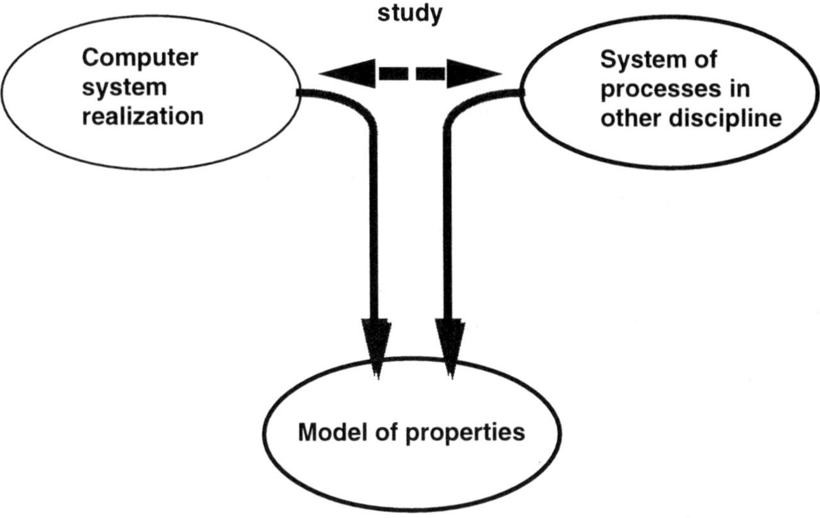

Figure 2 Dynamic models of reality.

We are used to modelling the world in static symbols. But informatics allows us to construct executable symbols (Van Weert, 1988) embodying complex dynamic conceptual models of reality; informatics allows us to build a virtual reality. Modelling then becomes 'programming' in conceptual application oriented or discipline specific executable modelling languages. Problems are analysed and solutions developed as dynamic models, brought to life on a computer, using methods and techniques of informatics.

5.3 Informatical disciplines

When specialized information processing tools or discipline specific executable modelling languages are required, the applicants must have both discipline specific and informatics know-how. The development of the computer algebra systems Maple and Mathematica can be taken as an example. In such cases particular scientific questions within the domain of a discipline can only be answered when informatics methods and techniques are applied. This integration gives rise to the informatical disciplines mentioned in subsection 3.4 (in this case informatical mathematics).

The relationship between informatics and an informatical discipline is pictured in Figure 3.

6 THE INFORMATICAL PROFESSIONAL

'Informatical professional' is a generic term used for those who practice an informatical discipline. Specific instances are for example: the informatical economist, business consultant, psychologist, linguist, chemist, mathematician, mechanical engineer and the informatical medical expert. The informatical professional has a solid background in a specific discipline, different from informatics, but also is familiar with methods and techniques from (application oriented) informatics. The tasks of the informatical professional complement those of the (application oriented) informatician. The informatical professional is able to communicate on a high level about these tasks with application oriented informaticians.

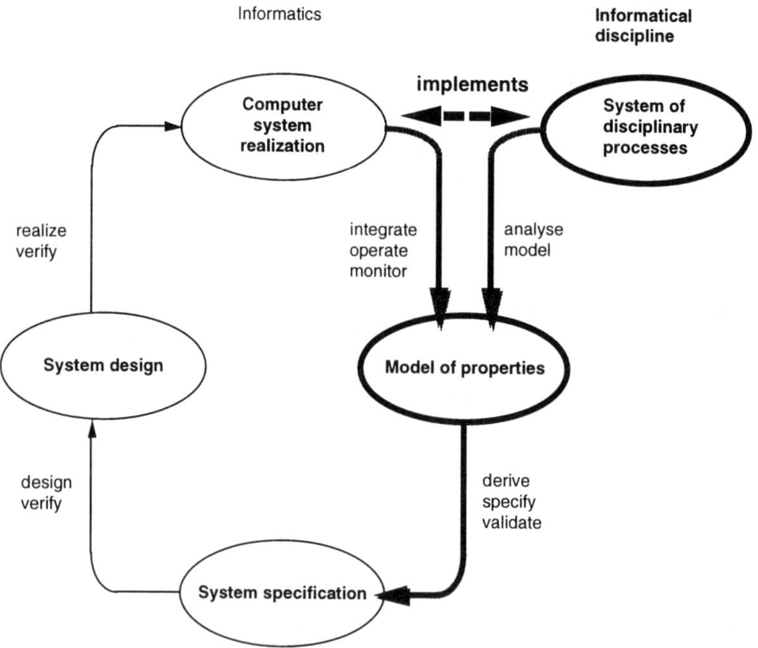

Figure 3 Relationship between informatics and informatical discipline.

The required competencies of informatical professionals can be derived from Figure 3. The informatical professionals must have their core competencies ('know how') in four of the six competency fields mentioned for the informaticians in section 4:

- problem analysis and modelling;
- specification;
- integration;

- activity control.

Two competency fields are of secondary nature ('know about', 'know how' in simple cases):

- design;
- realization.

7 EDUCATION OF INFORMATICAL PROFESSIONALS

Discipline specific and informatics know-how are integrated in an informatical discipline. Therefore educational programmes in informatical disciplines will contain three components: elements from the 'adopting' discipline, elements from (application oriented) informatics and integrative elements.

Typical core subjects from application oriented informatics are:

- process modelling and specification methods and techniques;
- human-computer interaction modelling and specification;
- software engineering.

Modelling and interfacing also appear as integrative elements. Familiar informatics subjects as the design of data bases and programming methods and techniques are of secondary nature for the curriculum.

7.1 Some examples

At Nijmegen University education in informatical disciplines is found in several departments (Van Weert, 1992). For example: informatical business administration, cognition science and language, speech & informatics, and also informatical medicine, physics and chemistry. Please note that in the referenced paper the adjective 'informational' is used instead of 'informatical'.

In Shaw (1991) computing specialists in disciplines outside information technology are mentioned as an example of people working in informatical disciplines. Shaw refers to programmes at Carnegie-Mellon University, George Washington University, the University of Illinois, the University of Colorado and the University of Toronto.

Informatical chemistry was presented as an example of an informatical discipline at the IFIP working conference 'Visualisation in scientific computing: Uses in university education' (Weber *et al.*, 1994).

7.2 A detailed example: cognitive science

The structure of the Master's programme of cognitive science at the Faculty of the Social Sciences of Nijmegen University is given in some detail as an example of an educational programme in an informatical discipline. Only elements from application oriented informatics and hybrid elements are presented.

Application oriented informatics (about 10% of the full programme)

- programming (top-down development of algorithms);
- programming (bottom-up development, data structures);
- information systems development;
- symbolic programming in Lisp.

An element missing in this programme is software engineering.

Hybrid topics (about 25% of the full programme)

- introduction to artificial intelligence (AI);
- programming paradigms for cognitive modelling and AI;
- computational psycholinguistics;
- introduction to expert systems;
- AI in education;
- knowledge elicitation for expert systems;
- human-computer interaction;
- information ergonomics;
- Master's thesis.

8 CONCLUSION

In this paper a conceptual framework has been presented which positions informatics in relation to other disciplines, especially in the context of education.

Informatics and informaticians

Informatics is the discipline dealing with programmed computer systems which embody (generic) systems of interacting processes. The modelled processes are from informatics itself. There is little interaction with application areas or other disciplines. The professionals are informaticians. The education is aimed at competencies, needed to realize generic systems (see section 4).

Application oriented informatics and informaticians

Application oriented informatics deals with programmed computer systems which embody specific systems of interacting processes from particular broad application areas, possibly in other disciplines. There is medium interaction with the application areas with visible results. The professionals are (application oriented) informaticians having additional expertise in a specific application area, possibly in another discipline. Education of these professionals is aimed at competencies needed to realize specific systems for broad application areas (see section 4).

Informatical discipline and informatical professionals

An informatical discipline is a field where (application oriented) informatics is integrated into a specific other discipline. The modelled processes are specific for the 'adopting' discipline and are described in discipline specific executable modelling languages. The scientific questions addressed belong to the domain of the adopting discipline, but can only be treated using informatics. Thus there is a strong interaction between informatics and the other discipline with visible results. The practitioners are called informatical professionals, underlining that they must have their roots in the adopting discipline, complemented and mixed with additional expertise in a core of (application oriented) informatics (see section 7).

Other disciplines and their professionals

What remains are all the other disciplines, in which various applications of informatics and its technology can be manifest or conceivable. Information processing tools, generic as well as application specific, support the problem solving. The scientific questions change under the influence of the use of this technology. The interaction with the technology of informatics is strong and its effects are highly visible. The professionals have their education in the specific discipline, which however includes the use of information processing tools within that discipline. There is no need for a generic informatics component in the curricula.

9 REFERENCES

Commissie Hoger Onderwijs InformaticaPlan (1986) *Eindrapport.* HBO-Raad, Den Haag, 13-16 [in Dutch].

Coulter, N.S. [ed.] (1991) Update to the Computing Reviews Classification System. *Computing Reviews,* **32** (1), 5-50.

Denning, P.J. *et al.* (1989) Computing as a discipline. *Communications of the ACM,* **32** (1), 9-23.

Gould, H. [ed.] (1971) *IFIP Guide to concepts and terms in data processing.* North-Holland Publishing Company, Amsterdam.

Hammer, M. and Champy, J. (1993) *Re-engineering the corporation.* Nicolas Brealy Publishing, London.

Mulder, F. and Hacquebard, A.E.N. (1998) Specifying and comparing informatics curricula through UCSI, in *Informatics in higher education: Views on informatics and noninformatics curricula* (eds. F. Mulder and T.J. van Weert), Chapman & Hall, London.

Shaw, M. (1991) Informatics for a new century: computing education for the 1990's. Special issue of *Education & Computing*, **7**, 9-17.

Van Weert, T.J. (1988) Literacy in the Information Age, in *Children in the Information* Age (eds. Bl. Sendov and I. Stanchev), Pergamon Press, Oxford, 109-122.

Van Weert, T.J. (1992) Application Oriented Informatics and Informational Disciplines: A symbiosis bridging the gap, in *Information Processing 92, Volume II* (ed. R. Aiken), Elsevier Science Publishers BV, Amsterdam, 144-150.

Weber, J. *et al.* (1994) Visualising microscopic molecular worlds in chemical education, in *Visualisation in scientific computing: Uses in university education* (eds. S. Franklin and A. Stubberud), Elsevier Science Publishers BV, Amsterdam, 9-24.

Wegner, P. (1997) Why interaction is more powerful than algorithms. *Communications of the ACM,* **40** (5), 80-91.

Wupper, H. and Meijer, H. (1998) Towards a taxonomy for computer science, in *Informatics in higher education: Views on informatics and noninformatics curricula* (eds. F. Mulder and T.J. van Weert), Chapman & Hall, London.

10 BIOGRAPHY

Tom J. van Weert is director of the undergraduate School of Informatics (Computing Science) of the Faculty of Mathematics and Informatics of the University of Nijmegen, The Netherlands. He also teaches management of large software projects to informatics students developing real software applications in multi-disciplinary teams. Previously he has worked in teacher education, teaching mathematics and informatics, and prior to that as a computer system engineer in an academic environment. His background is in applied mathematics. He has been active within several IFIP Working Groups and is currently chair of IFIP Working Group 3.2 on university education.

Informatics in curricula for noninformatics students: engineering and science

Roland Vollmar
Lehrstuhl Informatik für Ingenieure und Naturwissenschaftler
Universität Karlsruhe, Am Fasanengarten 5, D-76128 Karlsruhe
Germany, e-mail: vollmar@ira.uka.de

Jozef Gruska
Faculty of Informatics, Masaryk University, Botanicka 68a 60020 Brno, Czech Republic, e-mail: gruska@informatics.muni.cz

Abstract

In this paper three key issues are discussed concerning the role of informatics in science and engineering curricula. The first issue is that informatics is a fundamentally new methodology of key importance for the future. The second is the dramatic increase in basic information technology skills of freshman which makes treatment of more advanced informatics subjects possible and requires a change in teaching skills. The third key issue is that informatics education should concentrate on fundamental ideas thereby supporting life-long learning.

Keywords

Informatics, natural sciences and engineering, university education, continuing education, noninformatics majors, curriculum (general), curriculum (core), role of CIT

Informatics in Higher Education F. Mulder & T. van Weerts (Eds.)

1 INTRODUCTION

The ever increasing role which informatics plays in society, does not need discussion. Some catchwords already are sufficient to get the right association: Internet, multimedia, electronic banking, electronic commerce, electronic warfare, etc. These, however, only touch the surface of the enormous progress we are witnessing. When discussing educational issues, informatics must be recognized as the new fundamental methodology for science and engineering which can help solve many key problems of science, engineering and mankind. The insights, methodsand tools of informatics are of such great importance in science and engineering that informatics should be seen as giving rise to a third fundamental scientific methodology, taking its place besides the experimental and the theoretical methodologies which have been very successful for centuries. For a more detailed discussion of informatics as a methodology see another paper by Gruska and Vollmar (1997). In each of the scientific and engineering disciplines concepts, methods and topics have emerged which can only be handled with methodologies that informatics, including computing and communication technologies, can provide.

It is obvious that this development must have repercussions for the corresponding curricula. Up to now students of science and engineering have only been taught the very basic skills for working with very basic computing technology. This is far from sufficient. Students and graduates should be able to make use of informatics as a methodology during their studies and afterwards. Fortunately, due to the rapid spreading of Internet communication and information services, one may assume that in the immediate future high-school graduates will have the basic knowledge to work with Internet and to use basic word processing, graphical and database facilities of personal computers. This will allow university education to concentrate on the development of skills in using more advanced technology and, especially, to focus on fundamental issues.

The increase in experience of the coming generation of freshmen will also allow us to concentrate on issues of key importance for life-long process of (re)education. One of the current main obstacles will slowly disappear, or at least diminish significantly: insufficient practical experience and motivation of students which make it impossible to really appreciate and grasp more fundamental concepts, methods and results.

This paper puts forward some thoughts and observations concerning basic engineering and science studies at universities. Its main ideas can also be applied on such newly emerging subjects as 'computational sciences'. We will not discuss in depth the specifics of various combinations of (sometimes very different) subject areas. This would force us to differentiate between a plethora of studies. In the following we will first describe the background and the framework into which the courses of informatics have to be embedded. The topics we consider as fundamental will then be discussed in more detail. And to finish we will present an estimation of the necessary number of hours needed for special informatics subjects.

2 ENVIRONMENT

The following thoughts and comments are of a quite general nature. This is because we are not competent to discuss either the different cultures of the disciplines or the various levels of higher education in various countries. Therefore we restrict ourselves to university curricula in general.

We will try to be realistic, and not assume that it is easy to change current curricula overnight and add many hours for special courses on informatics. In all fields the development is very fast and therefore there is a continuous struggle for more hours in the curriculum. In addition, at least in some countries, universities are under a permanent pressure from government and industry to shorten the overall time students spend in education. We are aware that in this setting informatics has to compete.

Let us make another general remark about university education. It is not possible and also not meaningful to acquire all (or even most of) the knowledge needed to act in a particular profession during university education. Rather the basics and the methodology should be mastered. Professional knowledge has for the most part to be learned during the professional career. Universities have to lay a fundament which makes continuing education possible. This conviction is at the basis of the following and only minimum requirements for change will be advocated.

3 PROPAEDEUTIC

What can we expect in the next few years of the knowledge and skills in information and communication technology which all students will have at the start, and in the worst case at the end, of their first year of study? Just as students are accustomed to utilize telephones and copiers, they will soon have the know-how for using the infrastructure of data processing. They will know how to operate a personal computer (PC) or a workstation. How to use text processing, basic graphical, spreadsheet and presentation software. How to use e-mail as a basic communication tool and how to use the Internet as a basic information searching tool. Those few beginners who will still lack this know-how, will be able to get it at a central university institution, such as the university computing centre, where the newest information about hardware and software systems will be available.

During their whole study students should follow a variety of extra courses to test and improve their skills in dealing with more advanced technology. As a side-effect, such courses may also very well support an introduction into scientific work as such. As Krüger(1987) mentions, education about data and information bases is less concerned with questions of the computer use, but more with problems of searching, ordering, structuring and combining large amounts of information, i.e. with methods of modern scientific work.

The mastering of these skills in using computing and communication technology should be obligatory for all university students. However, programming is not necessarily among these skills. Yet , the situation may be much different from one discipline to another. In at least some disciplines - for example in electrical engineering, physics, chemistry and biology - students should be able to write more or less sizeable programs, while in other areas - for example civil engineering - students should just use finite element method tools.

With respect to the teaching of programming we are faced with a dilemma which is dependent on the view we take. On the one hand, one can assume that at least some fundamental know-how of programming is already present. In that case a basic course on programming could be combined with, for example, a course on calculus. On the other hand such a basic programming course could be offered as part of an introduction into informatics. Because at least some simple programming skills should be already mastered in the first semester, we recommend the first approach mentioned in combination with laboratory work in programming, especially for those students who have to learn programming from scratch.

4 THE CORE

Is it at all possible to detail the contents of courses, if there is such a rapid development of informatics as is claimed by various persons?

Citation from Tucker (1996)

Computer science remains a rapidly evolving discipline [...], which places considerable pressure on the [computer science and engineering] curriculum. The emergence of new tools, techniques and paradigms forces a continual re-evaluation of the topics covered and the pedagogical approaches used. Maintaining an up-to-date curriculum is particularly difficult for institutions because the pace of change in the discipline is so fast. As a result, the [computer science and engineering] curriculum quickly becomes outdated as the technology advances.

We take the same view, but nevertheless are convinced that there are basic topics of informatics which each engineering and science student should learn in an introductory course on informatics. These topics may be considered to be part of (general) literacy, but the fact that these act as fundament for further courses and continuing education is of larger importance.

Informatics as a new methodology should enter curricula in two different ways. First of all there should be some special 'inherently informatical' courses where basic insights, concepts, methods and skills are taught and practised. Secondly - and this is perhaps even of larger importance - informatics as a methodology should enter practically all courses; with respect to both what is taught and how this is taught. It is of key importance that informatics as a new methodology gets 'under the nails' of all students. As for example reported by Kelemen (1996) the contents of informatics courses also very much defines the perception of informatics as a science and a new methodology. We are convinced that a distorted perception of the discipline may lead to the wrong understanding of the potentials and the applicability of informatics concepts, methods and tools.

The basic topics in informatics which should be mastered by all science and engineering students are:

- basic potentials and limits of the algorithmic approach;
- basics of efficient and feasible computing, including randomized and approximation methods;
- basic concepts and methods concerning security in information processing, including basic concepts and systems of cryptography;
- basic concepts, methods and pitfalls of systems (programs) validation and reliability;
- principles of data base (and expert) systems.

Students who have mastered these basic topics, should have general knowledge about the fundamentals of informatics and, expressed in a more goal-oriented way, should be able to make decisions on which of their problems to tackle by computer and how much effort this will cost. They should also be able to look for adequate software and hardware tools. As mentioned above we only refer to the minimum number of topics necessary to reach the overall educational goal. Much more advanced would be basic courses on simulation and visualization methods. These, however, should be integrated in the core study of the particular subject.

4.1 Specific approaches: fundamentals

Let us now discuss some specific ways to achieve the goals mentioned above. Of central importance is the notion of 'algorithm'. An analysis of the potentials and the limits of the algorithmic approach is needed. This may be done in various ways. We prefer an introduction by Random Access Machine (RAM). First, the principles of the von Neumann computer have to be explained, then a simple microcomputer can be presented. By the reduction of its set of operations and by neglecting the restrictions concerning the number and the size of registers, the desired simple form of a RAM can be obtained. And from this it is a natural step to a parallel RAM (PRAM) and to the introduction of some basic ideas of parallel computing and programming.

In order to grasp the right understanding of the algorithmic approach awareness of its limitations is necessary. What can and what can not be computed should be explained and various examples should be given. In this connection the notion of computational complexity, especially time and space complexity, should be introduced. (Here programs in a higher language might be more suitable than

Random Access Machines). The following hierarchy should be made clear: non-computable problems - unfeasible problems (not belonging to NP) - NP (-complete) problems - feasible problems (belonging to P). Especially NP-complete problems and ways how to cope with NP-completeness deserve attention. Students should also learn that one has to search for an efficient algorithm to solve a problem, and be aware of the difference between efficiency and effectiveness. The solution of difficult problems through heuristics, approximation and probabilistic algorithms should be explained.

Another important topic is problem specification. Examples may illustrate the advantages of formal descriptions for finding algorithms and developing of software. Students should learn that such a formalization will result in well-understood algorithms and associated data structures. Appropriate specification models are finite automata and regular languages, also allowing basic concepts of syntax and semantics of (programming) languages to be presented. Modelling of dynamic and concurrent systems can be done by Petri-nets. It should also be emphasized that there is no fully automated method for the design of formal specifications.

4.2 Specific approaches: software

The amount of software in technical products is rapidly increasing. All engineering and science students should have at least some basic understanding of problems and pitfalls in software development. They should have a basic notion of software specification, modular and hierarchical structures, correctness, validation, documentation and maintenance.

Because of the processing power which is available today, one might think that it is not longer meaningful to teach about algorithmic efficiency and software engineering because each correct program - also an unnecessarily complicated one - will terminate in a reasonable time. However, in all mature engineering areas efficiency and correctness are always of major concern. Students should at least be aware that only modular and hierarchically structured programs can be reasonably easily understood. Students should also learn two basic principles of good software design: a program has to be correct and should be easy to modify because frequent requirements for change are a fact of life. They should also know that software validation techniques should be used and that thorough documentation has to be delivered. A piece of software without detailed documentation should not be released. Also engineering students should be aware that nowadays more and more software is used in safety-critical applications.

Even well-validated and widely sold software packages can often only be used by graduates who understand their technical merits and aims. The corresponding knowledge will be part of informatics methodology taught by the departments of engineering or science. Graduates should be able to make plausibility estimations about the correctness of the results obtained using algorithmic methods and software packages, and they should be acquainted with the problems of numerical stability.

As mentioned before students should have some experience with the programming of numerical problems. But they should be aware that nonnumerical data processing has at least the same importance and that processing of big amounts of data brings additional problems. The principles of data bases should be presented and also how expert systems work and what their limitations are. Security of information exchange and storage is another key issue in this era of modern communication and students should learn some basic concepts of cryptography and its protocols and of information security. Ethical questions should be posed and discussed, not as a separate topic, but integrated in the whole course. There are no definite answers to these problems , rather it has to be pointed out that ethical problems exist.

5 COMPARISON WITH OTHER APPROACHES

It may be useful and interesting to make a detailed comparison of our proposals with the topics which have been suggested in various other undergraduate curricula in informatics, but this would go beyond the scope of this paper. Let us just make a few remarks.

From the nine subject areas in Denning *et al.* (1989) only a minor part is covered by these recommendations. We think that some of the other ones should be incorporated in the curricula of the various disciplines. For example, electrical engineering students who have to design or maintain computers, should have much deeper knowledge in informatics than those students who only use computers as a tool. Architecture and programming languages are indispensable topics for mechanical engineers who deal with the development of embedded systems. For some of them a course on artificial intelligence and robotics could play a crucial role. A lot of work of civil engineers is done with graphics tools; for them more knowledge about computer graphics and human-computer communication would be helpful. And for physicists numerical and symbolic computation will be important.

All these topics should be taught in special courses, not being part of the proposed 'minimum curriculum' which should only contain the most important subjects common for all engineering and science students. This also holds for other topics not included in the list above, e.g. for such an important subject as parallelism. Here we have to restrict ourselves - according to Tucker *et al.* (1991) - to the goal to 'prepare students to apply their knowledge to specific, constrained, problems and to produce solutions. This includes the ability to define a problem clearly; to determine its tractability; to study, specify, design, implement, test, modify, and document that problem's solution; ...'.

6 CONCLUSION

The suggestions in the preceding sections should be considered as a collection of topics which can be viewed along three stages:

- problem analysis;
- algorithm design;
- program realization.

It seems appropriate to start with easily described every-day problems, to demonstrate the usefulness of formalization and then to develop algorithms. In our experience, graph theory problems and algorithms are very instructive for this. Many of such problems and their solutions are easy to grasp and, moreover, very useful for applications. Our suggestion is to connect theory, software and applications in the educational process (see for example Gruska and Vollmar (1997)).

To present the core material in a not too compressed form about 60-80 hours are necessary. In addition about 25-30 hours for laboratory work should be planned. Not included is the time needed to teach the material mentioned in the section on the propaedeutic. More important than the overall number of teaching hours is the atmosphere in which the topics are taught and the approach to informatics which professors of engineering and science show. If they are convinced that methods and tools of informatics are valuable for their disciplines and if they are passing this attitude on to their students, good results may be obtained even in a shorter time.

7 REFERENCES

Denning, P. *et al.* (1989) Computing as a discipline. *Communications of the ACM*, **32**, 9-23.

Gruska, J. and Vollmar, R. (1997) Towards adjusting informatics education to the information era, to be published in a book from Springer-Verlag.

Kelemen, C. (1996) *Public understanding of Computer Science and first courses for non-majors*. http://www.bowdoin.edu/allen/sdcr/kelemen.html, World Wide Web.

Krüger, G. (1987) Informatikgrundlagen in der Lehre an Hochschulen, in *Informatik-grundlagen in der Lehre* (ed. Bundesminister für Bildung und Wissenschaft), 105-113.

Tucker, A. B. (1996) Strategic directions in computer science education. *ACM Computing Surveys*, **28**, 836-845.

Tucker, A. B. *et al.* (1991) A summary of the ACM/IEEE-CS joint curriculum task force report: Computing curricula 1991. *Communications of the ACM*, **34**, 68-84.

8 BIOGRAPHY

Roland Vollmar was born in 1939. He received his diploma in mathematics from the University of Saarbrücken (Germany) in 1964 and his Dr.-Ing. degree from the University Erlangen-Nürnberg in 1968. Since 1965 he was affiliated with several institutes for computer science and with an industrial company. From 1974 to 1989 he was full professor in theoretical computer science at the Technical University of Braunschweig and since 1989 he has a same position at the University Karlsruhe. His main research interests include parallelism, especially cellular automata. He is author and. co-author of three books on these topics and of numerous articles.

Jozef Gruska graduated in mathematics in 1958 at the Comenius University in Bratislava and received his Ph.D. in computer science from the Slovak Academy of Sciences in Bratislava. He is professor in computer science at Masaryk University in Brno, Czech Republic, and has had a variety of long-term visiting research and teaching positions at universities in Europe, the USA and Africa. His research interests are: scientific computing, theory of automata and descriptional complexity, parallel automata and systems, and foundations of informatics. For a long time he has been heading the research seminar in Bratislava. He is the author of various books and curricula. His main international activities are: council member of EATCS (1985-91), country representative in IFIP-TC2, member of the advisory board of IFIP-TC12, chairman of the IFIP Specialist Group on Foundations of Computer Science(1989-96).

22

Informatics for noninformatics majors

Stanislaw Waligorski
Institute of Informatics, Warsaw University, 002097 Warsaw Banacha 2, Poland, e-mail: waligor@mimuw.edu.pl

Abstract

This paper gives a brief overview over education of informatics majors as implemented in Poland. The relationship between this education and that of informatics for noninformatics majors is discussed. Several problems and limitations are indicated which deserve attention. Various aspects of the situation of informatics education in society are also taken into consideration.

Keywords

Informatics, higher vocational education, professional training, continuing education, noninformatics majors, professional profiles

1 INTRODUCTION

As was the case in the past with other new and quickly developing important phenomena, the rapid development of informatics and of communication technologies has raised a great deal of vivid interest in society and amongst people. This also holds for informatics education, which can be seen as a gateway to a newly developing science and to new jobs and careers.

How does the general public perceive and appreciate this new situation?

- People with adequate informatics skills have no problem with finding jobs which suit them personally.
- More and more job opportunities connected with the new technology are opening and there is a common belief that this trend will last, at least in the nearest future.
- The jobs are considered to be (and often are) well-paid and are believed to offer good professional perspectives.

Informatics in Higher Education F. Mulder & T. van Weerts (Eds.)

- The offers of noninformatics jobs of many kinds that existed before are now accompanied by requests or requirements with respect to the 'ability to use computers with specific office software for word processing etc.', or even the 'ability to work with databases', to quote the modest ones.
- Such job opportunities may gradually become less accessible for those who can not use at least elementary tools of modern communication and management technology.

This creates a growing pressure on the whole educational systems of many countries (Van Weert and Tinsley, 1994). Schools which include computing into their curricula, are more competitive and have better chances to get adequate funding for further investment and development. The darker side of the picture is that many schools which can not attract good and fully qualified teachers may tend to hire someone anyway. Sometimes this results in full satisfaction of the community served by such a school, but in the worst case the results are regrettable. Such problems and temptations may plague every level and kind of education.

Dealing with such dilemmas is a bit easier when there is a good system of qualification standards. Its most important virtue is that it may serve as guidance for planners. Compared with that, its power in a prohibitive sense may be of less importance. Personally I believe that such systems or regulations must incorporate positive actions, such as the creating and supporting of solutions that may be examples for others.

2 EDUCATION OF INFORMATICS PROFESSIONALS

At the beginning of the nineties new curricula for vocational tertiary informatics education were introduced in Poland (Waligorski *et al.,* 1992). Below follows a list of the courses offered with short comments added.

1. mathematics (mainly mathematics of computation);
2. introduction to informatics (mainly introduction to algorithms and related topics);
3. programming (methods of structured and object oriented programming, Pascal and C++);
4. computer hardware (how to use hardware in a clever way, including networks);
5. operating systems (how to use these systems in a clever way);
6. business applications (including management and accounting);
7. databases (relational databases, SQL);
8. information systems (life cycle, CASE-tools, system analysis, design of small systems);
9. software systems (selected application software).

On the whole these schools for vocational tertiary education provide the maximum amount of informatics knowledge and skills that can be achieved in two years in any pre-university form of education in Poland. In general in these schools you will not find teaching of just theory, nor teaching just by demonstration which keeps students passive. The graduates will in general have hands-on experience in all areas of the curriculum. There is, however, no room in such a short curriculum for details. Graduates who enter the curriculum from secondary school with a sufficient level of knowledge and skills, usually are able to finish the two-year course without great difficulty and can then be considered as really competent starting professionals.

This curriculum was received very well and with great interest. Sometimes the reaction was even too good. A very reputable school decided to open an informatics department and ran it very well. Because of this it received very good publicity and it was a real success. All graduates of the first two-year course got immediately after their graduation employment at a nearby bank. But so did also their best teachers. The informatics department of the school survived this operation only with great difficulty.

Fortunately this school was not the only one in the country. The number of such departments in vocational schools skyrocketed during the last few years. It seems that now a point of saturation has been reached: the situation has become more stable and there are no more such stories to tell. Things seem to be running well, although it is very hard work and qualified people are needed. Many of these are young and proud of what they are doing. The weakest organizations, perhaps run by novices, have disappeared because of lack of teachers and students, but this is quite natural. The best schools are examples for others and in this way a new standard has been (hopefully) set.

A couple of years ago new versions of the curriculum for the education of informatics majors have been introduced. After that many schools and continuous education centres broadened their activities and provided informatics education of majors as well. Since everything happens within a framework defined by the same curriculum, the general picture is quite uniform.

Students, however, may have various motivations for following this education. Those who already achieved a certain amount of informatics skills as a result of 'on the job' training, now may try to improve these further and at the end of the process graduate with a certificate of technician in informatics. Others may wish to change their former profession to informatics and obtain the same certificate. The less the informatics knowledge at the beginning, the more difficulties are encountered before graduation. On the other hand we all are surrounded now by products of informatics and therefore the amount of informatics knowledge of interested persons is very rarely nil. In any case strong motivation, perseverance and ability to learn are of great help.

3 INFORMATICS EDUCATION OF NONINFORMATICS MAJORS

For those who do not need to graduate in informatics and have or will have another profession there are various intermediate forms, but this is quite another story

(Syslo, 1996). Generally speaking every profession needs both an amount of general informatics knowledge and certain specific informatics tools suited to its particular needs. Another important issue is that students for other professions prefer to be instructed by tutors who - of course - know the basics of informatics but - importantly - combine this with the ability to use the terminology of the students' (prospective) profession and to present examples taken from connected areas of application. Otherwise the content of instruction may unnecessarily be received as too abstract or too difficult.

The variety of noninformatics majors in question is too big to discuss in general, so let us take just one more example. Let us assume that we are talking about professionals from many areas, who have achieved certain positions and do not intend to change their professions. They do not have much time for any form of education except for 'on the job' training. Because of their positions they might prefer to attend 'seminars' rather than classes. The environment of such activities and the naming may matter. After getting familiar with new methods and achieving new skills which they see as necessary and/or interesting, they will want to maintain contacts with professionals in similar situations who deal with similar professional problems. They will also welcome opportunities for updating skills once acquired and for hearing about new problems and new achievements in the area of their interest.

This example shows that it may be worth to consider more complex models of organization which may be received more favourably by the people in question. Experience shows that these forms do not need to be more expensive than the most standard and uniform solutions. Such other forms of organization may develop a spirit of cooperation, foster the creation of informal groups of common professional interest and encourage informal exchange of knowledge and professional information.

4 NONINFORMATICS MAJORS IN THE EDUCATIONAL SYSTEM

Let us finally change our point of view and look at any nation-wide educational system as a whole. Key persons in education and training of any specialists are teachers. They also must be educated and trained. And education also needs managers, coordinators, organizers, members of consulting services etc.

Simple calculation shows that in the period of time we have had for the introduction of modern informatics into the educational system of our countries, in many cases there has been no possibility to provide sufficient informatics education and training for so many teachers, managers and other personnel, as was needed (Dalek, 1992). Naturally the top people will come from various professions and very often professional informaticians will be the minority. There is no doubt that many noninformatics majors will strongly influence further developments in the application of this new technology in education. This is only one of many reasons why informatics education and training of noninformatics majors is so important.

6 REFERENCES

Dalek, J. (1992) On education of school teachers of informatics, in *Proceedings of the Tenth Methodological Seminar in Informatics* (eds. J. Zabrodzki *et al.*) [in Polish].

Syslo, M.M. (1996) Computers in schools, concepts and reality, in *Computers in Schools, Proceedings of the XII Annual Conference* (ed. M.M. Syslo) [in Polish].

Van Weert, T.J. and Tinsley, D. [eds.] (1994) *Informatics for Secondary Education, a Curriculum for Schools.* UNESCO.

Waligorski, S. *et al.* (1992) *Curriculum for Tertiary Vocational Schools for technicians in Information Technology.* Approved by Committee for Science and Ministry of Education [in Polish].

7 BIOGRAPHY

Stanislaw Waligorski is professor of informatics at Warsaw University. He earned his Master's degree in Communication Engineering in 1959, his Doctorate in Mathematics in 1964 and his professorship in 1975. From 1959 to 1968 he worked as a computer designer and research programmer. From 1968 on he was with the Institute of Informatics of Warsaw University. From 1974 to 1977 he acted as head of the Department of Informatics of the Ministry of Science and cooperated in the creation of departments of informatics at selected universities in Poland. Since that time he has taken part in several projects connected with informatics education. He is member of the IFIP TC-3 Committee for Education, president of the Polish Olympiad in Informatics and member of the International Committee of the International Olympiad in Informatics.

23

Towards a taxonomy for computer science

Hanno Wupper
Computing Science Institute, Faculty of Mathematics and Informatics, University of Nijmegen, Toernooiveld 1, 6525 ED Nijmegen, The Netherlands, e-mail: Hanno.Wupper@cs.kun.nl

Hans Meijer
Computing Science Institute, Faculty of Mathematics and Informatics, University of Nijmegen, Toernooiveld 1, 6525 ED Nijmegen, The Netherlands, e-mail: Hans.Meijer@cs.kun.nl

Abstract

This paper tries to capture the essence of information technology and computer science. The principal goal of an information technologist is the same as that of any technologist: to create machines with certain properties. To achieve this an abstract schema of the machine's structure is invented or developed from an abstract specification of the problem. It is the information technologist's principal task to prove that the schema satisfies the specification. Computer scientists support or even enable this by developing the required mathematical and physical means. This paper proposes a consistent set of notions, together with a consistent terminology, which may clarify the relation of information technology and computer science to other scientific disciplines and which also may give rise to new ideas about computer science education.

Keywords

Informatics, university education, informatics majors, taxonomies, academic requirements

Informatics in Higher Education F. Mulder & T. van Weerts (Eds.)

1 INTRODUCTION

Terminology

In computer science agreement on terminology is limited. For its name alone one has the alternatives 'computing science' and 'informatics'. Fundamental terms in computer science, like 'state' or 'automaton' or 'specification' or even 'program' may have different meanings in different contexts. It may very well be the case that only the term bit qualifies for having a universally accepted meaning. This situation is an inevitable reflection of the fact that there is no common understanding of the core of this particular branch of science, let alone a basic understanding among the general public.

This paper tries to answer the question what information technology, by which we refer to the actual, professional manufacturing of applications, is all about and what computer science has to do with it. We try to establish a set of fundamental notions for which we hope to find consistent terms. Here the notions - not the terms - form the important issue.

Frameworks

In our approach we refine and detail a basic, abstract and general observation. This observation is based on a development cycle related to the various forms of the ubiquitous software life cycle in software engineering, but it tries to unify and normalize these. An important goal is to generalize the development cycle to the whole area of information technology. We take the notions 'computer science' and 'information technology' in their widest possible sense, that is respectively the science and the technology of the use of computers and computer applications, of the creation of such applications, of the specification of customers' requirements, the proofs of correctness of applications, etc.

In the next three sections we employ and explain three different frameworks: a formula, a diagram (resembling the software life cycle), and a tetrachotomy of theory, method, language and tool.

2 INFORMATION TECHNOLOGIST'S PRINCIPAL TASK

2.1 Machines with properties

We start from two fundamental notions which refer to the real world.

Definition: machine

A machine is some physical object (or 'substantial' object, see Bunge (1977)) which has been intentionally constructed from certain parts for some well-defined purpose.

Definition: property
A property is a physical phenomenon which can be ascribed to a physical object.

A machine is said to 'have a property', which expresses the proposition that that property is ascribed to that machine. Simple examples of properties are weight, speed or colour. However, in the context of information technology one is mainly interested in complex, dynamic properties like 'controlling a nuclear reactor's temperature' or 'navigating an aeroplane'. We are primarily interested in externally observable properties. The property 'structure' is given a special role below.

We deliberately propose to restrict the term machine to objects of the real world. A watch is a machine, so is a computer with or without software, but a formula or a computer program is not. A computer program only 'helps' to let a machine have certain required properties.

In information technology functional correctness and efficiency have traditionally been considered to be important properties of (machines executing) computer programs. Other properties like time constraints or reliability, which earlier seemed too difficult to deal with, can now be reasoned about in a more uniform framework.

Adequacy
Whether a machine actually has all required properties, is the problem of adequacy. This problem may be very hard or even impossible to decide. One may simply not know particular laws of nature, or one may be blocked by fundamental inaccuracies or uncertainties of measurement. But even if the physics are easy, the machine may still be too complex. In the sequel (see Figure 1) we are dividing the problem of adequacy into three subproblems, that of:

- meaning;
- structure;
- (formal) correctness.

2.2 Specification and schema

A basic notion being the descriptive mirror image of 'property', is 'specification'.

Definition: specification
A specification is a statement of properties, in some suitable language.

A specification is said to 'state a property': the property is to be obeyed or fulfilled. Whether a specification states particular properties is the problem of meaning.

A machine is said to 'fulfil a specification' if, for each property from a sufficiently well-defined collection, the machine has this property whenever the specification states it. Whether a machine fulfils a specification is the problem of acceptance.

Given a specification, the problem of adequacy may now also be decomposed into two subproblems (see Figure 1), that of:

- acceptance;
- meaning.

The descriptive counterpart of 'machine' is 'schema'. A schema also is the concrete counterpart of a specification, just as a property is the abstract counterpart of a machine.

Definition: schema
A schema (of arity $n \geq 0$) is a pair (s, X) where s is a sequence of n specifications and X is a structure description containing n numbered 'place holders' for components.

In the term schema we want to capture the description of the (detailed) structure of a machine. According to the Oxford English Dictionary structure is 'the mutual relation of the constituent parts or elements of a whole determining its particular nature or character'. In other words, a machine's structure is the specific or even characteristic way in which it is assembled from its parts - and a schema is a description of such a structure. Molecules, for example, are 'machines' assembled from atoms by means of 'chemical binding'. Chemistry studies the structure of molecules, taking (only) the properties of atoms into consideration. Chemistry is not primarily interested in living cells, computer chips or plastic toys, which are 'assembled' from particular molecules. Whereas many sciences, like chemistry, seem to confine themselves to a more or less homogeneous class of parts, computer science studies a whole hierarchy of parts: gates, processing elements, instructions, programs, languages, computers, information systems, control systems and networks.

Structure

A machine is said to 'be assembled from a collection of n parts conforming to a structure description X', if it is faithfully built according to X, with each part set in the position of the correspondingly numbered place holder. A machine is said to be a realization of a schema (s, X), if it is assembled conforming to X from a numbered collection of n machines which fulfil their correspondingly numbered specifications in s. Whether a machine is a realization of a schema is the problem of structure. Note that a machine contains particular parts, whereas a structure description only contains place holders to which a schema assigns requirements by way of specifications. The schema treats the machine parts as 'black boxes' of which only properties are prescribed, not the internal structure; the structure itself is a 'glass box'.

2.3 Formula of the task

Summing up the foregoing yields:

- a machine has or is supposed to have certain properties;
- a specification is a description of (these) properties;
- a schema is a description of the (precise) structure of a machine, relative to the specification of the properties of its parts.

A schema is said to 'satisfy a specification', if every machine which is a realization of the schema fulfils that specification. This leads to the formula, in words:

> a schema (s, X) satisfies a specification S if any machine that can be built according to X using parts fulfilling s, fulfils S

or, in symbols:

$$(\forall \mathrm{i}: 1..\#s.\ m_i\ \textbf{\textit{fulfils}}\ s_i) \Rightarrow (m\ \textbf{\textit{assembled}}\ X)\ \textbf{\textit{fulfils}}\ S$$

Since specifications and schemata are mathematical objects (descriptions of properties and structure), we may now capture the essence of an information technologist's task in mathematical terms. In order to build a machine with certain properties the technologist must produce a specification S, a schema Y and a proof p, such that p is a proof that Y satisfies S. Then, if S states the required properties, the required machine is a realization of Y.

The proof p may be any mathematically acceptable proof, including fully formal proofs as well as sufficiently precise reasoning. When information technologists discuss their product, be it finished or in development, with colleagues, their superior or a customer, they will primarily argue in favour of their schema satisfying the specification. This argument can only be interpreted as a try to establish a proof, however sloppy it may be. The only alternative to proof seems to be belief in some form of higher authority (based on power, experienced knowledge or intellect) or an insight by which the truth of a statement is immediately clear.

Correctness

Whether a schema satisfies a specification is the problem of correctness, which is particularly hard because of its complexity. A schema is a description of the structural composition of parts of which specifications are given. This makes it possible to treat most of the complexity of the adequacy problem in the mathematical domain: only the meaning of the specification and the physical realization of the structure defined by the schema cannot be dealt with mathematically.

This also admits a reduction of the complexity problem by hierarchical decomposition. One may initially restrict the schema to large parts which are optimally chosen to allow simple specifications and an easy structure description, and then repeat the same activity for the parts. This is referred to as the 'Chinese Box Principle', where the box is composed of boxes which are composed of boxes, etc. This procedure avoids the problem of capturing all complexity at once, but only if and when the specifications of parts hide (abstract from) details which exist only locally. Another gain is that parts may be reused (spatially as well as temporally). A striking example is the programmable computer where the 'architecture' or 'programmer's model' is a relatively simple specification of a very complex part and one 'only' needs to deal with the complexity of the other part: the program.

3 PROFESSIONAL ACTIVITIES

The four notions defined in the previous section (machine, property, specification, schema) are the 'cornerstones' of the diagram in Figure 1. The five characteristic problems introduced in the previous section (adequacy, meaning, acceptance, structure, correctness) appear in the diagram as relations (double sided arrows) between these cornerstones referring to particular objects, i.e. instances of the respective notions.

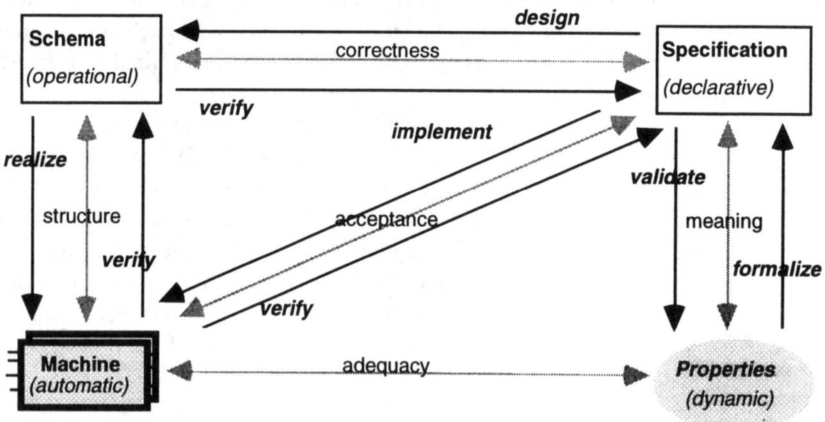

Figure 1 The diagram of professional activities of the information technologist.

Between (nearly) every pair of objects there further can be drawn arrows which capture quite disjoint professional activities. These arrows we believe to cover all essential activities of an information technologist. The diagram is a reworked version of the well-known software life cycle which is an Escher-like variant of the 'waterfall model' (Sommerville, 1996). It is also an idealized diagram in the sense that in practice the activities are not normally performed in strict sequence, but iterated, backtracked, etc. Definitions of the activities depicted in the diagram are given in an appendix (section 8).

4 COMPUTER SCIENTIST'S PRINCIPAL TASK

The professional activities shown in Figure 1 are those of an information technologist, not of a computer scientist. The computer scientist's primary activity is to do research which results in some form of support for the professional activities mentioned before.

Often such support results in a software package, a new language or 'paradigm'. This may well hamper dissemination and acceptance of research findings, if one cannot afford an expensive software package or cannot switch to a new programming language. However, one may still benefit from research results by using underlying theory or methods developed. It seems useful to make complex research results more accessible by dividing these into four classes being defined below.

Definition: theory
A theory is a collection of scientific laws or theorems ('true statements'), usually generated by a finite collection of deduction rules from a finite collection of axioms.

Most theories are infinite, in which case one needs a proof and a decision procedure to establish whether a statement is true.

Definition: method
A method is a collection of notions, rules and procedures which may help to systematically find a solution for a given problem.

Definition: language / formalism
A language or formalism is a collection of terms (or sentences, or sequences of symbols) with well-defined syntax and semantics (which maps each well-formed term to its 'meaning' in some physical or mathematical model, usually following its syntactical structure).

Definition: tool
A tool is a computer system automating parts of professional activities.
The fact that most tools which support information technology, are themselves prime examples of products of that same technology causes what one might call a 'strange loop of computer science' (Hofstadter, 1979). Of course many technologies (engineering as an example) do produce their own tools, but it seems that in information technology it happens at an overwhelming scale. The fact that initially software tools are the results of research by computer scientists (TEX for

example), causes an intricate intertwining of computer science and information technology which is one of the primary causes of the terminological chaos referred to in the introduction.

5 CONCLUSION

Every professional activity in information technology archetypally consists of:

- writing down a problem in some language (the specification);
- developing a solution (a schema) for it using some method, while writing down the partial or intermediate solutions in that same or some other language;
- proving - on the fly or afterwards - that the schema satisfies the specification, by showing that our formula when applied to that specification and schema is a theorem in an appropriate theory;
- employing tools in doing so.

It is the principal task of a computer scientist to provide the necessary languages, methods, theories and tools. These may be associated with the elements in Figure 1 in a systematic way.

- Languages have their role in the mathematical objects 'specification' and 'schema' with all possible intermediate objects.
- Theory deals with the mathematical modelling of the physical objects 'machine' and 'properties' and with the five basic relations between the objects together with their associated problems, thereby laying the foundation for the formula in subsection 2.3.
- Methods and tools support the arrows, i.e. the professional activities, in particular those done by hand or automatically.

Scientific understanding is impossible without abstraction. Moreover, abstraction of reality into mathematical models enables reasoning about reality by mathematical means. However one may need to be very careful about the appropriate level of abstraction. In many fields of computer science one may identify a machine with the schema of its software ('the program is the true result'), in some other fields one may identify a schema with its specification ('the program is an executable specification'), but negligent use of such abstractions may be very confusing.

The following aspects should be discerned:

- the mathematical description of a computer program (the specification);
- the bit pattern representing that program inside the computer (the schema);
- their physical combination whilst executing (the machine);
- the effects of this in the real world (the properties).

These aspects are present on the very abstract level of our diagram. When they are not separated, the Babylonian confusion pervading computer science will persist, with at least the following consequences.

- Technical terms may have (slightly) different meanings in different research areas which situation does not favour communication among scientists.
- Computer scientists, particularly young ones and students, may have difficulties in putting the results of others in the right context.
- It may be unnecessarily difficult to relate the results of computer science to those in other disciplines.
- It is very hard to explain to the general public or the authorities what computer science is all about and which benefits may be expected from research programmes.

Systematically applying Ockham's razor we have touched upon a number of divide-and-conquer-like classifications which may help in explaining computer science, for instance to students:

- physical - mathematical;
- meaning - correctness - complexity - structure;
- formalize - design - realize;
- act - verify;
- theory - method - language - tool;
- professional activities - scientific research.

We hope that our approach also clarifies the relationship with other scientific disciplines. Computer science may learn a lot from the 'development cycle' in engineering disciplines as well as from the 'verification cycle' in the natural sciences. The role of induction versus deduction points to an 'equal opportunity' status for experimental methods. Mathematics will of course teach us how to handle the central correctness problem and how to deal with its complexity.

Finally, we have experienced that our taxonomy helps students of information technology - the future makers of software - to distinguish essential concepts from everyday's whim and to see their own future profession in a broad perspective. Our taxonomy may well help them understand why they have to learn new methods, among other things, during their whole professional life. It may help students of computer science to see more clearly what their theories, languages, methods and tools are good for. Scientific as well as professional education should be methodological and we hope that our framework contributes to that.

6 ACKNOWLEDGEMENTS

We wish to thank Henk Barendregt, Guy Debrock, André van den Hoogenhof, Toine Tax, Huub van Thienen, Frits Vaandrager, Tom van Weert, and all other colleagues who contributed to this paper with their ideas, criticism and sharp questions.

7 REFERENCES

Hofstadter, D.R. (1979) *Gödel, Escher, Bach: an Eternal Golden Braid.* Basic Books, New York.

Sommerville, I. (1996) *Software Engineering.* Addison-Wesley, Reading, Massachusetts.

Bunge, M.A. (1977) *Treatise on Basic Philosophy, vol. 3: Ontology I.* Reidel Publishing Company, Dordrecht, Holland.

8 APPENDIX

Information technologist's professional activities defined

Definition: formalize
To formalize is to write a formal specification which states exactly the required properties.
This activity comprises subactivities like their actual formalization in some language and their structuring for purposes of presentation, reuse, etc.

Definition: validate
To validate a specification is to establish that the specification indeed states the required properties.
To this end one must become sure about what will be the case when the specification is made true. This can be done basically by:

- insight, when the specification is so clear that we comprehend it immediately;
- prototyping, where the prototype is tested or measured;
- reasoning, where additional properties are mathematically proven.

Definition: implement
To implement is to physically make a machine which fulfils a given specification.
This is either accomplished rationally, by designing and realizing a schema, or by putting parts together intuitively.

Definition: verify a machine against a specification
To verify a machine against a specification is to ensure that a machine fulfils a given specification.
If a correct schema of the machine cannot be produced, verification must be performed inductively (or in 'black box' style) where as many hypotheses as possible are derived from the specification and are verified by experiments. Information technologists call this testing.

Definition: realize
To realize is to physically make a machine which is the realization of a given schema.
This involves picking up the required parts and putting them together in the right way. In the case of pure software systems, we assume - by using the word 'pure' - a programmable machine to be used as part. As a consequence the realization of the machine as a whole is trivial: loading a machine-readable representation of the schema into it. In the case of a machine in hardware one may want to let the realization be performed automatically.

Definition: verify a machine against a schema

To verify a machine against a schema is to ensure that a machine is a realization of a given schema.
Note that a verification is (only) necessary if the machine is made by an untrustworthy device, in particular a human - in which case the verification consists of checking whether the right parts are assembled in the right way. When the machine is very complex or cannot be opened (e.g. without breaking down), it may be the case that one can only verify the machine against its specification.
Definition: design
To design is to elaborate a schema which satisfies a given specification.
In our framework this means no more and no less than finding a suitable schema (s, X) such that our formula in subsection 2.3 becomes true. Apart from small 'toy' cases this activity is too complex to be performed without computer support. On the other hand the activity cannot in general be fully automated. Designing is a creative mathematical activity which comprises finding a theorem and, if necessary, strengthening its assumptions until it can be proven.

Definition: verify a schema against a specification
To verify a schema against a specification is to prove that a schema satisfies a given specification.
This verification must be performed deductively (or in 'glass box' style). The automatic part of the design will not need a proof as long as the used tool is trustworthy. The part by hand may be elaborated systematically and stepwise; each step will need to be proven. Or the schema may be 'invented' in which case it must be proven to be correct from scratch.

9 BIOGRAPHY

Hanno Wupper studied mathematics and informatics at the Ruhr-University Bochum, where after his graduation in 1974 he was responsible for system development and maintenance. In his group one of the first fully machine and device independent graphical programming systems has been developed. He defended his doctoral thesis in informatics in 1984 at the University of Oldenburg and has been assistant and associate professor at the University of Nijmegen since 1986. His research interests are methodology and embedded systems.

Hans Meijer graduated from Delft University of Technology in 1971. He joined the University of Nijmegen in 1974, where he received his doctorate degree in 1986. Currently he is a senior lecturer / associate professor in programming methodology. His current research interest is transformational programming and its relation to automatic proof checking and computer algebra.

PART THREE

Short Papers

Learning from other disciplines: pedagogic models within computer science and from elsewhere

Sally Fincher
Computing Laboratory, University of Kent at Canterbury, Kent CT2 7NF, England, e-mail: S.A.Fincher@ukc.ac.uk

Abstract
This short paper deals with the similarities (for teaching) between computer science as a discipline and other disciplines: for example it is like maths in one way and like medicine in another, and like English in yet another. The paper addresses the question as to how - as teachers - we can (and should) use examples from the teaching of those disciplines to enhance our own.

Keywords
Informatics, other disciplines, curriculum (general)

1 BACKGROUND

Teaching within computer science (CS) has traditionally been accomplished by the delivery of a large quantity of knowledge-based lectures supplemented with practical laboratory sessions and, increasingly, small-group and project work. This pedagogic pattern is not confined to CS, but is common across cognate disciplines (Hativa and Marincovich, 1995): mastery of facts, presented in incremental stages, from simple to complex, each stage building on the last, is the common paradigm for teaching.

Whilst this lecture-based pattern guarantees the efficient *presentation* of material, it frequently does not address other learning issues; for example, learner autonomy and synthesis of knowledge (Van Heuvelen, 1991). This is a particularly potent question for CS where we aim not only to equip the students with a coherent

Informatics in Higher Education F. Mulder & T. van Weerts (Eds.)

corpus of material, but also to have them acquire particular skills throughout their undergraduate career. For CS is not just a knowledge-based subject. As well as producing graduates with subject knowledge, we also expect them to have the ability to practice, especially with regard to the skill of programming.

2 WHAT IS DIFFERENT ABOUT CS AS A DISCIPLINE?

Programming requires a combination of applied knowledge and practical skill. It is: conceptually challenging, requiring a high level of analytical skill to break down a given problem into patterns which can be effectively mapped into an implementation language. And it is complex, involving both technical and design knowledge to create a program which not only works, but makes efficient (and, in the best examples, elegant) use of the given resources. It is also continually demanding, set in the context of a young and rapidly changing technology which affects technical objectives, requiring that a skilled programmer achieves an ever-evolving attitude and skill set. This combination of requirements is not so frequently seen in the 'hard' sciences from which CS grew, where the application of learned knowledge often *is* the practice of a discipline.

3 EXISTING ADOPTION AND INTEGRATION

CS already borrows teaching models from some other disciplines. For example, the teaching of CS is like management science in its real-world subject matter. Almost all CS work (excepting the most formal aspects) is required to exist in the world, interacting with other systems, both human and electronic. The use of case studies by management scientists (whether 'real' or constructed as a teaching tool) which model the complexity of interactions that can occur in real-life systems are increasingly being adopted within the teaching of CS.

Architecture and engineering, like CS, also build things and these things must work both within themselves and within the world. Those CS educators who adopt the label 'software engineers' recognize an affinity here and borrow pedagogic practices - for example test suites and benchmarking - as well as those teaching objectives which relate to design concerns (and constraints) working to combine functionality with aesthetics. All these are concepts which are familiar to our practice.

These 'borrowed' models undoubtedly already enhance the teaching and learning which occurs within CS. However, these models are in fact the easy ones: they cross over where the intent of the teaching is the same. In some instances, they have crossed from the practice of their originating discipline with the practitioners, who take up the teaching of CS as a supplementary or alternative subject to that in which they were trained. Indeed, this is the same way that the 'traditional' models were transferred, from the home disciplines of the first generation of CS educators which, in general, were maths, physics and engineering (although often these educators are not aware of subsequent changes in the educative models of those original fields).

4 OTHER DISCIPLINARY MODELS

However, as the discipline of CS develops and matures into its own shape, distinct from the disciplines in which it originated, so other educational models become appropriate. It is unlikely that these models will transfer with practitioners in the same way; this time we shall have to seek them out. For example, those skills which programming requires, whilst unusual in scientific subjects, are not infrequently found in, and are sometimes traditional to, the teaching and learning in other subject areas. Law, for example, has long recognized the difference between learning law and being a lawyer and pedagogy in that discipline reflects this objective. A simple example of this is the practice of moots, where cases must be demonstrated and argued in a public arena. Medicine, too, is a content-dense subject which additionally attempts to deliver high-level skills of learner autonomy and synthesis (in the case of medicine these skills are manifested in areas such as diagnosis) and have adapted their teaching practices to reflect this (McMaster, 1997).

Although less frequently identified, there are also, perhaps, common approaches between the teaching of CS and some of the disciplines within the humanities. A poem uses a language. What makes language poetic is the approach which informs the use; the conventions of form, the density of meaning and the deliberation of the construction. Once a student is in command of language (the knowledge base) then methodologies from the teaching of English - critical approach and deconstruction of texts - might be seen to have an applicability. Perhaps especially so with regard to the 'reading' of programs written by others, a difficult process requiring both interpretative skills and commentary.

5 A FINAL OBJECTION

It might be argued that the intent, the educational objectives, which pertain in these other disciplines are too far removed from ours. If teaching methods were adopted from maths and physics and engineering, it was because they were relevant to the intent of our teaching in a way which these other areas are not.

This seems to me to be a poor argument, because intent is never identical, but it can be analogous. To use examples I have cited here, we are already teaching that learning CS is not the same as being a computer scientist and that the construction of (and appreciation of) a good program is formed by rules and informed by commentary. However, our existing educational models and methods are tools not well adapted to these tasks and our educational objectives would be better served, our teaching enhanced and the learning of our students facilitated, by models which have been developed to address them, informed by the successes of other disciplines.

6 REFERENCES

Hativa, N. and Marincovich, M. [eds.] (1995) *Disciplinary Differences in Teaching and Learning: Implications for Practice*. New Directions for Teaching and Learning no. 64. Jossey-Bass, San Francisco.

McMaster (1997) *The "McMaster" Model of Medical Education*. The Education Section of the McMaster Faculty of Health Sciences: gopher://fhs.csu.McMaster.CA:70/11/edu.

Van Heuvelen, A. (1991) Learning to think like a physicist: a review of research-based instructional strategies. *American Journal of Physics,* **59** (10), 891-897.

7 BIOGRAPHY

Sally Fincher holds degrees from the University of Kent (BA) and Georgetown University, Washington DC (MA). She currently is working as teaching development officer within the Computing Laboratory at the University of Kent at Canterbury from where she runs the UK Computer Science Discipline Network (CSDN) and manages project EPCOS (Effective Projectwork in Computer Science). She is a member of the conference of Heads and Professors of Computing Learning Development Group.

25

Classifying information systems education by method engineering

Karel Lemmen
Faculty of Engineering (Informatics), Open University, PO Box 2960, 6401 DL Heerlen, The Netherlands, e-mail: karel.lemmen@ouh.nl

Fred Mulder
Faculty of Engineering (Informatics), Open University, PO Box 2960, 6401 DL Heerlen, The Netherlands, e-mail: fred.mulder@ouh.nl

Sjaak Brinkkemper
Baan Company, R&D, Orgware Development, PO Box 250 6710 BG Ede, The Netherlands, e-mail: sbrinkkemper@baan.nl

Abstract

Method engineering (ME) deals with the selection and assembly of situation-specific methods for information systems development. In this short paper we propose to use ME with an educational goal, that is to evaluate information systems curricula.

Keywords

Information systems, curriculum (general), taxonomies, educational profiles

Informatics in Higher Education F. Mulder & T. van Weerts (Eds.)

1 INTRODUCTION

Developing information systems (IS) requires a sensible selection of methods from a broad spectrum of various possible methods for design, project management, quality management, information planning, etc. Method engineering (ME), being part of the informatics discipline, offers approaches to do such a selection for specific situations on a solid basis. ME also facilitates the assembly of situation-specific methods (e.g. see Brinkkemper *et al.*, 1996). In this way ME can be helpful for IT-professionals in their practice of systems development.

On the other hand educators are confronted with the question: 'How should a curriculum in informatics or more specific in IS be in order to educate state-of-the-art IT-professionals?' We have seen quite a number of influential proposals in the past thirty years. However, not much effort has been put into comparing and characterizing the different model curricula in a systematic way. This can be useful not only for the educators themselves but also for the potential students and for the professional field which receives the graduated students as input. An example of such a study for informatics curricula in a broad sense is Mulder and Hacquebard (1998) where an instrument is used called UCSI (Unified Classification Scheme for Informatics). In this short paper we focus on the IS development area only. We apply ME based upon a framework for IS development as a classification tool by which one can show in detail the completeness and specific emphasis in the IS part of a curriculum.

2 METHOD ENGINEERING: THE A/L-FRAMEWORK

ME frameworks are meant to give an overview of the process of IS development and are mostly based upon a combination of empirical experience and theoretical views. Over the years several frameworks have been proposed mainly related to the analysis and design process in IS development. This limited scope also holds for our A(spect)/L(evel)-framework (Figure 1) which is based on the work of Essink (1988).

	goal structure	environmental interaction	functional structure	entity structure	process structure	system dynamics	allocation aspect	realization aspect
OSM								
CIM								
DSM								
IPM								

OSM = Object System Modelling
DSM = Data System Modelling
CIM = Conceptual Information System Modelling
IPM = Implementation Modelling

Figure 1 The A/L-framework.

Each element of the A/L-framework stands for one particular aspect (A) on a specific modelling level (L) of IS development. The framework has 8 x 4 = 32 entries. We indeed observe that the A/L-framework concentrates mainly on the analysis and design aspects of IS. The strength of the framework is that it forces the same set of aspects at each modelling level.

The four modelling levels are:

- OSM, describing the part of the organization for which an IS should be designed and realized (the 'why' question);
- CIM, viewing the IS as a set of (functional) components by which the information requirements of the users should be fulfilled (the 'what' question);
- DSM, considering the IS as a data processing system (the 'how' question);
- IPM, viewing the IS as a concrete, operative and maintainable system (the 'with what' question).

With respect to the eight different aspects we can conclude that five of them (the shaded area in the framework) concern the architecture of the system, starting from a conceptual view (OSM, CIM) up to and including the implementation view (DSM, IPM). The remaining three aspects: goal structure, allocation and realization, should be considered in order to be able to identify the goals, meaning and feasibility of the chosen architecture and to view the system as an operational and functional system. More details on the framework can be found in Lemmen *et al.* (1993).

Now using the A/L-framework ME proceeds as illustrated in a simplified way in Figure 2.

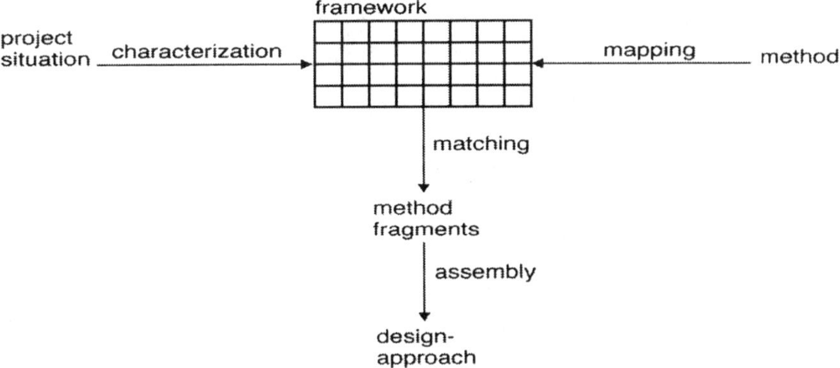

Figure 2 ME based on the A/L-framework (simplified view).

The A/L-framework is used in different ways. First of all in a generic sense the existing methods for IS development are mapped onto the framework. Second in a specific sense each particular project situation is to be characterized through the framework. And finally the project situation can be matched within the framework with the range of available methods resulting in a 'best fit' method or mostly 'best fit' construct or assembly of parts of different methods.

3 CURRICULUM EVALUATION

Each entry in the A/L-framework defines an important step in designing IS as viewed from the field of ME. Accepting this view leads to the statement that each IS curriculum should pay attention to any of these topics. As an example we evaluate the recently published IS'97 undergraduate curriculum (Davis *et al.*, 1997).

On the basis of an overview of the recommended body of knowledge, IS'97 can be mapped globally onto the A/L-framework. Figure 3 shows the result. It can be concluded from Figure 3 that IS'97 mainly concentrates on the architecture of IS. There is for example less attention for the organizational context (OSM), the goal structure and the allocation and realization aspect. On the other hand IS'97 contains two curriculum areas that go beyond the scope of the A/L-framework: project management and interpersonal skills (teams). And of course the IS'97 curriculum assumes prerequisites in computer use skills, presentation skills, quantitative and qualitative analysis and organization functions.

	goal structure	environmental interaction	functional structure	entity structure	process structure	system dynamics	allocation aspect	realization aspect
OSM								
CIM								
DSM								
IPM								

– Project Management
– Interpersonal skills (teams)
IS'97

Figure 3 IS'97 mapped onto the A/L-framework.

We could perform a similar evaluation for other curricula and then draw comparative conclusions. This will be done in a future paper.

4 CONCLUSION

In our opinion ME is promising with respect to evaluating IS curricula. Similarly ME could also be used as a tool for designing IS curricula. It would be natural then to give ME a prominent position in the curriculum as a topic itself. Future research will concentrate on a further elaboration of ME in an educational setting.

5 REFERENCES

Brinkkemper, S., Lyytinen, K. and Welke, R.J. [eds.] (1996) *Method Engineering: Principles of method construction and tool support*. Chapman & Hall, London.

Davis, G.B., Gorgone, J.T., Couger, J.D., Feinstein, D.L. and Longenecker, H.E., Jr. (1997) IS'97: Model Curriculum and Guidelines for Undergraduate Degree Programs in Information Systems. *Data Base*, **28** (1), 1-94.

Essink, L.J.B. (1988) A Conceptual Framework for Information Systems Development Methodologies, in *Eurinfo '88, Proceedings of the First European Conference on Information Technology for Organizational Systems* (eds. H.J. Bullinger *et al.*), North Holland, Amsterdam.

Lemmen, K.A.M., Punter, H.T. *et al.* (1993) *Methodologie van informatiesysteem-ontwikkeling*, Open University of the Netherlands, Heerlen [in Dutch]. A summary can be found in: Punter, H.T. and Lemmen, K.A.M. (1996) The MEMA-model: Towards a new approach for Method Engineering. *Information and Software Technology*, **38** (4), 295-305.

Mulder, F. and Hacquebard, A.E.N. (1998) Specifying and comparing informatics curricula through UCSI, in *Informatics in higher education: Views on informatics and noninformatics curricula* (eds. F. Mulder and T.J. van Weert), Chapman & Hall, London.

6 BIOGRAPHY

Karel Lemmen studied mathematics at the Technical University of Aachen in Germany. He has taught informatics in higher professional education before he went in 1985 to the Dutch Open University (Faculty of Engineering). He has specialized in information systems and databases and has chaired course teams and developed course material in those areas. His research interests are: IS curricula, method engineering and the application of IT in an educational setting. He is preparing his dissertation on the first two themes.

Fred Mulder is working at the Dutch Open University from its start in 1983 and is full professor in informatics education since 1991. He holds a Bachelor's degree in chemical engineering and an Engineering degree in applied mathematics, both from the University of Twente (NL). He received his Ph.D. degree in theoretical chemistry from the University of Nijmegen (NL). After a postdoc research project in Canada, he went to teach informatics and mathematics in higher professional education, prior to his OU period.

Sjaak Brinkkemper is a senior product architect at Baan Company, a leading vendor of Enterprise Resource Planning (ERP) software, based in the Netherlands. Before his industrial career he has held academic positions at the Universities of Nijmegen (NL), Austin (US) and Twente (NL). His research interests are production of packaged software, method engineering, CASE tools and workflow management.

26

Impacts of interdisciplinary dialogue to computer science education

Veijo Meisalo
Department of Teacher Education, PO Box 38, FIN-00014
University of Helsinki, Finland, e-mail: meisalo@cc.helsinki.fi

Erkki Sutinen
Department of Computer Science, PO Box 26, FIN-00014
University of Helsinki, Finland, e-mail: sutinen@cs.helsinki.fi

Jorma Tarhio
Department of Computer Science, University of Joensuu
PO Box 111, FIN-80101 Joensuu, Finland
e-mail: tarhio@cs.joensuu.fi

Abstract

Based on our experiences in an interdisciplinary research group, we propose more flexibility in those areas of computer science education which are interesting also to other disciplines.

Keywords

Informatics, other disciplines, informatics majors, noninformatics majors, curriculum (core), role of CIT

Informatics in Higher Education F. Mulder & T. van Weerts (Eds.)

1 DIALOGUE EDUCATIONALISTS AND COMPUTER SCIENTISTS

The categorical organization of the university makes professionals working on the same topic from different backgrounds alien to each other. The area of computer-supported learning environments is an example of this. Educationalists and computer scientists do not know, and hence respect, each others' theoretical background or methods. Although the principles of designing computer-aided learning environments encourage teamwork and close cooperation,the implemented software is seldom balanced. Usually either a computer scientist or an educationalist is the dominating partner.

If an educationalist is the originator of the software, the result might be recognized by its inflexible implementation, possibly making the student a passive browser of a book-like organized file. The educationalist's poor programming and implementation skills may lead to a disastrous result, although he is an expert in activating teaching methods. The solution does not necessarily make use of the computer's potential: the role of the computer is obscure or taken as given. The code may be scattered, consisting of goto statements from one page to another.

The problems of the software, made by a computer scientist, are quite opposite but at least as serious. Often, a computer scientist does not think of his product from the learner's point of view: in educational software, this is reflected in vague pedagogical goals. Moreover, the computer scientist is seldom an expert in evaluating the software from the user's perspective.

2 INTERDISCIPLINARY RESEARCH

In 1995, we started an interdisciplinary project of animation-aided problem solving (AAPS). The participants came from Computer Science (CS) and Education. The aim of the project is to develop computer-supported methods for creative problem solving, similar to those developed earlier for automatic algorithm animation by the computer scientists (Lahtinen *et al.*, 1996). Creative problem solving is needed in various areas of education (Kuitunen and Meisalo, 1996).

Although the research topic was relevant to both the disciplines, it required several meetings to understand each others' vocabulary, methods, and perspectives, even the way of doing things together. The meetings were necessary to make each participant a genuine contributor of the group. The dialogue, with concurrent development of new computer-aided learning tools, gave us a clear view of the problems of computer-mediated education. In general, cooperation of computer scientists and educationalists is essential in making pedagogically sound, technically advanced, and innovative computer-aided learning environments.

3 UNCOVERING THE CORE OF COMPUTER SCIENCE

The dialogue has enforced each participant of the research group to evaluate his role in the whole project. From a computer scientist's perspective, the question is: 'What has computer science to offer to the interactive learning environments?'

This question has made us think of computer science as a problem solving science. Traditionally, CS education has concentrated on closed problem settings instead of open ones. However, any genuine research starts from a wonder, with no explicit and well-formulated questions.

Furthermore, a computer scientist is an expert in the area of discrete structures. These are an important element of any learning environment where the active user is allowed to manipulate graphical objects, representing his mental models, for example as concept maps. The fact that the learning environments do not give much to an active learner is due to the programmers with no expertise in efficient implementation of advanced structures, which belongs to the core of computer science.

4 SUGGESTIONS FOR RENEWING COMPUTER SCIENCE CURRICULA

A dialogue between computers scientists and other professionals, carried out together with a common project, provides new horizons in understanding computer science as a discipline. It also clarifies questions of the role of CS in the area of computer uses in education which has traditionally been the duty of educationalists. In addition, it offers practical consequences on how and what aspects of CS to teach to nonmajors.

The dialogue has made clear the importance of skills, like those of creative problem solving, to enhance the traditionally knowledge-centered CS curricula. For nonmajors, we emphasize the importance of programming skills.

Based on our experiences in using creative problem solving methods in CS research, we will teach a course on this topic. This course not only sketches various problem solving methods and encourages the students to apply them, but also challenges the students to design software to promote problem solving.

To employ their expertise in activating the learners with the help of computers, the educationalists should know the required technologies. Therefore, a course in computer-aided learning environments for educationalists should consist not only of applications and pedagogical theories, but also of programming and software implementation skills.

The dialogue has shown that it is also possible to bridge the gap between research and education. We organized a data structures laboratory for CS majors of the third year, utilizing group processes and creative problem solving methods (Meisalo *et al.*, 1997).

5 REFERENCES

Kuitunen, H. and Meisalo, V. (1996) The LOTTO project: Creative problem solving for schools. Group processes and creativity in action, in *Proc. XIII Research Symposium on Mathematics and Science Education* (ed. M. Ahtee *et al.*), Report 162. University of Helsinki, Department of Teacher Education, Helsinki, 61-70.

Lahtinen, S.-P., Lamminjoki, T., Sutinen, E., Tarhio, J. and Tuovinen, A.-P. (1996) Towards automated animation of algorithms, in *Proc. Fourth International Conference in Central Europe on Computer Graphics and Visualization 96* (eds. N. Thalmann and V. Skala), University of West Bohemia, Department of Computer Science, 150-161.

Meisalo, V., Sutinen, E. and Tarhio, J. (1997) CLAP: teaching data structures in a creative way, in: *Proc. ITiCSE '97, Integrating Technology into Computer Science Education*, ACM, Uppsala, 117-119.

6 BIOGRAPHY

Veijo Meisalo is an associate professor and Dean of the Faculty of Education at the University of Helsinki, Finland. His research interests cover group processes and creative problem solving in science education.

Erkki Sutinen is a researcher in the Department of Computer Science, University of Helsinki, Finland. His main interests are algorithms, especially approximate string matching and designing computer-based tools for active learning, like concept mapping and algorithm animation.

Jormo Tarhio is an associate professor in the Department of Computer Science at the University of Joensuu, Finland. His research interests are in the areas of string algorithms, animation and computer-supported concept mapping techniques.

27

Internet-studies communication and information technology (CIT)

Sigrid E. Schubert
Technical University of Chemnitz, Faculty of Computer Science
D-09107 Chemnitz, Germany, e-mail: ssc@informatik.tu-chemnitz.de

Abstract

About 300 students taking the extension study course Communication and Information Technology (CIT) are studying exclusively via the Internet. New forms of communication using the Internet were developed and implemented, replacing all the traditional study components. The content of the CIT subject provides its own teaching aids. Students describe their experiences with the Internet-studies very positively and colleagues and friends join the course.

Keywords

Communication and networks, role of CIT

1 DEVELOPMENT

In 1995 the first 56 full-time employed postgraduate students commenced a new way of studying in a course conducted by Professor Dr U. Hübner, holder of the chair of ‘Computer Networks and Distributed Systems’ at the Faculty of Computer Science. The lectures were provided in the form of hypertexts with links to chosen Internet sources, and were distributed via monthly e-mail packages. According to their own statements, the students required approximately ten hours per week to work through the study material at home on their own computer. This included four hours per week on Internet exercises, the so-called on-line time. For every ten students one personal tutor was provided to support the e-mail exercises. The students sent their solutions to the exercises and questions on the subject matter to the tutor.

Informatics in Higher Education F. Mulder & T. van Weerts (Eds.)

2 APPLICATION OF CIT IN THE INTERNET STUDIES

Computer science is especially innovative in the field of development and the application of modern tutorial systems (Schubert, 1995) and CIT in the educational domain. Providing lectures in form of hypertext documents can be considered as the first step to extensive multimedia applications. But this mode of delivery is still clearly limited by the domestic equipment possessed by the students. The exchange of experience via internal e-mail lists for purpose of study is completely new. The students' need to talk and take part in technical discussion on a large scale is made possible by the use of e-mail. This application of CIT proved to be very sensitive with respect to the number of participants as well as to the required technical guidance. In an extreme case there is no discussion at all. This can happen equally with groups that are too small or too large. In particular, hasty correcting by the tutors has a demotivating effect.

A new initiative is the self-assessment of individual study progress through test files. After initial resistance to the use of electronic supervision the tool is accepted and intensively used. The self-study program is designed to prepare the students systematically for the demands of the examination by solving measured quantities of exercises within a given time. To expand the self-study program, answers to exercise questions can be entered into an answer scheme analogous to a database. The tutors use the tool to assess the students' answers or to add corrections. In part two of the study, the main emphasis is on experiments in the laboratory of the Technical University Chemnitz via Internet. Therefore, the project part 'Teleguided experiments' is the subject of the research project 'Internet distant study'. Even now this part permits the learning environment for network management and planning in an isolated experimental environment that has no connection to the rest of the network. A defined initial position can be guaranteed for each practical participant even after massive control defaults of preceding students (Schubert, 1997).

3 EXPERIENCES WITH THIS FORM OF STUDYING

Very time intensive

The time required for the development of interactive teaching aids is often seriously underestimated. For the present there is no saving of staff or administrative expense for the university. The expenditure on preparation is many times the preparation time for a conventional lecture or exercise. The high expenditure on student assistance cannot be covered by the planned four hours per week for ten participants. The triple expenditure of time has been watched during complicated study phases, e.g. the beginning of the first part.

Rewards

Why does the university teacher face such burdens for apparently unattractive tasks? The author sees two arguments.

- The scientific engagement in the reconnaissance and the exploration of new ways of studying through the application of CIT.
- We are encouraged by the positive response and results from the special target group of students for which any other form of studying is out of question. The study success rate of the first graduates is approximately 80%, which is very good for employed postgraduate students.

Communication problems

Because there is a demand for postgraduate university qualifications, students from almost all professional groups - from the young graduate to the university professor - are studying in this extension study course. This produces communication problems resulting from the different technical languages and previous knowledge. Even the age difference (from 23 up to 63 years) produces new demands for education. The group discussion of one study year makes those variations in experience of life and communication habits very clear. Because at the moment the largest group has 129 participants it is an important task to overcome carefully the reluctance of the majority of the students to express ideas publicly for fear that they might contain mistakes.

E-mail as a leveller

The e-mail of a student does not show the age and qualifications of the writer. In addition, there is approximately the same amount of knowledge and ability in the subject being studied, giving rise to a kind of communal spirit. The students help each other.

4 REFERENCES

Schubert, S.E. (1995) *Innovative Konzepte für die Ausbildung*. Springer-Verlag, Berlin.

Schubert, S.E. (1996) Basismechanismen der Informationssicherheit. *Informatische Bildung und Computer in der Schule - LOGIN,* **16** (5/6), 10-15.

Schubert, S.E. (1997) Internetstudiengang Informations- und Kommunikationssystemen. *AUE - Informationsdienst Hochschule und Weiterbildung,* (1/97), 37-41.

5 BIOGRAPHY

Sigrid Schubert is an assistant professor in the Department of Computer Science at the Technical University of Chemnitz, Germany. She studied mathematics, physics and education at Chemnitz and Dresden (Master's degree 1972). After teaching twelve years in secondary and vocational education, she became head of the Didactics of Computer Science Group at the Technical University of Chemnitz, after having received her PhD in didactics (in 1988). Her research interests are the development and evaluation of new learning and teaching environments. She has been active in the German Federation for Information Processing (GI) and in IFIP Working Groups on education.

Collaborative work on informatics education of noninformatics students: a pilot project proposal

Eric W. van Ammers
Department of Informatics, Wageningen Agricultural University
Dreijenplein 2, 6703 HB Wageningen, The Netherlands
e-mail: Eric.vanAmmers@users.info.wau.nl

Abstract

This short paper actually is a proposal for a pilot project to set up a database for the field of informatics that can be used in various 'tailored' ways through the Internet by the informatics educational community. The implementation of such a database, preferably in an international context, requires a range of activities that are identified in this proposal.

Keywords

Informatics, informatics majors, noninformatics majors, curriculum (general), role of CIT

1 STATEMENT

Teachers would be greatly served if they could compose their curricula by drawing material from a database. This is even more effective when standards have been set on the level of knowledge the students are to attain.

Desirable features of the database are that the material should be:

- available electronically in a form that is optimized for import into the more popular document processing systems;
- divided into *independent* elements requiring say at most 8 hours to master;

Informatics in Higher Education F. Mulder & T. van Weerts (Eds.)

- easy to adapt for a teacher to fit the local didactic context, i.e. no specific didactic principles should be imposed.

It would be worthwhile to set up such a database for the field of informatics and make it available to the informatics educational community through the Internet. Its primary audience will be those who are involved in teaching informatics, but it will also be highly useful to noninformatics majors.

The database would allow the efficient construction of educational material tailored to a particular learning situation. It would stimulate the transformation of teachers from *originators* of to *managers* of teaching material.

2 ACTIVITIES

The implementation of an *Informatics Curriculum Database* looks like an impressive effort. Roughly speaking it involves the following activities.

- Identify disciplines to be served (e.g. medicine, law, physics, biology, etc.).
- Identify levels of depths and competence the material has to expose. Most likely students in higher vocational institutions will be taught on a more shallow level than university students.
- Divide the outlined curriculum into individual learning elements subjected to the following restrictions:
  > the time an average student needs to study an element is limited to say 8 hours;
  > elements are independent of each other, i.e. they do not refer to (parts of) other elements;
  > every element supplies a list of concepts considered a prerequisite to understand the material presented;
  > an index relating individual concepts to associated learning elements should be made available;
  > every element is illustrated by at least one specific example for every discipline;
- Work out the learning elements into documents that:
  > supply an explanation of the particular element to be used by teachers as a starting point for their own statement of the matter;
  > are 'neutral' in style (i.e. not strongly biased to some didactic form);
  > will be reviewed for acceptance by a committee;
  > are written by means of an agreed upon standard text processing system;
- Scan the Internet for existing material that qualifies (possibly after some adaptation) for the database.
- Set up a glossary to standardize the terms of the database.

- Transform the accepted elements into the text formats for distribution purposes and add the element to the database.
- Design procedures to maintain the database and to deal with matters of royalties.
- Set up a server to take care of Internet access to the database.

The database should be *certified* to a certain extent. That is its users should be confident that the entries of the database are refereed by a team of recognized experts. Evidently it would be wise to run a pilot project first on a sample of the curriculum.

3 ACKNOWLEDGEMENTS

The idea for this project germinated from A.K. Dewdney's book *The Turing Omnibus: 61 Excursions in Computer Science*, published by Computer Science Press (1989).

4 BIOGRAPHY

Eric W. van Ammers got involved with programming through his physics studies at the Groningen State University in the sixties. After his graduation he joined the Software Department of the Philips-Electrologica Company. He joined the Wageningen Agricultural University in 1977. His activities consist mainly of curriculum development and lecturing. His research remains focused on programming methodology. He conducted early experiments with literate programming. Van Ammers has published papers on programming methodology and he has designed two tools to support the techniques of literate programming.

INDEX OF CONTRIBUTORS